Hans Bernhard Schmid, Daniel Sirtes, Marcel Weber (Eds.)
Collective Epistemology

EPISTEMISCHE STUDIEN
Schriften zur Erkenntnis- und Wissenschaftstheorie

Herausgegeben von / Edited by

Michael Esfeld • Stephan Hartmann • Albert Newen

Band 20 / Volume 20

Hans Bernhard Schmid, Daniel Sirtes,
Marcel Weber (Eds.)

Collective Epistemology

ontos

verlag

Frankfurt I Paris I Lancaster I New Brunswick

Bibliographic information published by Die Deutsche Bibliothek
Die Deutsche Bibliothek lists this publication in the Deutsche Nationalbibliographie;
detailed bibliographic data is available in the Internet at http://dnb.ddb.de

North and South America by
Transaction Books
Rutgers University
Piscataway, NJ 08854-8042
trans@transactionpub.com

United Kingdom, Ire, Iceland, Turkey, Malta, Portugal by
Gazelle Books Services Limited
White Cross Mills
Hightown
LANCASTER, LA1 4XS
sales@gazellebooks.co.uk

Livraison pour la France et la Belgique:
Librairie Philosophique J.Vrin
6, place de la Sorbonne ; F-75005 PARIS
Tel. +33 (0)1 43 54 03 47 ; Fax +33 (0)1 43 54 48 18
www.vrin.fr

©2011 ontos verlag
P.O. Box 15 41, D-63133 Heusenstamm
www.ontosverlag.com

ISBN 978-3-86838-106-1

2011

Printed on acid-free paper
ISO-Norm 970-6
FSC-certified (Forest Stewardship Council)
This hardcover binding meets the International Library standard

Printed in Germany
by CPI buch bücher.de

Content

PART I

Introduction

DANIEL SIRTES, HANS BERNHARD SCHMID, AND MARCEL WEBER

"The parliament believes that public expenditure-based stimulus plans are a better means for revitalizing the economy than tax cuts"; "the company knew about the risks of their product long before the incident"; "current philosophers doubt that the existence of the external world can be proven." This kind of statements is not at all unusual in everyday talk. In other words, it is commonplace to treat aggregates of people, organizations, or groups as holders of such attitudes as beliefs, knowledge, or doubts. However, to the philosophically trained ear, they may seem somewhat sweeping or vague – who exactly are the 'believers', 'knowers' or 'doubters' in these cases? Thus, the common practice of attributing epistemic states to collectives is in stark contrast to the predominant view in most of received epistemology, where, until recently, it was usually taken for granted that only single individuals can be the subject of cognition. Part of the reason for this is that received epistemology has largely been normative rather than descriptive. In the received view, individuals are the only true 'knowers' there can be, and the fact that individuals are members of groups and tend to be socially embedded, is only taken to be explanatory as a possible source of error and deviation from the epistemic goals rather than a positive feature of epistemic agents. Social relations might be *causally* necessary for people in order to attain knowledge; but they do not play a *constitutive* role. This tendency can be seen most clearly at the very beginning of epistemology in René Descartes' *Meditations.* In order to answer the question of the possibility, the limits and scope of knowledge, Descartes deems it necessary to withdraw from social life and retreat to his lonely castle, where no customs, traditions and authorities can interfere with his quest for truth and contaminate the ultimate source for the justification of true knowledge, which is to be found within his own individual self (Descartes 1993, 13). It is true, however, that not all of received epistemology is strictly anti-social. Thus, it has been argued repeatedly in the history of epistemology that social relations can be instrumental for individuals to attain their epistemic goals, if only these relations are of the right kind. Most prominently, Charles Sanders Peirce (1878) has argued that the pursuit of knowledge is a genuinely social venture that involves mutual cognitive support among the participants within an extended community of communication. Knowledge, Peirce argues, is the regulative ideal of a universal consensus which is to emerge from unlimited critical debate among all actual and potential cognizers – a view that can be found in Edmund Husserl's (e.g. in Husserl 1995, 5th Meditation) late phenomenology as well as, more recently, in Jürgen Habermas's (1981) work. The same kind of debate can be found in the philosophy of science of the 20th century. Reichenbach's (1938) distinction of context of justification vs. context of discovery has been taken to shield the pure philosophical questions about knowledge and its justification from the 'dirty' social and cultural mess of knowledge production. This Cartesian route epitomizes in Laudan's 'arationality assumption', according to which *"the sociology of knowledge may step in to explain beliefs if and only if those beliefs cannot be explained in terms of their rational merits"* (Laudan 1977, 202, italics in original). On the other hand, Neurath was concerned to encompass and comprehend the practical complexities of reliance on scientific testimony (see Uebel 2005). Finally, Kuhn saw the scientific community as the real subject of scientific rationality. He claimed that the diversity of the community members and thus the different responses to novel ideas and evidence within the leeway provided by shared epistemic values is crucial to the progress of scientific knowledge (Kuhn 1977). Opponents of "socialized" epistemology or philosophy of science objected that the notion of sociality implied in these views is not only highly idealized, but also grossly over intellectualized. Real social actors – even scientists – tend to pursue non epistemic goals as well as epistemic ones; sometimes, people prefer convention, consensus or successful publication over truth, and regularly, people advocate those views that best serve their aims. Some have even taken these insights to suggest that the process of knowledge acquisition is to be understood solely in terms of interests and power while truth and epistemic values can be discarded on the trash heap of the history of ideas. This disregard to the truth or falsity of the theories advanced in science was coined as the 'symmetry principle' by David Bloor (1976). Thus, the following two questions arise: First, is it possible to make sense of the notion of social, socialized, or collective knowledge and its production and, second, if this notion does make sense, is it possible to understand and characterize the *positive role of sociality* in knowledge acquisition? The answer to the latter question had better be consistent with the assumption that real individual social agents are largely driven by mundane non☐epistemic interests.

We take it that these two questions are at the center of current research on collective intentionality, social epistemology and their recently emerging combination, labeled 'collective epistemology' by Margaret Gilbert (2004), among others. In order to see how collective epistemology contributes to a new understanding of the role of the social in the acquisition and attribution of knowledge, it is necessary to have a closer look at each of these fields. The perhaps more widely used term "social epistemology" has been serving as an umbrella for a wide variety of philosophical endeavors. A common ground of all of them is that it accepts that knowledge and knowledge production is a social endeavor where the social aspect has been neglected thus far in epistemology. Furthermore, most approaches sailing under the label "social epistemology" attempt to answer the latter of the aforementioned questions: What kind of positive role does sociality play in the production, justification and dissemination of knowledge? (e.g., (Kitcher 2001; Goldman 2002b; Longino 1990; Fuller 2002)) Thus, by stressing the social nature of science, while believing in the possibility of distinguishing between 'positive' and 'negative' epistemic values and social constellations, social epistemologists reject both Laudan's 'arationality assumption' and Bloor's 'symmetry principle'. They try to show a third way, a way out of the science wars between rational science-dogmatists and radical science-relativists. The dichotomy of rationality versus sociality itself is rejected (Longino 2001) as individuals need not be purely epistemically driven for knowledge to emerge. Resembling Adam Smith's invisible hand, non-epistemic interests may be beneficial for the division of cognitive labor and, hence, conducive to the attainment of knowledge. In a similar vein, M. Solomon (2001) argues that even if all scientists were driven by non-epistemic concerns, the consensus of scientific communities could still be rational if it is reconstructable as being based on empirical grounds. Longino, however, is not concerned with reconstruction, but rather with the explication of social norms such as equality of intellectual authority which should be followed in order to produce objective scientific knowledge. A different route is taken by the externalist epistemologist Alvin Goldman, arguing for reliablist assessments of social knowledge production mechanisms (Goldman 2002a). However it may be, social epistemologists are concerned with knowledge as attained by a group, rather than by an individual. However, this kind of group level analysis of knowledge demands an answer to the other question of collective epistemology, namely how knowledge can be attributed to a collective in the first place. This is the question that collective intentionalists have worked on, mostly ignored by social epistemologists. Research on collective intentionality originated in the analysis of the intentionality involved in joint action. Authors such as Raimo Tuomela, Michael Bratman, John Searle, and Margaret Gilbert have developed detailed accounts of what it means for people to act jointly. They agree that for a complex to instantiate joint action, it has to be jointly *intended.* Most of these authors start out from an analysis of individual intention, and try to extend it to the special case of joint intention. In spite of this joint focus and shared extensional strategy, there are persisting differences among the leading proponents of the analysis of collective intentionality, which reach down to the most fundamental issues. One of the most interesting issues in this debate concerns the relation between joint and collective agency. It seems natural to say that whenever individuals act together, there is a sense in which that action can be attributed to the participating individuals collectively – "as a body", as it were –, because the individual action involved in these cases is of the participatory kind. In other cases, however, collective agency and individual agency come apart; this is particularly true in cases in which there are non-operative members of collective agents. Among the philosophers working on collective intentionality, Margaret Gilbert and Raimo Tuomela are special in that they have broadened their analyses to include intentional states of the cognitive (and, in Gilbert's case, affective) kind. The idea is that not only intentions, but other intentional attitudes such as beliefs can be collective, too. Summative accounts hold that for a group to believe p it has to be true that (most of) its members believe p (Quinton 1976). Against this, it has been argued that there is a sense of group belief where it is not assumed that the individual members hold corresponding beliefs (Gilbert 1987). There are two ways to interpret this phenomenon. Most authors hold that such attitudes are not proper beliefs, but acceptances (Tuomela 2000; Meijers 2002; Wray 2003). Other authors defend the view that such attitudes are beliefs (Gilbert 2002; Tollefsen 2003). The matter is complicated by the fact that there is no agreed upon distinction between beliefs and acceptance in the literature. In general, acceptances tend to be seen as pragmatically motivated attitudes, which are adopted voluntarily for the purpose of the attainment of some non-epistemic goal. In contrast, beliefs tend to be seen as purely truth-tracking devices which are neither influenced by the agent's interests, nor subject to voluntary control. In actual fact, however, this distinction might not be as clear-cut as that. Picking up on Tuomela's (2000) distinction between pragmatic acceptance and acceptance-as-true (which is held on an evidential base rather than for prudential reasons), (Hakli 2006) argues that the distinguishing feature between beliefs and acceptances is that the latter are under the voluntary control of the members, i.e. that they can be directly adopted, revised, or rejected at will (even though they need not be acquired in this way), and he argues that the belief-type attitudes that are ascribed to collectives are of this type rather than proper beliefs. If apparent cases of group beliefs are really a matter of voluntarily adopted attitudes, and if the attitudes in question are not to be of the sort of pragmatic interests, then the question of the *reasons* for having these attitudes comes into the focus.

The present volume collects selected contributions from a workshop on Collective Epistemology which was held at the University of Basel in October 2008.[1] This workshop pursued three goals. The first aim was to take the debate on collective epistemology one step further by giving some of the leading philosophers in the field the opportunity for discussion and exchange. The second goal was to open up the field of collective epistemology for related fields in general epistemology for the purpose of cross-fertilization, such as the analysis of epistemic agency, the epistemological role of testimony, and virtue epistemology. Both of these topics are of great importance for collective epistemology, and vice versa. Third, the aim was to situate collective epistemology in the closely related fields of philosophy of science and sociology of knowledge, as well as in the wider context of the analysis of collective intentionality. The chapters of this volume reflect this threefold aim. The essays collected in Part I of this volume focus on some of the notorious problems of collective intentionality and epistemology. How can we understand the group as an agent? Deborah Tollefsen analyzes the question of the potential role of groups as testifiers. Can groups be the source of testimony? And what status could that testimony have? Tollefsen argues that while some groups can be testifiers, others cannot. Kay Mathiesen focuses on the question whether or not groups can be epistemic agents. She thereby suggests following a general trend in current epistemology not to define knowledge in terms of some or another quality of beliefs, but in terms of certain qualities of the potential belief holders. Anita Konzelman Ziv follows up on this by focusing on the potential bearings of virtue epistemology for the question of group knowledge. In particular, she addresses the issue of whether or not individual vice can be instrumental for collective epistemological virtue. The contributions in Part II focus on the nature of justification of group beliefs and group knowledge, Raimo Tuomela and Raul Hakli present and discuss the latest state of their work. Tuomela takes on the task of characterizing group

[1] The editors wish to acknowledge generous support from the Swiss National Science Foundation and from the Freiwillige Akademische Gesellschaft Basel for this conference.

knowledge and its justification in a variety of constellations. A matrix of properties is introduced on the group, joint-member and individual member level and their permutations are explored. Thus, a rich framework of social epistemology is introduced such that knowledge can be characterized as a social institution in the sense that the "epistemic" practices (gathering of knowledge, acceptance of something as the group's view, relevant inferences and action on its basis, and the justification of acceptances) in a group are governed by its ethos, thus by its normative epistemic standards. In this manner, knowledge – as opposed to mere reason-based belief – can be understood as having special institutional status.

Hakli pleads for a disambiguation of different kinds of beliefs and importantly that their justification should be assessed with different kinds of theories of epistemic justification. He argues that while *involuntary* beliefs (which can be individual or summative group beliefs) could be assessed epistemically on externalistic grounds, i.e., by assessing the reliability of the causal mechanisms that produced them, individual and group *voluntary* beliefs (i.e. *all* non-summative group beliefs) or acceptances presuppose the ability of giving *reasons* to defend the upheld acceptances. However, voluntary beliefs should not be deemed unjustified if the agent could not defend it from *any kind* of challenge: this would make attaining knowledge too difficult or maybe even impossible. Acceptances should rather be understood as embedded in a *process* of dialectical justification that is necessarily relative to the community that raises the concrete challenges. Thus making voluntary beliefs and all non-summative group beliefs inherently contextual and social. The papers in Part III are devoted to exploring the wider context of collective epistemology. Don Fallis argues that the analysis of the collective epistemic goals pursued by mathematicians substantiates the claim that inductive and probabilistic considerations should be given more weight in mathematics.

Bob Evans, a sociologist of science, enriches the discussion by showing that different kinds of actors are involved in epistemic groups. Seeing the acquisition of expertise as a process of socialisation within the experiences of specific social groups makes it possible to see that different kinds of expertise can be distributed in different ways.

Marcel Weber takes up an attempt by Samir Okasha to cast theory choice problems in science by an analogy to social choice problems. Okasha examined an interesting connection between Kuhn's concept of incommensurability and Kenneth Arrow's impossibility theorem in certain social choice problems. Weber shows that, at least in experimental sciences such as genetics, this problem does not arise. He also tries to make sense of Kuhn's idea that while there is no unique algorithm that could determine theory choice at the individual level, the whole community manages to select the theory that is most fruitful.

The final contribution by Caroline Baumann exemplifies the potential fruitfulness of the combination of collective intentionality and social epistemology. Baumann criticizes Gilbert's proposal on norm-guided behaviour. Gilbert argues that it is rational for people to act according to social norms irrespective of their individual preferences. This is so because the normativity of social norms is grounded in a joint commitment and rationality requires people to enact the joint commitments they are parties to. Baumann's arguments for the rejection of Gilbert's position should have direct bearing on Longino's proposal of social norms for objective knowledge.

Although the intricate relationships between the two research fields that this workshop has brought together are still a *terra incognita*, this volume shows that the analysis of these questions has both the relevance and the focus to develop into *collective epistemology*, an independent field of research in the near future.

Bibliography

Bloor, D. (1976), *Knowledge and Social Imagery*. London: Routledge.

Descartes, R. (1993), Meditations on First Philosophy: In Which the Existence of God and the Distinction of the Soul from the Body Are Demonstrated. Trans. Donald A. Cress. 3rd ed. Hackett Publishing Company.

Fuller, S. (2002), *Social Epistemology. Second edition.* Bloomington: Indiana University Press.

Gilbert, M. (2002), "Belief and Acceptance as Features of Groups". *Protosociology* 16, 35-69.

——— (1987), "Modeling Collective Belief". *Synthese* 73, 185-204.

——— (2004), "Collective Epistemology". *Episteme* 1, 2, 95-107.

Goldman, A. I. (2002a), *Pathways to knowledge. Private and public.* Oxford: Oxford University Press.

——— (2002b), "What Is Social Epistemology? A Smorgasbord of Projects". In: *Pathways to Knowledge*, January 31, 182-224.

Habermas, J. (1981), *Theorie des kommunikativen Handelns.* Frankfurt (Main): Suhrkamp.

Hakli, R. (2006), "Group beliefs and the distinction between belief and acceptance". *Cognitive Systems Research* 7, 2, 286-297.

Husserl, E. (1995), Cartesianische Meditationen. Eine Einleitung in die Phänomenologie. 3rd ed. Meiner.

Kitcher, Ph. (2001), *Science, Truth, and Democracy.* Oxford: Oxford University Press.

Kuhn, T. S. (1977), "Objectivity, Value Judgment, and Theory Choice". In: *The Essential Tension. Selected Studies in Scientific Tradition and Change.* Chicago: University of Chicago Press, 320-339.

Laudan, L. (1977), *Progress and its Problems: Toward a Theory of Scientific Growth.* Berkeley and Los Angeles: University of California Press.

Longino, H. E. (1990), *Science as Social Knowledge.* Princeton: Princeton University Press.

——— (2001), *The Fate of Knowledge.* Princeton: Princeton University Press.

Meijers, A. (2002), "Collective Agents and Cognitive Attitudes". *Protosociology* 16, 70-86.

Peirce, C. S. (1878), "How to Make Our Ideas Clear". *Popular Science Monthly* 12, 286–302 (reprinted CP 5.388-410).

Quinton, A. (1976), "Social Objects". *Proceedings of the Aristotelian Society* 76. New Series. 1-27.

Reichenbach, H. (1938), *Experience and Prediction.* Chicago: University of Chicago Press.

Solomon, M. (2001), *Social empiricism*. Cambridge Mass.: MIT Press.

Tollefsen, D. (2003), "Rejecting Rejectionism". *Protosociology* 18/19, 389-405.

Tuomela, R. (2000), "Belief versus Acceptance". *Philosophical Explorations* 3, 2, 122.

Uebel, Th. E. (2005), "Epistemic Agency Naturalized: The Protocol of Testimony Acceptance." Ed. Alan W. Richardson. *Aristotelian Society Supplementary Volume* 79, 1 (7), 89-105.

Wray, K. B. (2003), "What Really Divides Gilbert and the Rejectionists?" *Protosociology* 18/19, 363-376.

Groups as Rational Sources

DEBORAH TOLLEFSEN

1. Introduction

This paper explores what it means to be a testifier, and by extension what it means for a group to be a testifier. The current discussions of testimony focus on the verb *to testify*, and they offer theories of the nature of testimony. These theories generally take the form: "S testifies that p if and only if" or "A statement p counts as testimony if and only if" and so on. Testifying *is* an action—a speech act. But you have to be the right sort of being to perform this sort of act. Not just anyone can testify. My focus, then, is on the *testifier* rather than the testimony.

Another way of describing the focus on this paper is this: I want to try to say what it means to be a rational source. The phrase "rational source" comes from Tyler Burge's work on testimony (Burge 1993). I use the phrase a bit differently than he does. He defines a rational source as being an agent with the capacity to reason or with a rational faculty.[2] "Rational sources are sources that themselves are a capacity to reason or are rational beings" (1993: 470). However, the ability to reason cannot be sufficient for being a testifier because animals have the ability to reason (at least given a certain conception of reason) but they aren't typically conceived of as testifiers, or capable of offering us testimony. I use "rational source" as synonymous with testifier. To testify is to engage in a certain form of epistemic agency. In several papers I've argued that groups can be epistemic agents (2004; 2006) and in a more recent papers I have argued

---

[2] Burge wants to leave open the possibility that computers could be a rational source but does not acknowledge computers as rational agents. A computer is not a rational being but involves processes that are themselves rational, though derivatively so. See Burge, 1998.

that testifying, a paradigm case of epistemic agency, is something groups do too (2007; 2009). We receive testimony from research groups, search committees, government agencies, task forces, and so on. And often times the testimony of a group cannot be understood in a summative fashion as the testimony of all or some of the group members. The argument for the non-summative account of group testimony resembles arguments for the non-summative nature of group belief. When groups form beliefs it is often done so via consensus and it is very possible that the group's belief does not reflect the majority of beliefs regarding the matter. Rather, group belief is often the result of collective acceptance of some proposition (though the group can still, in my view[3], be said to genuinely believe). The testimony offered by a group via its spokesperson or via written document similarly resists a summative approach. It simply does not follow that because group G says "There are weapons of mass destruction in Iraq" that all or most of the members (or that any member) of the group would testify similarly. In many cases, when a group testifies, the group itself will be the source of the testimony. Reflection on our common practice of citing groups as the source of information offers some confirmation of this. This isn't to say that group testimony is always to be given a non-summative analysis. In some cases what a group testifies to may be exactly that to which each would testify. My point here is that it need not and, indeed, there exist lots of actual cases of group testimony that resist a summative analysis.

But the fact that groups issue intelligible statements either in writing or via a spokesperson seems to me now not sufficient to say that they, themselves, are testifiers. Testifying involves a certain relation between speaker and hearer. In particular, it involves a normative relation. Rational sources are not just sources of information but agents that can be held responsible for the information that they give. In this paper, I focus on the issue of whether groups have what it takes to engage in full-fledged testimonial exchanges. In section II, I begin with a discussion of the nature of

---

[3] See Tollefsen (2002a; 2002b) for a defense of the attribution of intentional states to groups.

testimony. I focus on what I take to be the most compelling account of its nature - the assurance view of testimony. In section III, I turn to the issue of whether groups are rational sources.

2. The Nature of Testimony

Testimony is a specific type of speech act and there has been an ongoing debate in the epistemology of testimony regarding the nature of this speech act. Conservative views of testimony define it in terms of the speaker's intention to present evidence to an audience on a matter that is known to be in dispute or for which the audience is in need of evidence (Coady 1992). More liberal accounts of testimony define it as "tellings in general" with no restriction on the domain (e.g. E. Fricker 1987; 1994; 1995; Sosa 1991). More recently Jennifer Lackey has developed what I will call the disjunctivist account of testimony. According to Lackey: S testifies that p by making an act of communication a if and only if (in part) in virtue of a's communicable content, (1) S reasonably intends to convey the information that p, or (2) a is reasonably taken as conveying the information that p (2006: 193). This account allows for the fact that many times an utterance will convey information and hence, offer us testimony, even when the speaker does not intend to testify, as in the case of posthumously published work from which we obtain information about the deceased's life. But it also tries to accommodate the intuition that testifying very often seems to be something people do intentionally.

In addition to these approaches to testimony there is a view about the nature of testimony which highlights the normative relation between speaker and hearer. Those who advocate an *assurance view* of testimony argue that what makes testimony a unique type of speech act is that when one offers testimony to another they are lending their assurance that the testimony is true. It isn't that one gives testimony and then says "I assure you." The act of testifying and the assurance are one and the same. To testify is to invite another to trust you. This doesn't mean that one cannot give false testimony. There is such a thing as a false assurance. But it does mean that testimony is essentially interpersonal. When I testify I invite another to trust me and because of this my interlocutor has expectations that exist only because I testified. With an assurance comes an entitlement. The hearer is entitled to question me if p turns out to be false. To testify, then, is to appreciate your role in an epistemic relation and to be aware that this relation opens up the possibility of being called to question. It is helpful here to consider what happens when we do hear false testimony or when another leads us astray. We rebuke them, question them, and insist they explain themselves. The existence of this sort of response suggests that testimony is a normative relation and that subjects who are unable to appreciate these norms (and even flout them by lying) are not testifiers. I do not have time here to defend the assurance view in detail. It has been developed and defended more thoroughly by Richard Moran (2006) and Benjamin McMyler (2007). I'm inclined to think that the assurance view captures something essential about the act of testifying and the nature of the agents that engage in testimonial relations. There are various sorts of agents that can give us information or *indicate* things to us. My thermostat indicates the temperature in my house; my cat indicates that she is hungry by exhibiting certain types of behavior. But there is a difference between indicating and testifying.

It should be noted that the assurance view does not appear to be in conflict with the conservative view of testimony or something like Lackey's view. Indeed, I think the assurance view can be accommodated within these accounts by emphasizing the link between assertion and truth. But the liberal view seems unable to accommodate the intuition that testifying is essentially interpersonal. Testifying like marrying can't be done by oneself. Thus, the diary that is found that offers information about the dead author is not testimony (though it still might convey information) and this is precisely because the author never gave his or her assurance to anyone that the contents were true. They never opened themselves up to scrutiny. Indeed, the idea of going to a person and saying "You wrote in your diary that you had an affair with Elvis, but I know that to be false. How could you lie to me like that?" is absurd. If the notion of "telling" were developed in a more robust fashion such that the posthumous diary case was not a form of testimony (perhaps it is a case of indication), then I think they too can accommodate the idea that testimony is essentially an interpersonal affair and that it is an affair that is deeply tied to epistemic responsibility. To give one's assurance is to take responsibility for what you have said, for its impact on another, in the act of testifying you acknowledge another's dependence on you.

Given the link, then, between testifying and epistemic responsibility, what sorts of epistemic qualities does an agent have to have in order to be a testifier? I will argue here that one of the essential features is doxastic stability. Miranda Fricker discusses doxastic stability in her recent book *Epistemic Injustice* (2007) and it was after reading this that I began to think about the prerequisites for being a testifier and whether or not groups meet those prerequisites. Fricker builds on Bernard Williams' discussion of the process of "steadying the mind." Williams discusses the process by which a subject comes to sort his wishes into either belief or desires as follows:

> "The basic mechanism depends on the fact that there are others who need to rely on our dispositions, and we want them to be able to rely on our dispositions because we, up to a point, want to rely on theirs. We learn to present ourselves to others, and consequently also to ourselves, as people who have moderately steady outlooks or beliefs." (Williams 2002: 192).

Fricker highlights the role of steadying the mind in the context of testimony. Our practice of relying on the word of another presupposes that the other has a steady mind. Consider how we would treat an epistemic subject whose testimony constantly changed or was subject to change on a whim. You ask your friend Paul the time of day: He reports 2:00 p.m., but then says "Wait, actually, it is 1:30." A few moments later, he says "No, it is 12:30." Such a testifier would exhibit a great deal of unreliability. Even if, in the end, Paul provided the correct time, you would not be justified in believing what you were told. But it is because of our reliance on others and our awareness that they expect us to be stable, that forces us to avoid expressing mere wishes and attempt, instead, to offer the truth.

> "We might say, then, that trustful conversation with others is the basic mechanism by which the mind steadies itself. Such dialogue pressurizes the subject into having attitudes of belief towards only those propositions that merit it. It draws the subject away from assertoric caprice and towards doxastic stability." (Fricker 2007: 52).

And again Williams:

> "The subject is engaged in trustful conversation with another who relies on him, and the question is whether he can give that person to believe the proposition. In doing that, he may well, in such a case, give himself to believe it as well. It is the presence and needs of others that help us to construct even our factual beliefs." (Williams 2002: 192).

The importance of a steady mind cannot be overstated. As Fricker points out, the steadying of the mind is essentially tied to personal identity and notions of the self:

> "William suggests that this process of settling the mind is the most basic mechanism whereby we come to be who we are. It settles not only one's mind, but thereby one's identity too. As not only our beliefs and desires, but our opinions and value commitments settle themselves through social dialogue into more or less stable states, so an important dimension of our identity thereby takes shape." (Fricker 2007: 150).

Doxastic stability, then, is required to be a testifier and it is the acknowledgement that others rely on you to form beliefs that fuels this stability. The expectation of doxastic stability on the part of hearers points to the importance of epistemic responsibility in testimonial exchanges. If Paul constantly changed his testimony in the ways described above we would not hold him responsible for misleading us. Indeed, after a point, we would treat him as exhibiting a sort of epistemic pathology. He would be excused and we wouldn't rebuke him for his unreliable testimony. Our practice of holding others responsible for their testimony presupposes that others have a steady mind.

3. Groups as Rational Sources

What does this discussion tell us about the capacity of groups to testify? Do groups engage in the steadying of their minds and are they capable of acknowledging their epistemic responsibilities? In what follows, I discuss two cases that I think exhibit a steadying of the group mind. The steadying was done precisely because group members realized the fact that others were depending on the group to speak its mind and that they had a responsibility to say something definitive and take collective responsibility for what was said. The first is from the history of science and I owe the example to John Beatty. In "Masking disagreement among experts" (2007), John Beatty provides us with a fascinating case that clearly exhibits the non-summative nature of group testimony. In 1956 a distinguished panel of geneticists formed by the U.S. National Academies of Science (NAS) issued a report on the genetic hazards of radiation exposure. The details of this case and the group deliberation leading to the issue of the report are fascinating because they reveal the ways in which these scientists felt the need to provide a unified story to the public rather than reveal their dissenting opinions. There was a great deal of controversy regarding radiation exposure and its long term effects. The Atomic Energy Commission (AEC) seized on this and used it as a way of rebutting charges that radiation exposure would have long term genetic effects. The perception of disagreement among the public was of great concern to those who formed the NAS panel. If the panel did not provide a unified voice, it risked undermining the public's trust in science. They also were deeply concerned that, if they did not provide some testimony regarding the long term genetic effects of radiation, someone else would. They wanted to avoid, for instance, the AEC issuing its own report regarding the hazards of radiation exposure. As Beatty notes this wasn't just that they were concerned some other group would usurp their expert status or undermine their authority, they were deeply concerned that some other group, one less reliable, might issue false or misleading information.

But offering a unified statement was not easy. There was considerable disagreement within the panel. The issue of the maximum permissible dosage was particularly contentious. One geneticist on the panel even refused to report anything regarding a permissible dose because of his belief that the issue was indeterminable. Despite the clear differences of opinion, all the geneticists signed the report and "in so doing very publicly agreed to let it stand as the committee's position" (Beatty 2006: 64). The report of the NAS panel is a paradigm case of group testimony. The testimony of NAS cannot be understood summatively. NAS also engages in a steadying of its "mind." It was the presence and needs of other epistemic agents which forced NAS to achieve a consensus regarding the information they wanted to convey to the public. The doxastic stability of NAS was necessary in order to maintain the image of science (or the subgroup-physicists) as a rational source. I would go further and say that it wasn't just necessary to maintaining the *image* of science (or a sub group of science) as a source of truth, but it was necessary for it to be a rational source. Doxastic stability is constitutive of testimonial agency. To be a testifier (individual or group) one must exhibit doxastic stability to a certain degree. This stability sought precisely because there is an acknowledgement that others depend on you for knowledge and that that dependency opens you up to possible scrutiny if the testimony is inaccurate or otherwise uninformative.

The second case of steadying of the group mind involves an unusual collective agent—Wikipedia. By Wikipedia I do not mean the website or the computer program that makes mass collaboration possible. I mean the Wikipedia community. That this community is a group and is capable of engaging in rational deliberation is something I have argued for elsewhere (Tollefsen 2009). What is interesting about Wikipedia is its somewhat childlike status—unsteady and unwilling to accept epistemic responsibility at times but clearly undergoing the process of steadying the mind. It is for this reason that certain entries on Wikipedia can be viewed as the testimony of the Wikipedia community rather than simply the testimony of some individual or some set of individuals who offered independent testimonial statements. The process of steadying the Wikipedia mind was done in direct response to concerns over the ways in which people are relying on Wikipedia as a source of information.

The democratic nature of Wikipedia is, by now, well known. Anyone, regardless of expertise, can write and edit Wikipedia articles and they can do so anonymously. In addition to authors and editors, there are over 1500 administrators that check articles to make sure that they conform to Wikipedia guidelines and policies. Techies are able to develop and contribute software programs that are used to rectify vandalism and other anomalous contributions. All of the participants are subject to the guidelines and policies developed by contributors, via the consensus approach.

Wikipedia entries begin with the submission of an individual or a small group of individuals who co-author the entry (a *stub*). The entry is then added to or edited by others. Any change made to the article is tracked and made public. Changes are often the topic of discussion and these discussions are also made public. There is, therefore, a great deal of joint deliberation that takes place in the course of the development of an article. Because such deliberation often is heated, there are conflict resolution processes to resolve disputes regarding the content of an entry. Though administrators do sometimes appeal to straw votes to resolve disputes, most decisions regarding the content of an article, policies and procedures, and the general workings of Wikipedia are made via a consensus. The existence of a decision making process (the use of discussion boards, and then, if need be conflict resolution tools) suggests that there is a mechanism in place for the forming of group illocutionary intentions (Tollefsen 2009).

Consensus regarding the content of an article and its quality is reached over time, however, and some times it is a lengthy discussion period. In the meantime, the content of articles can change quite a bit and if, disputes are heated, articles can change randomly from day to day. This sort of doxastic instability should lead us to question the status of Wikipedia as a testifier. Recall the case of Paul. Paul was subject to random changes in his beliefs and, as a result, his testimony. We would not rely on him and moreover if he exhibited this behavior across contexts and for a lengthy time, we would probably be reluctant to label him as an epistemic agent. Paul isn't just an unreliable testifier; he isn't a testifier at all. Likewise, the doxastic instability of many of Wikipedia's articles makes it difficult to see it as a rational source, a testifier.

But Wikipedia itself admits the immaturity of many of its articles. Wikipedia notes that the origin of an article is often a singular perspective. But those that become the topic of discussion among multiple people gradually are transformed to represent a more neutral, plural perspective. Here is Wikipedia's description of the process:

> "… many articles start their lives as partisan, and after a long process of discussion, debate and argument, they gradually take on a neutral point of view reached through consensus. Others may for a while become caught up in a heavily unbalanced viewpoint which can take some time — months perhaps — to achieve better balanced coverage of their subject. In part, this is because editors often contribute content in which they have a particular interest and do not attempt to make each article that they edit comprehensive. However, eventually additional editors expand and contribute to articles and strive to achieve balance and comprehensive coverage." (http://en.wikipedia.org/wiki/Wikipedia:About).

In order to identify those that have reached or are near to reaching a comprehensive, verifiable, and neutral point of view, Wikipedia has distinguished two categories: featured articles and good articles. Articles in each category go through a lengthy review process and are subject to the approval of the Wikipedia community. The fact that Wikipedia articles, at least in their infancy, are constantly changing or subject to change, suggests that these articles do not express the "mind" of the Wikipedia community. The more mature articles, however, those that go through a lengthy process of discussion and review and which are then featured as those meeting the ideal of Wikipedia scholars, do. These articles, of course, are still subject to revision but much less so. They are maintained by those who check for vandalism. And though discussions continue about their content, substantial changes to content happen relatively infrequently. To this extent the mature articles are no different than the steady states of individuals. Steadying the mind does not mean that beliefs are never changed or altered when new evidence becomes available. Rather, it means that beliefs have, as Fricker put it, "a life expectancy" and changes, if they occur, are a result of responsiveness to reasons. I submit that the practice of selecting good and featured articles is a method of steadying the Wikipedia mind and this steadying was a direct result of the community's awareness of the status Wikipedia was gaining as a source of information. Wikipedia has taken responsibility for those articles that are labeled good and featured. Those that have not gone through a thorough review process have a disclaimer—read with care.

4. Conclusion

To be a testifier one has to be the right sort of agent. One needs to maintain a level of doxastic stability and has to exhibit a capacity for taking responsibility for the truth of what they say. I've argued that certain groups exhibit both doxastic stability and epistemic responsibility. It is the very acknowledgement that others are dependent on them epistemically that causes some groups to steady the "group mind." Groups can be rational sources. But clearly not all groups do exhibit such a capacity. Wikipedia appears to be in a developmental stage. Other groups are more like epistemic infants and may remain so indefinitely. If we intend to gain knowledge from groups we ought to be very careful to identify the testifiers from the mere indicators, the mature from the infantile.[4]

Bibliography

Beatty, J. (2007), "Masking Disagreement among Experts". *Episteme* 3,1 (2006), 52-67.

Burge, T. (1993), "Content Preservation". *The Philosophical Review* 102, 4.

---

[4] The status of infants and young children as potential testifiers and testifiers in training is the subject of my current research.

——— (1998), "Computer Proof, Apriori Knowledge, and Other Minds: The Sixth Philosophical Perspectives Lecture". *Noûs* 32, Supplement: Philosophical Perspectives, 12, Language, Mind, and Ontology.

Coady, C. A. J. (1992), *Testimony: A Philosophical Study.* Oxford: Oxford University Press.

Fricker, E. (1987), "The Epistemology of Testimony". *Proceedings of the Aristotelian Society Supplementary* 61, 57–83.

——— (1994), "Against Gullibility". In: B. K. Matilal and A. Chakrabarti (eds.), *Knowing from Words.* Boston: Kluwer, 125–161.

——— (1995), "Critical Notice: Telling and Trusting: Reductionism and Anti Reductionism in the Epistemology of Testimony". *Mind* 104, 393–411.

Fricker, M. (2007), *Epistemic Injustice: Power and the Ethics of Knowing.* Oxford: Oxford University Press.

Lackey, J. (2006), "The Nature of Testimony". *Pacific Philosophical Quarterly* 8, issue 2, 177-197.

McMyler, B. (2007), "Knowledge at Second Hand". *Inquiry* 50, 5, 511-540.

Moran, R. (2006), "Getting Told and Being Believed". In: J. Lackey and E. Sosa (eds.), *The Epistemology of Testimony.* Oxford: Oxford University Press, 272-306.

Sosa, E. (1991), "Testimony and Coherence". In: B. K. Matilal and A. Chakrabarti (eds.), *Knowing from Words.* Boston: Kluwer, 59-67.

Tollefsen, D. (2002a), "Organizations as true believers". *Journal of Social Philosophy* 33(3), 395-411.

——— (2002b), "Collective intentionality and the social sciences". *Philosophy of the Social Sciences* 32, (1), 25-50.

——— (2004), "Collective epistemic agency". *Southwest Philosophy Review* 20 (1), 55-66, 2004.

——— (2006), "Collective Epistemic Agency and the need for Collective Epistemology". In: K. Schulte-Ostermann, P. Stekeler-Weithofer, and N. Psarros (eds.), *Facets of Sociality: Philosophical Approaches to Co-Operative Action.* Frankfurt: Ontos-Verlag, 309-330.

——— (2007), "Group Testimony". *Social Epistemology* 21 (3), 299-311.

——— (2009), "Wikipedia and the Epistemology of Testimony". *Episteme: Special Issue on the Epistemology of Mass Collaboration* 6 (1), 2009.

Williams, B. (2002), *Truth and Truthfulness.* Princeton: Princeton University Press.

Can Groups Be Epistemic Agents?

KAY MATHIESEN

Abstract

In this paper, I confront an objection to group epistemic agency that has been posed in two separate papers (Meijers 2002 and McMahon 2003). They argue that groups are never "independent" epistemic agents. I discuss a number of cases where the beliefs of groups and of their members may diverge. I argue that these cases show that groups may be independent epistemic agents. We can conclude from this that work on "agent centered" epistemology should focus on groups as well as individuals.

1. Introduction

Recent work in epistemology has brought the status of epistemic agents to the fore. Work on virtue epistemology, for example, has us look, not to the nature of the beliefs held by agents, but to the nature of these agents themselves. Work on virtue epistemology has us ask whether the epistemic agent is wise, open-minded, etc. (Greco 2008). Work on social epistemology has us look at other epistemic agents as a source of information and has us consider what might be the unique status of testimony as a source of knowledge (Adler 2008).[5] Work on epistemic rationality and epistemic utility focuses on epistemic agents as rational choosers of epistemic actions such as believing, seeking evidence and weighing evidence (see e.g., Goldman 1999; Levi 1977; Maher 1993).

Can we ask these sorts of questions about groups, such as corporations, scientific and other research groups, or even communities? Or, will we need to look at the members of such groups and how social connections

---

[5] This is not to say that this is the only project in social epistemology. For an overview of the full range of projects, see Goldman 2004.

affect the epistemic agency of the individuals and thereby of the group? This is not simply a question for those working on collective epistemology, it is an important question for anyone interested in applying the work in epistemology to questions of knowledge management, philosophy of science, and a number of other areas where groups of persons working in concert produce knowledge. If groups are epistemic agents in their own right, then we can ask questions regarding epistemic responsibility, virtue, and choice about group epistemic processes. Thus, this question has important methodological implications for how enquiry in a number of fields ought to proceed.

In a previous paper (Mathiesen 2006), I argued that group beliefs may be properly understood as epistemically directed—that is, that there is nothing inconsistent or problematic about the idea that a group's beliefs and group epistemic processes may be appropriately truth tracking. There is an objection to group epistemic agency, however, that needs to be addressed further than I was able to do in that paper. It has been argued that, with regard to properly epistemic beliefs, there can be no difference between what the group believes and what all of the members believe. Thus, there is no prima facie reason to suppose that group beliefs (at least in the epistemic sense) are anything more than simply a restatement of what all the members of the group believe. (Below I call this the "non-divergence" argument.)

In what follows, I argue that indeed the properly epistemic beliefs of a group and its members[6] can diverge and thus we have good reason for treating groups as epistemic agents in their own right. I begin by contrasting what I call "pragmatic beliefs," that are not open to the non-divergence argument, and epistemic beliefs which are open to it. I provide a case of group epistemic belief and ask whether it is ever possible for the beliefs of the members and the group to diverge. I consider a number of

---

[6] By "member" here I simply mean the individual person who is a member of the group. When I mean to be referring to the person qua their role in the group, I will use the locution "qua member."

cases where the group accepts a proposition, while the members either reject or withhold judgment on the very same proposition. While the first four of these cases are enlightening as they illustrate the complex relationship between individual and group acceptances, they are open to serious objections. It appears that in each of these cases there is either a failure of epistemic rationality on the part of the members, on the part of the group, or the case is not one of genuine *group* belief or acceptance. I argue, however, that the fifth case presented, where the group and the members have differing epistemic risk settings, is not open to such objections. If this argument succeeds, we will have overcome a major obstacle in the way of philosophical acceptance of group epistemic agency.

2. Groups as Believers

A common argument put forward to show that the views held by the group are not simply reducible to the views that the members hold qua individuals is what I will call the "divergence argument" (see e.g., Gilbert 2002; Tollefsen 2002; Tuomela 1995). To see how the divergence argument works consider the following case:

Example 1: The Parents

Susan and John are parents of a pre-teen daughter. The daughter wants to know when she can start dating. Susan thinks that 14 is old enough to start dating. John thinks that anything younger than 18 is a mistake. They think it is best for their daughter if they show a "united front." So, they decide to split the difference. They tell their daughter, "We think that you will be mature enough to date when you are 16." They continue to hold their individual beliefs, but act on and enforce their group position as parents.[7]

---

[7] This case is inspired by a slightly different case of disagreeing (but collectively believing) parents discussed in Gilbert 1994: 249-250.

Since neither Susan nor John actually believe that 16 is the proper age to start dating, the statement "We think you will be mature enough to date when you are 16" is not merely shorthand for "I believe and you believe," or even, "We together believe."[8] Rather, so the argument goes, in order to account for such cases we need to accept the concept of a genuinely *group view*, that is not reducible to the beliefs of the members.

Some (e.g., Gilbert 2002; Tollefsen 2002) have characterized such group views as group *beliefs*. Still others have raised the concern that these views do not have many of the features traditionally associated with belief. [9] For our purposes, we can sidestep much of this debate insofar as it is concerned with whether groups have all the *psychological features* of belief that an individual would have. Since the focus here is whether groups can be epistemic agents, we can focus purely on the epistemic features of belief.[10] Indeed, we can sidestep the whole issue of whether groups can "really" believe, by using the term "acceptance" for both individual and group doxastic attitudes.[11] With this as our starting point, we can then focus solely on the sorts of doxastic states we are interested in for the purposes of epistemology (as opposed to philosophy of psychology, ontology, or philosophy of mind).

---

[8] Others, including Gilbert (1989), Searle (1995), and Tuomela (1995) have given extended arguments that such group intentional states are not always reducible to aggregations of those of the individual members. If you remain unconvinced by the discussion here, see their valuable work.

[9] This is the main point of contention in the "rejectionist" vs. "believers" debate. Rejectionists, who reject the possibility of genuine group belief, include Hakli (2006), McMahon (2003), Meijers (2002; 2003), and Wray (2001; 2003). Believers, who argue that there is a sense of belief that applies equally to groups and individuals, include Gilbert (1987/1996; 1989; 1994; 1996; 2000; 2002; 2004), Preyer (2003), Schmitt (1994), Tollefsen (2002a; 2002b; 2003), and Tuomela (1992; 1995; 2000; 2004).

[10] For a further discussion of this point, see e.g., Mathiesen 2006.

[11] Note that a "categorical belief" model is being used here. That is, rather than merely assigning degrees of belief in propositions, it is assumed that epistemic agents accept, suspend judgment, or reject propositions. For discussions and defenses of the categorical belief model, see e.g., Levi 1962 and Maher 1990.

In what follows I use Keith Lehrer's characterization of this epistemic form of acceptance. According to Lehrer, "There is a special kind of acceptance requisite to knowledge. It is accepting something for the purpose of attaining truth and avoiding error with respect to the very thing one accepts" (Lehrer 1990: 11). In the case above the parents are not engaging in an epistemic acceptance of the proposition "16 is the proper age to begin dating." They are not accepting this proposition "for the purpose of attaining truth and avoiding error."[12] Rather, in this example, they are accepting the proposition for the purpose of solving a particular practical problem.[13]

We can call an agent that adopts doxastic states for the purpose of pursuing a practical goal a "practical doxastic agent." The parents form a practical doxastic agent, which accepts propositions for the purpose of achieving certain practical goals. Since it is typically better to act based on the truth, they may often accept propositions that are true, but this is merely a means to their practical ends. If they cannot agree on which proposition is true (or closest to the truth), if they have no particular views on the matter, or if accepting a true proposition will not help them meet their goals, then they may choose to accept propositions that one or both do not personally believe to be true.[14]

In contrast with such practical agents, we can call those agents who accept propositions "for the purpose of attaining truth and avoiding er-

---

[12] Of course, it is possible for two people to "take the average" of their beliefs on the view that it is more likely to be the truth, as I discuss in section three. But, we are assuming this is not the case here.

[13] One might think that the parents do not accept the proposition in an epistemic sense for a further reason: there is no truth of the matter about what the appropriate age is for dating. And, it might further be argued that it is only in cases where there is no fact of the matter that we will find (non-irrational) non-epistemic acceptance. If so, then the standard divergence argument for group belief is weaker than has been thought. This, however, does not impact my argument here, which is to show that there may be cases of divergence in cases of *epistemic* acceptance.

[14] Admittedly, not any old belief about the appropriate age will do. It is not that they could just pick a number at random between 1 and 100. They would each agree to the proposition that 16 is better than 10 on the one hand, or 25 on the other, for example. Perhaps we ought to say they are not *sufficiently* interested in avoiding error.

ror..." "epistemic agents." The parents do not form an *epistemic* agent, at least with regard to their acceptance of this proposition. It seems unproblematic that groups may be epistemic agents. Groups may form precisely to pursue epistemic interests, e.g., research groups, fact finding committees, expert panels. However, some have argued that such epistemic groups do not have "beliefs of their own." On this view to say that an epistemic group accepts a proposition is simply be shorthand for saying that each of the members individually accepts the proposition.

One might wonder why, if we can show that groups accept propositions qua practical agents, we could not also show that a group accepts propositions qua epistemic agent. To see the difficulty recall how the divergence argument for practical group belief goes. In order to show that groups may be distinct doxastic agents we showed that a group may have accepted a proposition p where that is not equivalent to saying that all or most of the members accept that p. This argument proceeds by showing that there may be cases where the group accepts p, while the members do not personally accept p.[15] We would expect that if groups have epistemic agency of their own, then we should be able to make the same move. That is, that we should be able to devise a case where the group accepts a proposition while the members do not.

To see whether we can make this argument with regard to group epistemic agents, we will need a clear example before us. In the rest of the paper I will use an example I will call "the hiring committee." The set-up is a bit more complicated than that of the parents. So, I will need to spend a little time describing its features. Suppose that a philosophy department has been given permission to hire an assistant professor. The department then forms a sub-committee of three persons, who constitute the hiring committee. The department gives the hiring committee a list of features that they are looking for in a candidate and the relative weighting that such features should be given. This list, along with the weightings, set the

---

[15] In what follows, "fail to accept" may mean either that the agent rejects or suspends judgment on the proposition in question.

standards of whether a candidate is qualified for the job. The job of the committee is to gather, sort, synthesize, and evaluate relevant information to make the determination of who is qualified for the position. What is being asked for is not their subjective judgments about who is qualified for the job. Rather, they are to judge whether the candidates meet the explicit standards provided by the department—they are what is called in a court of law the "finders of fact."[16]

The members of the hiring committee are epistemic agents, so they will do their best to accept true propositions, reject false propositions, and withhold judgment on those propositions where they have insufficient evidence to accept or reject. They have collectively agreed as a group to use epistemic practices that the members believe are effective in achieving the *epistemic* goal of accepting truths and avoiding falsehoods. In other words, the members have done their best to ensure not only that they are good epistemic agents, but that the group as a whole functions in an epistemically reasonable way, e.g., in ways that make it more likely that they will accept the true, reject the false, and withhold judgment when there is insufficient evidence.

Example 2: The Hiring Committee

The members of the committee have finished reviewing the information presented by Jones and are now considering the proposition, "Jones is qualified for the position." With regard to this proposition each of them may reject it, accept it, or withhold judgment. The outcome of the committee's decision process is as follows: The hiring committee accepts the proposition that "Jones is a qualified candidate." A majority of the members do not accept this proposition.

---

[16] In other words, there is no disagreement about what the standards are or what would count as meeting the standards. Thus, there is no ontological issue here about what counts as being "qualified." We are interested in epistemological disagreement here, not ontological disagreement.

Is this possible? If yes, we would have a prima facie case that groups are epistemic agents. If no, it would not prove that groups are *not* epistemic agents. It would, however, block what has been a successful argument for showing that there is group belief in the sense of acceptance by a practical agent. To show that groups may be epistemic agents, we would need to find a different argument.

It has been argued that such a situation is indeed impossible. James McMahon, for example, argues that "a collective belief of this sort [i.e., one that aims at truth] is formed when all the members agree that the relevant evidence supports a particular conclusion... If joint acceptance is acceptance in the epistemic sense, then *all the parties personally believe what is jointly accepted*, and this is common knowledge." (McMahon 2003: 353). So, according to McMahon, a group belief forms when, and only when, the members agree that there is sufficient evidence to accept the proposition in question. If a member agrees that the evidence is sufficient to warrant accepting a proposition (in the sense of actually assenting to it, not merely going along), then she must believe that there is sufficient evidence in support of the proposition. If she believes that there is sufficient evidence in support of the proposition, then she is rationally bound to accept the proposition—i.e., she will "personally" believe it.

Anthonie Meijers similarly argues that, "if only epistemic reasons for believing are taken into account, it is impossible that there is a difference in content between what I as an individual believe and what I believe as a member of the group, for epistemic access is not role bound" (Meijers 2003: 379). We can compare the case of the parents and the case of the hiring committee to illustrate his point. The parents, qua members of the parental team, each accepts that, "16 is the appropriate age to begin dating." When interacting with their daughter, they will reason, speak, and act in accordance with this view. In non-parental contexts, however, they may reason, speak, and act on their personal beliefs.[17] For instance, when chatting with his friends, John may vigorously defend his personal view that 16 is too young to begin dating. In other words, qua members of the co-parenting unit they accept this proposition, but qua individuals they do not accept it. Their beliefs are "role-bound." What they accept depends on whether they are acting as co-parents, or simply chatting with their friends in a discussion of differing parenting styles. For a group such as the hiring committee, which is making epistemic decisions, rather than pragmatic ones, it seems impossible for someone to believe that the evidence supports the proposition "Jones is qualified" qua hiring committee member, but not qua individual.[18] If the group is accepting propositions for good epistemic reasons, and the members believe that this is the case, then they should accept exactly the same propositions. If the evidence supports the acceptance of a proposition, then it should be accepted by all—both by the group and by the members qua individuals.

If McMahon and Meijers are correct, the divergence argument for group epistemic agency is blocked. On the other hand, if we can show that there are cases where the individual and group epistemic acceptances diverge, we will have opened up one path that may be used to argue for independent epistemic agency for groups.

Of course, there could be any number of non-epistemic reasons why the group and the members qua individuals diverge on what they accept—for instance, there may be so called "group think."[19] In the following, our goal is to find cases where the group and the individuals diverge on what they accept, while none may be said to be failing to act as *epistemic*

---

[17] Or, more properly, in contexts where they are not acting as part of this particular parenting team. That is, there may be a distinction between the general role of "parent," and the role of "member of a particular co-parenting team."

[18] Of course if a member had a different set of standards of what it is to be "qualified" than does the group, then this would be possible. However, we are assuming here that "qualified" in this context simply means that the person satisfies the criteria provided by the department.

[19] For a philosophical discussion of groupthink in relation to social epistemology, see Solomon 2006.

agents.[20] In other words, I want to show how an epistemically rational group agent may be composed of epistemically rational individual agents, and yet the views of these two agents will diverge.

3. Differing Evidence Sets

One reason that two epistemic agents might differ on what propositions they accept is that they have access to different evidence. Might a group and the individuals who form it fail to have access to the same set of evidence? Consider the following case:

Case A: After the previous meeting when the committee unanimously accepted the proposition "Jones is qualified," each of the members has received new information. This information contains a defeater for the proposition that "Jones is qualified." All of the individual members have updated their beliefs and now reject the proposition "Jones is qualified." However, the group's position is determined by what results from the appropriate group processes. Thus, before their next meeting when they can take into account the new information qua hiring committee, the group still accepts the proposition, "Jones is qualified."

In this case the group belief and the beliefs of the individuals do diverge. Nevertheless, the non-divergentist can argue that this is only because of an epistemic failure on the part of the group. If the group has not taken into account new information available to the individual members, then the group is failing as an epistemic agent. It is failing to do what is necessary to ensure that it accepts the true and rejects the false, i.e., it is failing to consider all the relevant available evidence. And, thus, case A fails to show that divergence is possible in the case of epistemic acceptance.

---

[20] As with agency simpliciter (see e.g., Pettit 2007), there is no bright line that distinguishes a *really poor* epistemic agent from something that fails to be an epistemic agent altogether. Here I show that both the group and the individual may be clearly good (though not perfect) epistemic agents, and yet differ on which propositions they accept.

In response to this argument it can be pointed out that being a slow epistemic agent does not mean one is not an epistemic agent at all. Suppose, for instance, that the signals from my sense of smell take a minute to be processed once they get to my brain. In that case, part of me may "have" information that would change my cognitive state, but it has not yet been taken into account. I would be a rather inefficient epistemic agent, but I don't see why in principle it would mean that I am not an epistemic agent at all. We can argue along similar lines that the group is a slow or intermittent epistemic agent. There are periods where it is not processing information and updating its beliefs. This being the case, however, one might argue that at the time of the purported divergence the group is failing to exercise its epistemic agency, thus, this is not a genuine case of divergence after all. Given these objections, let us put this sort of case aside.

Let's focus on the time at which all the members have whatever available evidence there is and they are deliberating as a group. Could it be that one or more of the individuals has access to evidence that the group as a whole lacks? We might ask how this is possible; how could it be that an individual member has information that the group does not? It would seem that the member is failing in her epistemic obligations to the group if she does not share her evidence with the group. However, this may not always be the case, for instance, consider the following scenario:

Case B: The hiring committee decides to use the following procedure for coming to their group decision. Each member is to give reasons in a discussion and come to a group consensus based on shared reasons. Suppose, however, that one or more of the individual members receives confidential information that is not available to the group as a whole.[21] The information contains a defeater for the proposition that Jones is a qualified candidate. Each agent reasons appropriately on the basis of the evidence they have. Qua members of the hiring committee the individuals collectively reason only on evidence available to the group as a whole. However, since they

---

[21] We can even imagine a case where all the members know the additional information, but this fact is not common knowledge.

are reasoning on differing evidence sets, the group accepts the proposition that Jones is qualified, while one or more of the members withhold judgment on the proposition, or perhaps even reject it.

The non-divergence advocate might object that, in this case, the evidence available to the individuals is excluded for a *non-epistemic* reason. So, one or more of the members of the committee does not believe that the procedures of the group are those that would lead to accepting the true and rejecting the false. If the members were committed to the group being as fully epistemically rational as they can make it, the group would be using all available relevant evidence in its deliberations. So, the divergence between the group and the individual is due to the failure of the group members to ensure that the group acts in an epistemically appropriate way.

This argument is not compelling. It is not true that, in order to act in an epistemically appropriate way, one must have access to all possible information. We in general accept that there are moral constraints on the sorts of information to which we may have access. This does not mean that no moral agent can be an epistemic agent. It just means that our epistemic agency, like our practical agency, is constrained within the bounds of morality. If we really thought that our highest duties were epistemic ones, then we would have no reason for research ethics, privacy laws, etc. Not only does it seem appropriate that enquiry and evidence gathering be kept within the constraints of morality, it does not strike me as in any way anti-epistemic to do so. To be an epistemic agent is not to be *only* an epistemic agent or to place the epistemic good above all other values.

Whatever one thinks of case B, we are not dependent on it to show that there may be divergence. Evidence may be excluded from group reasoning for purely epistemic reasons, as in the following case:

Case C: The hiring committee uses the same belief formation process as described above. Some piece or pieces of information possessed by the individuals have been excluded from consideration in the process of group reasoning, because the group's epistemic standards reasonably exclude such information. However, the individuals still form their beliefs based on the totality of the evidence they have been exposed to. Thus, the group may accept the proposition that Jones is qualified, while the individuals fail to believe that he is qualified.

This case needs a bit more elaboration, because it may be unclear why anyone would exclude evidence from consideration if the concerns were purely epistemic. Ought not a rational epistemic agent consider the totality of the available evidence? Not necessarily.

We see numerous examples of this in the legal system. For instance, juries are frequently asked to "disregard" certain information or are not given access to available evidence in the first place. While in some cases this may be for procedural reasons or to deter rights violations on the part of authorities (e.g., the exclusion of evidence from an illegal seizure), in other cases it is because such evidence is thought to be prejudicial. The rationale for excluding such evidence from consideration during the jury's deliberative process is that such evidence will actually make them *less* likely to come to the correct verdict (Goldman 1999: 292-295). However, while members may genuinely disregard information in their deliberations *as a jury* (e.g., by not presenting it in their group deliberations as a reason for or against, or by holding people accountable for their votes by requiring reasons based on admissible evidence),[22] they may not be able to do so "personally." That is, a juror may form the belief that the defendant is guilty based on some hearsay evidence that was inadvertently revealed during the trial. But, the juror may nevertheless feel bound to base his comments during deliberations and his vote as a jury member only on the evidence that the judge has said should be considered.

A similar sort of situation could arise in the case of the hiring committee. There is some empirical evidence that interviewing candidates in person actually leads to poorer hiring decisions than would be made if one restricted one's evidence to their written materials (see e.g., Bishop and

---

[22] Note that I am saying that juries are capable of doing this, not that they always will.

Trout 2005). Suppose then, that the hiring committee interviews Jones, and then reads the Bishop and Trout paper. They are convinced by Bishop and Trout's arguments and they now believe (individually and collectively) that the committee will make a better decision if the information gained through the interview is excluded. So, in their group reasoning they explicitly make an effort to disregard any information they gained from the interview. Nevertheless, as individuals they may not be able to force themselves to forget the impression they got from that interview. The familiar fact of doxastic involuntarism[23] that *human* epistemic agents are prey to makes this a plausible hypothesis.[24]

The non-divergentist might argue that, once again, some agents in this situation are failing to be epistemically rational. If evidence is misleading, then it should be excluded by the individuals in their personal reasoning as well as by the group. When individuals fail to exclude the information in their personal deliberations, then they are failing to act rationally as epistemic agents. Thus, as above, the only reason the group view and the individual views diverge is that one or the other is failing to be fully epistemically rational. In this case it is one or all of the individuals who are failing to be fully epistemically rational. Of course, this does not show that either the group or the members are failing to be epistemic agents. As noted above, epistemic agency does not require that one be a perfect epistemic agent. Nevertheless, it would be preferable if we could show that the group belief can diverge from the members' personal beliefs without either being open to the charge of an epistemic failure of this sort. Otherwise, we will be in the position of arguing that groups may form epistemic agents, but that when they do it is only in cases where there is some epistemic failure, either on the part of the group or on the part of the individuals.

---

[23] See e.g., Alston 1988.

[24] Bernard Williams (1973) has argued that what I have been calling an "epistemic agent" must be one whose doxastic states are involuntary: see Mathiesen 2006 for an argument against this view.

4. Time Lag

Suppose we limit ourselves only to cases where neither the group nor the individuals could be open to the charge of epistemic irrationality. If both the group as a whole and the individual members are not open to epistemic criticism, can the outcome of the group epistemic process differ from the views of the individual members? I believe that they can—consider the following case:

Case D: The hiring committee adopts a different procedure for combining their individual judgments. As part of this procedure; (1) the members do not discuss the case together, (2) each member is given access to the same set of evidence to consider, (3) each member's vote is weighted based on their past reliability and their confidence level in their vote.[25] The members are so confident in their group procedures that they reasonably believe that their collective judgments are likely to be more reliable than their individual judgments. The calculations are run by a computer, which delivers the results directly to the department chair. The members will have to check their e-mails before they know what the results of the calculations are. Two of the members take the "withhold judgment" position, while one takes the "accept" position. However, given the greater past reliability and confidence of the one member who says "accept", the weightings result in a group position of "accept."

It may be thought that once the individual members know the results of the procedure the members will update their beliefs. Given their reasonable confidence in the reliability of the group procedure, they will all personally accept the proposition. Thus, there will be no divergence. But, this is where the time-lag comes in. Before the individuals know the results the following situation holds: the group accepts the proposition, but two out of

---

[25] For a discussion of such weighted voting procedures, see e.g., Goldman 1999: 81-82.

the three members withhold judgment. Thus, there is a divergence between the epistemic acceptances of the individuals and the group.[26]

In this case the non-divergentist may argue that, while the department chair has information about the *result of a group process* that the hiring committee engaged in, the resulting proposition is not *the group's* view. The argument goes like this. For some agent to have a belief (or any doxastic state), at the very least, the belief must be available to the agent for orienting itself in the world—e.g., for further reasoning and acting. The only way that a group can act and reason is through its members. If the members do not even know what the group belief is, then the group cannot act and reason on the basis of this belief. Thus, until the members know what the belief is, the group does not believe it. In other words, a condition on group belief (or acceptance) is common knowledge on the part of the members of what the group belief is.

Based on this argument, the non-divergentist may argue that to say that a group accepts a proposition implies that there is common knowledge among the members of what is accepted. If there is such common knowledge, then the individuals will have updated their beliefs to agree with that of the group. Thus, there will be no divergence between the beliefs of the group and that of the individuals who form the group.

5. Differing Epistemic Risk Tolerance

Interestingly, the issues we are running into here are very similar to those discussed by philosophers who work on disagreement (see e.g., Kelly 2005, Christensen 2006, and Feldman 2006). If we think of the group and each of its individual members as distinct epistemic agents then our question is, how can equally epistemically rational agents end up with divergent views? In particular, can they end up with divergent views even though the

---

[26] If the members are not epistemically required to update their beliefs in this way, then this case would not rely on the time lag. This would strengthen my argument by adding a second case of divergence.

same evidence is available to them? Drawing from work on *epistemic value theory*, below I show how two or more fully epistemically rational agents with access to the same evidence may end up with diverging views on a particular proposition. Before proceeding, however, I will need to briefly discuss the idea of "epistemic risk."

In his 1962 paper "On the seriousness of mistakes," Isaac Levi describes two types of epistemic agents—those who "do not consider avoiding error to be very important at least as compared to the importance of eliminating doubt" and those who are "less anxious about getting an answer"(p. 56). He explains that, "The chief difference between the first truth seeker and the second is that the latter takes mistakes more seriously in relation to eliminating doubt than the first. We might describe the situation by saying that both individuals are attempting to replace doubt by true belief but that they exercise different 'degrees of caution' in doing so" (p. 56).[27] Others have called these different degrees of caution that epistemic agents may observe differences in their tolerance for "epistemic risk." While some have given models of epistemic agency that implicitly assume some particular epistemic risk profile, many have argued that there may be reasonable disagreement among epistemic agents about the preferred attitude toward epistemic risk taking (Fallis 2007).

In a recent paper, Joshua Riggs (2008) argues that this fact about reasonable differences in tolerance for epistemic risk may lead to reasonable differences in the doxastic states of epistemic agents. As Riggs puts it,

> "[T]wo fully informed and reflective people could rationally disagree about whether p. If one of them is more of an epistemic risk-taker than the other, then presumably there will be cases where the evidence is suf-

---

[27] Later in the paper (pp. 58-63), Levi describes these variable degrees of caution as the relative concern with type I or type II errors and how they factor into the setting of the significance level when looking at evidence from experiments. As Levi puts it, "a low significance level reflects the fact that the investigator takes mistakes very seriously relative to suspending judgment. On the other hand, a high significance level indicates that the investigator is anxious to relieve his doubts. Thus, the level of significance can serve as a rough index of the degree of caution exercised in search for the truth" (p. 63).

ficient to make belief in p rational for that person, yet would allow only suspension of belief for a more epistemically cautious person. If each were aware of their respective proclivities toward epistemic risk, it seems that each person could accept the other's doxastic stance toward p as reasonable, while under no rational pressure to change his own." (Riggs 2008: 8).

If we consider the group and the individuals as distinct agents, then it is possible that the epistemic risk tolerance of the hiring committee differs from the tolerance of its individual members. These differences in epistemic risk settings may be due to their different pragmatic interests. Epistemic risk settings may reasonably be shaped by such pragmatic factors (see e.g., Fallis 2006; Levi 1962: 57). As we saw at the beginning of the paper, there is little disagreement that groups may function as practical agents. A practical agent has certain goals or interests. In the case of the hiring committee, its practical goals have been determined by the charge from the departmental committee to determine a set of "qualified" candidates for the position. The practical goals of the members may be quite different from those of the group. For instance, the individuals may "personally" prefer to be very skeptical that anyone is truly qualified. But, given that *as a group* they need to present a set of names to the department, such skepticism would be out of place in group reasoning.

The hiring committee may, for example, find it better to either rule in, or rule out, a candidate than to simply withhold judgment. Since the practical job of moving forward with the search process only requires that *the committee* makes a judgment, the members have the luxury of playing it safe epistemically speaking and withholding judgment. Note that we are not saying that the committee is accepting the proposition for pragmatic reasons. They are accepting the proposition based on their goal to accept the true and reject the false, but their willingness to accept the epistemic risk of falling into error is higher than that of the members qua individuals. Thus, it takes less evidence to move them from withholding judgment to acceptance.

Now we are ready to consider our final case:

Case E: The members and group have different epistemic risk settings with regard to accepting the proposition, "Jones is a qualified candidate." These risk settings determine how much evidence is necessary for acceptance. So, while both the individuals and the group as a whole consider precisely the same evidence and they assign the same weight to the evidence, the group reaches its threshold for acceptance while no individual member has reached her threshold for acceptance. And, since there is no epistemically preferred threshold, both the group and the members are equally epistemically rational.

Conclusion

I have tried to present a plausible argument that groups may function as independent epistemic agents by showing that they can accept propositions, where that acceptance is not shorthand for saying that all or most of the members (personally) accept that proposition. If the above arguments are successful, a barrier in the way of accepting the view that groups can be epistemic agents has been removed. This opens up a broader field for the evaluations of epistemic agency. In particular, it gives us stronger reasons to think that we may treat groups (at least in some cases) as epistemic agents in their own right. As a result, we will need to develop more sophisticated ways of addressing group epistemic agency and to consider how group processes, and not just individual member attributes, may contribute to agents that perform in epistemically virtuous or rational ways. Take for instance, a group of scientists who, working together over a period of time, have been highly accurate in their collective findings. Suppose we want to understand what epistemic virtues are connected to their epistemic success. One way we can do this is by looking at the individual epistemic virtues of the members. This approach makes sense if what the group accepts is equivalent to what each member individually accepts. But, if what the group accepts is not so reducible, we should look at the *group's* epistemic

42

virtues.[28] This would require that we develop an account of group epistemic virtue. We would need to answer such questions as, what constitutes collective wisdom, creativity, and open-mindedness.

Bibliography

Adler, J. (2008), "Epistemological Problems of Testimony". *The Stanford Encyclopedia of Philosophy*, Edward N. Zalta (ed.), http://plato.stanford.edu/archives/fall2008/entries/testimony-episprob/.

Bishop, M. A. and Trout, J.D. (2008), *Epistemology and the Psychology of Human Judgement*. New York: Oxford University Press.

Christensen, D. (2007), "Epistemology of Disagreement: The Good News". *Philosophical Review* 116, 187-217.

Fallis, D. (2006), "Epistemic Value Theory and Social Epistemology". *Episteme* 2 (3), 177-188.

——— (2007), "Attitudes Toward Epistemic Risk and the Value of Experiments". *Studia Logica* 86 (2), 215-246.

Feldman, R. (2006), "Epistemological Puzzles about Disagreement". In: S. Hetherington (ed.), *Epistemological Futures*. Oxford: Oxford University Press, 216-236.

Gilbert, M. (1987/1996), "Modeling Collective Belief". In: *Living Together: Rationality, Sociality, and Obligation*. Maryland: Rowman and Littlefield, 195-214.

——— (1989), *On Social Facts*. Princeton: Princeton University Press.

——— (1994), "Remarks on Collective Belief". In: F. Schmitt (ed.), *Socializing Epistemology: The Social Dimension of Knowledge*. Lanham: Rowman and Littlefield, 235-255.

——— (1996), "More on Collective Belief". In: *Living Together: Rationality, Sociality, and Obligation*. Maryland: Rowman and Littlefield, 339-60.

——— (2000), "Collective Belief and Scientific Change". In: *Sociality and Responsibility: New Essays in Plural Subject Theory*. Maryland: Rowman and Littlefield.

——— (2002), "Belief and Acceptance as Features of Groups". *Protosociology* 16, 35-69.

——— (2004), "Collective Epistemology". *Episteme* 2 (1), 95-107.

Goldman, A. (1999), *Knowledge in a Social World*. New York: Oxford.

---

[28] See Lahroodi 2007 for a fuller discussion of collective epistemic virtues.

———— (2004), "What is Social Epistemology? A Smorgasbord of Projects". In: *Pathways to Knowledge: Private and Public*. Oxford: Oxford University Press, 182-204.

Greco, J. (2008), "Virtue Epistemology". The Stanford Encyclopedia of Philosophy. Edward N. Zalta (ed.), http://plato.stanford.edu/archives/fall2008/entries/epistemology-virtue/

Hakli, R. (2006), "Group beliefs and the distinction between belief and acceptance". *Cognitive Systems Research* 7 (2-3), 286-297

Kelly, T. (2005), "The Epistemic Significance of Disagreement". *Oxford Studies in Epistemology* 1, 167 - 96.

Lahroodi, R. (2007), "Collective Epistemic Virtues". *Social Epistemology* 21 (3), 281 - 297

Lehrer, K. (1990), *Theory of Knowledge*. Boulder, CO: Westview.

Levi, I. (1962). "On the Seriousness of Mistakes". *Philosophy of Science* 29 (1), 47-65.

———— (1977), "Epistemic Utility and the Evaluation of Experiments". *Philosophy of Science* 44, 368-86.

Maher, P. (1990), "Acceptance without belief". *Philosophy of Science Association* 1, 381–92.

———— (1993), *Betting on Theories*. New York: Cambridge.

Mathiesen, K. (2006), "Epistemic Features of Group Belief". *Episteme* 2 (3), 161-175

McMahon, C. (2003), "Two Modes of Collective Belief". *Protosociology* 18/19, 347-62

Meijers, A. (2002), "Collective Agents and Cognitive Attitudes". *Protosociology* 16, 70-85.

———— (2003), "Why Accept Collective Beliefs? Reply to Gilbert". *Protosociology* 18, 377-388.

Pettit, P. (2007), "Rationality, Reasoning and Group Agency". *Dialectica* (61) 4, 495-519.

Preyer, G. (2003), "What is Wrong With Rejectionists?" In: Interpretation, Sprache und das Soziale: Philosophische Artikel (Interpretation, Language and the Social: Philosophical Articles). Frankfurt am Main; Humanities Online, 237-255.

Riggs, W. D. (2008), "Epistemic Risk and Relativism". *Acta Analytica* 23 (1), 1-8.

Searle, J. (1995), *The Construction of Social Reality*. New York: The Free Press.

Schmitt, F. (1994), "The Justification of Group Beliefs". In: F. F. Schmitt (ed.), *Socializing Epistemology: The Social Dimensions of Knowledge*. Maryland: Rowan and Littlefield, 257-288.

Tollefsen, D. (2002a), "Challenging Epistemic Individualism". *Protosociology* 16, 86-117.

―――― (2002b), "Organizations as true believers". *Journal of Social Philosophy* 33, 395-410.

―――― (2003), "Rejecting Rejectionism". *Protosociology* 18-19, 389-405.

Tuomela, R. (1992), "Group Beliefs". *Synthese* 91, 285-318.

―――― (1995), The Importance of Us: A Philosophical Study of Basic Social Notions. Stanford: Stanford University Press.

―――― (2000), "Belief versus Acceptance". *Philosophical Explorations* 2, 122-137.

―――― (2004), "Group Knowledge Analyzed". *Episteme* 2 (1), 109-127.

Williams, B. (1973), "Deciding to Believe". In: *Problems of the Self: Philosophical Papers 1956-1972*. Cambridge: Cambridge University Press, 135-151.

Wray, K. B. (2001), "Collective Belief and Acceptance". *Synthese* 129, 319-333.

―――― (2003), "What Really Divides Gilbert and the Rejectionists?" *Protosociology* 18-19, 363-376.

Collective Epistemic Agency: Virtue and the Spice of Vice

ANITA KONZELMANN ZIV

Abstract

The paper evaluates Christopher Hookway's claim that individual epistemic vice can enhance the value of collective epistemic virtue. I suggest that this claim can be defended on the grounds of a dynamic account of collective intentional properties that is supplemented by an account of a spontaneous ordering mechanism such as the "intangible hand". Both these accounts try to explain how individual traits integrate into collective traits by way of aggregation. In this respect, they are different from normative and summative accounts of plural subjects. I argue that it is the repeatable and self-amplifying nature of character traits that calls for a dynamic account of collective virtues. With regard to epistemic virtues and their role in the acquisition of knowledge I hold that their dynamic and self-amplifying character warrants their reliability, since it is this character that bottoms out in repeated acts of epistemically correct behavior that constitute a 'responsible practice'. The successful appliance of the latter amplifies the attitude it origins from. If epistemic virtues construed along these lines are attributed to collectives, a dynamic aggregate account supplemented by an account of an "intangible hand" device might explain how an aggregate of virtuous efforts of individuals can not only absorb a certain amount of vice but be even enhanced by the 'spice' of some non-intentional epistemically vicious side effects of epistemically virtuous endeavor.

1. Introduction

With the rise of Virtue Epistemology, analyses of knowledge and requirements for justification refocus on epistemic subjects and their properties. Virtue Epistemologists claim that the normative dimension of knowledge is mainly aretaic in nature and needs to be accounted for in terms of responsible epistemic agents and their virtues. Virtue accounts generally agree on virtues being complex properties involving characteristic patterns of thought, appropriate emotions, and right actions. They further agree on virtues being gradual phenomena whose obtaining requires the features mentioned to be present in the right degree.[29] Virtues are characterized, for example, as being a "deep and enduring acquired excellence of a person, involving a characteristic motivation to produce a certain desired end and reliable success in bringing about that end" (Zagzebski 1996, 137) or as "acquired base of excellent functioning in some generically human sphere of activity that is challenging and important" (Roberts & Wood 2007, 59). For Virtue Epistemologists one such virtue relevant sphere is the whole of epistemic activity, which can be subdivided into the realms of acquiring, maintaining, communicating and applying beliefs (Wood 1998, 33-53). Lists of epistemic virtues therefore contain skills and traits applicable in these kinds of activity, such as open-mindedness, foresight, wisdom, prudence, understanding, creativity, discernment, discretion, love of truth, and so on.[30] Accordingly, gullibility, superstition, closed-mindedness, etc. count as epistemic vices. Some virtue theories further distinguish between "faculty virtues" and "character virtues", while other theories do not subsume faculties to the concept of virtue (Baehr 2006). It is commonly agreed that, roughly, people can be praised for displaying both these types

---

[29] * I would like to thank the participants of the conferences "Epistemic Agency" (Geneva, 25-26 April 2008) and "Collective Epistemology" (Basel, 3-5 October, 2008) for discussions on draft versions of this paper that helped me clarify some points. I also thank Marcel Weber for helpful comments on the present paper.

"Classical Greek philosophers distinguished between moral virtue, moral strength, moral weakness, and moral viciousness. Morally vicious persons are flawed in thought, word, and deed [...]. Morally weak persons suffer from what the ancients called *akrasia* (weakness of will). They [...] lack a motivational structure of sufficient strength and development to move them to act virtuously. Morally strong persons judge rightly with respect to moral matters but must nevertheless struggle with temptation and contrary inclination. Morally virtuous persons not only judge and feel appropriately but move easily to act in morally appropriate ways; for such persons doing the right thing constitutes a 'default mode'" (Wood 1998, 45f).

[30] Wood lists the *motivational* virtues of inquisitiveness, honesty, tenacity, love of truth and teachableness, as well as the *dialectical* and *pedagogical* virtues of insight, articulateness, creativity, precision, eloquence, charity, sincerity and humility, and the *organizational* virtues of administration, foresight, strategy and problem solving (*op.cit.*, 33-53).

of properties, while they can be blamed only for the absence of "character virtues" but not for the absence of "faculty virtues" (or faculties). This distinction is based on the assumption "that character traits are those dispositions over which we can exercise certain types of control" (Lahroodi 2007, 284).

In this paper I shall investigate the question of whether and how a virtue epistemological account can be extended to collective agents. This question arises when Virtue Epistemology meets Collective Epistemology, which is another recently opening field within theories of knowledge. Collective Epistemology explores the view that epistemic agency is not restricted to natural individuals, but extends to groups and institutional collectives as well. Reasons given for this view draw on a conception of epistemic agents as "deliberators", being "subject to epistemic assessment" and, consequently, "subject to the immediacy that is characteristic of reason" (Tollefsen 2004, 55f.). Epistemic assessment implies the possession of a "rational point of view" from which epistemic agents can "assess their own attitudes for consistency, truth, and intelligibility" (op.cit., 56). This rational point of view is considered a "unique locus of power and responsibility", marked by the first person concept (ibid.). Given that the first person concept admits not only for singular but also for plural specification, so the argument goes, the plural specification "we" enables this locus of epistemic power and responsibility to shift from oneself to a group (op.cit., 64, note 11). In scientific research and other epistemic processes that involve joint individual contributions the rational point of view is distributed "within and across" collectives to the effect that certain reasons become salient "from the first person plural perspective" of group goals and, as such, have "immediacy" for individuals in function of their group membership (op.cit., 60).

Collective agency and plural subjecthood in general have been extensively discussed in the last 30 years, often under the label of Collective Intentionality. The central difficulty with attributions of intentionality to collectives is resumed in the question of how to integrate individual intentional states into collective intentional states. This question becomes particularly salient when we turn to affective intentionality, since feeling is considered to be one of the most intimate ways in which an individual person experiences herself.[31] While a number of philosophers are ready to concede the possession of genuine conative and cognitive states to collective subjects, many of them shy away from attributing genuine affective states in the same way.[32] With these preliminaries in mind, let us now turn to the question of whether the conception of collective epistemic agency reasonably allows reference to virtuous character traits, given that the latter essentially involve affectivity. This question comes to the fore in the following passage of Christopher Hookway's paper *How to be a Virtue Epistemologist* (2003):

> It is easy to see that communities may also possess virtues – facilitating debate and regulating the progress of investigations – which may not be reducible to the virtues of the individuals who belong to them. [...] What would be vices in individual inquirers may be virtues when possessed by members of a team (Hookway 2003, 189).

Let me resume this quote in the following twofold claim:

i)   Collectives possess genuine (epistemically relevant) virtues;

ii)   Through their integration into collective virtues individual vices (or virtues) might undergo a transformation of value.

It seems to me that the claim is not very controversial or interesting if virtues were construed as skills or faculties for the absence of which one can-

---

[31] Hans Bernhard Schmid takes it that "individualism about feeling is a deep-seated conviction that permeates not only most theories of affectivity, but large part of our pre-theoretical views (i.e. folk psychology) as well" (Schmid 2008, 68). He outlines three different versions of individualism about feeling, namely ontological, epistemical and physical individualism, and shows how these attitudes contributed to the deep "research lacuna" with regard to collective affective intentionality (*op.cit.*).

[32] Attributing possession of genuine intentional states to collectives roughly means considering collectives as instances of a kind which counts the possession of irreducible intentional states among its characteristic properties.

not be blamed. For the following discussion of Hookway's claim I will, therefore, assume a meaning of "virtue" in terms of character traits. This requires a reformulation of i) and ii):

i') Collectives possess genuine (epistemic) character traits;

ii') Through their integration into collective character traits individual character traits might undergo a transformation of value.

Claim i') calls for a discussion of epistemically relevant traits and the role they play in the acquisition of knowledge. Claim ii') focuses on the polarity and gradual nature of such traits, relating these two features to the problem of integrating individual states into collective states. Accordingly, I will treat, in a first step, some features of epistemic virtues that seem relevant to me with regard to their possible applications to collective subjects. In a second step, I will present two accounts of collective subjects and point out why the second seems better suited to meet the conditions for character trait ascriptions. The concluding part is intended to show how such an account could justify Hookway's twofold claim.

2. Epistemic virtues and collectivity

"The central claim of virtue epistemology is that, Gettier problems aside, knowledge is true belief which results from a cognitive virtue" (Greco 1993, 413). According to this statement of one of the main proponents of Virtue Epistemology, the added value of knowledge over true belief is due to specifically cognitive virtues involved in the generation of the belief. It is argued that epistemically virtuous behavior is a necessary and in many contexts even a sufficient condition for knowledge attribution if the virtue "plays a *critical* or *salient* role in getting a person to the truth, [...] if it *best explains* why a person reaches the truth" (Baehr 2006, 198). Virtue Epistemology assumes that the force of epistemic virtue will rule out the imponderabilities inherent in inductive reasoning, to the effect that the involvement of virtue can justify attributions of knowledge in contexts the settings of which are not essentially probabilistic. On the other hand, the account forbids attributions of knowledge in cases where beliefs are *only* accidentally true, that is when the processes leading subject S to a true belief do not encompass any virtuous epistemic behavior on the side of S.[33]

For a better appraisal of the significance of epistemic virtues I will briefly discuss a few central issues coming into play here. Firstly, it is worth noting that it is still an open question whether epistemic virtues shall count as subclass of moral virtues or whether they are categorically distinct from the latter. While Linda Zagzebski, another main proponent of Virtue Epistemology, defends an Aristotelian inspired unified view of moral and epistemic (or intellectual) virtues, Julia Driver argues that invoking the goal of a good human life for both kinds of virtues is construing too broadly the concept of unification. Driver holds that the moral and the epistemic mode of normative evaluation are fundamentally different, in spite of their structural similarities and intersections. Her argument mainly draws on cases of genuine conflict or incompatibility between moral and intellectual virtue, on cases of (moral) "virtues that require ignorance, or rest on epistemic defect" (Driver 2000, 131). The examples given include modesty which "requires the agent to *underestimate* self-worth", or charity which may "sometimes rest upon the agent overestimating the good in others". Here, epistemic virtue is put on a level with "full awareness" of certain qualities relevant for the appropriate evaluation of a situation (*ibid.*). In contrast, the unified view considers epistemic virtues as moral virtues manifested in activities that are specifically truth-directed.

A classical example for a virtue that regularly appears in discussions of epistemic virtuous behavior is courage. The unified account takes it that if a person S is courageous she will also display courage if, for example, she has to defend a truth against strong but bad counterarguments. Courage displayed in a situation where the challenge is of specifically epistemic nature is epistemic courage, hence an epistemic or intellectual virtue. The upshot of this view is that a person who lacks epistemic courage in

---

[33] For a detailed discussion of these issues see Greco 2003.

comparable situations is to be blamed. In general, a unified view takes it that "we criticize others for their beliefs as well as for their actions" and that we are more inclined to criticize beliefs than feelings or desires (Zagzebski 1996, 5). According to Zagzebski "such criticism is much closer to *moral* criticism than the criticism of bad eyesight or poor blood circulation" for which standard "non-moral labels" are used (*ibid.*). Against the unified view it has been argued, however, that we are naturally much more hesitant to blame people for epistemic than for moral shortcomings.[34] This fact seems to imply that either we consider epistemic matters not as morally relevant matters, or we take epistemic virtues to be similar to natural faculties and talents, rather than to character traits. The latter option was prevalent in the early days of Virtue Epistemology which then was dominated by reliabilism and its concern for the role of reliable processes in matters of justification and knowledge. Ernest Sosa and other pioneers in the domain used the term "virtue" almost synonymously with "faculty". In the meantime, the increasingly 'responsibilist' tendency in the domain of Virtue Epistemology made shift the term's meaning more to the end of a character trait.[35] My taking side for a *character trait* account of epistemic virtues basically rests on the assumption that the term "virtue" is generally applied to character traits such as honesty or courage, but not to faculties such as good memory or good eyesight.[36] Even if the latter contribute in

---

[34] "[T]here does seem to be a difference in how we praise and blame when invoking epistemic versus moral norms. We are more forgiving for epistemic defect" (Driver 2000, 132).

[35] For more details on the development of responsibilist Virtue Epistemology see, for instance, Axtell 2000b and Baehr 2006.

[36] Jason Baehr points out an epistemically more important difference between character virtues and faculty virtues: "There is a natural correspondence between particular faculty virtues and particular fields of propositions. [...] it makes good sense to speak of 'visual propositions', 'introspective propositions', 'a priori propositions', 'memory propositions', and the like. But character virtues are fundamentally different from faculty virtues in this respect. [...] This is due to certain uniquely 'situational' aspects of these traits. [...] The virtues of intellectual caution and carefulness, for instance, might be required in one situation to reach the truth about a proposition which in another situation could be known only via an exercise of intellectual courage and perseverance. [...] In contrast with faculty virtues, the relevance of a character virtue to a particular

relevant ways to epistemic success, I would not label them "epistemic virtues". Epistemic virtues understood as character traits definitely have ethical implications, while other epistemically relevant properties have not.

Secondly, I take it for uncontested that epistemic virtues – like all virtues – are dispositional in nature, and that, functionally, they are motivational states. Virtues differ, however, in their structure from many other kinds of dispositions. One important point is that we ascribe a good many dispositional properties on purely counterfactual reasons. For example, there is no difficulty in stating and believing that a certain crystal glass is fragile, even if the glass in all the years it belongs to the family never ever gave a proof of its fragility. With virtues, the case is different. We would hardly say that S is courageous if we never saw S behaving courageously or otherwise came to know that S was behaving so. Ascriptions of a character property C to person S seem to require some recordings of S's factually displaying C. A second and apparently related feature of character traits is the fact that displaying character trait C – that is manifesting disposition C – is repeatable and usually amplifies property C in its bearer S. By contrast, dispositions such as fragility or solubility are not repeatable for a given object, and many other dispositions that are repeatable – such as the disposition of a door to be opened – are not substantially modified by their manifestations. Virtues, in contrast, are dynamic and self-amplifying dispositions to act in accordance with an internally hold value. Courage, for example, is the property motivating a person to take a risk for, say, the value of justice or – in epistemic contexts – for the value of knowledge.

It seems, then, that virtues have to be accounted for not only in terms of their being dispositional but also of their being realized in adequate virtuous behavior. Attributing a virtue V appears to be attributing a complex of characteristic patterns of thought and appropriate emotions, together with a record of V-pertinent actions A_V. The set of doxastic and emotional

---

field of propositions is not given by the content of the propositions themselves. This is reflected in the fact that it makes little sense to speak of 'intellectual courage propositions', 'fair-mindedness propositions', etc." (Baehr 2006, 208).

dispositions that constitute a complex disposition to act in a certain way given certain circumstances provides the evaluative and motivating force of a virtue V. Actualized, this complex disposition leads to a behavior that 'closes', so to speak, the motivation opened by the occurrence of V-specific circumstances. Satisfying the motivation fueled by V, the virtuous action A_V and its rightness are well-founded in V.

Thirdly, like all virtues epistemic virtues are gradual properties with a positive and a negative polarity. If courage becomes too strong, it tends to turn into the vice of daredevilry; if it is too weak it is likely to drift towards the vice of cowardice. Lists of epistemic virtues mirror this conception of polarity and conceptual vagueness, opposing traits such as open-mindedness, foresight, wisdom, prudence, understanding, creativity, discernment, discretion, love of truth, etc., to traits such as gullibility, superstition, closed-mindedness, etc., listed as epistemic vices. Without going in all details of epistemic virtue approaches here, it is worth noting that the emphasis on virtues in the genesis of knowledge highlights the idea of agency and personal responsibility in epistemic matters, as well as the fact that there are choices in the epistemic realm that will influence the causation of correct beliefs. Stressing the role of motives to behave in an epistemically upright way, a virtue account further emphasizes the import of the values held in one's epistemic community.

A last feature I wish to point out concerns the reliability of epistemic virtues. In epistemological contexts, the reliability of belief generating processes is invoked to ensure a systematic link between the truth conditions of the proposition asserted in a belief and the belief. Reliability here is understood to circumscribe the high regularity of law guided processes that are generally not disturbed in any significant manner. Alternatively, the term 'reliability' seems to integrate the 'all things considered' clauses of inductive generalizations. The reliability of law guided mechanisms in belief producing processes is supposed to warrant knowledge by ruling out those cases of conformity between a truth T and a belief 'T' in which conformity obtains for purely random reasons. The merit of reliabilism goes hand in hand with its drawback: while it succeeds in ruling out Gettier problems for knowledge ascription, it rules out as well the subjective component of knowledge. The epistemic subject S of a reliably justified belief may – subjectively – have wanting reasons to believe T. Whether S attributes to herself the state of knowing T or not, in the reliabilist view she would be justified in doing so even if the justifying process is not transparent to her. This is an epistemically unsatisfying result that responsibilist versions of reliabilism try to remedy by building (at least part of) the knowledge relevant reliability into cognitive virtues. Epistemic virtue thus not only captures the condition of indispensable subjective responsibility for appropriate knowledge ascription but also brings the condition of reliability – so to speak – under adequate subjective control. Cognitive virtues, then, give rise to knowledge because they are reliable and their reliability results from epistemically responsible doxastic practices.

This characterization stresses, on the one hand, the interdependence between a virtue and certain practices and, on the other hand, the claim of an internal relation between the reliability of a virtue and actual responsible behavior. It loops back, so to say, to the second point I made with regard to epistemic virtues, namely that the truth conditions of virtue ascriptions seem to involve some recordings of the virtue being factually displayed. I further assumed that – in contrast to many other dispositional properties – displaying a virtue is repeatable and self-amplifying. In the light of the aforementioned we could say, then, that the dynamic and self-amplifying character of epistemic virtues warrants their reliability, since it is this character that bottoms out in repeated acts of epistemically correct behavior. Repeated acts of epistemically correct behavior constitute a "responsible practice" the successful appliance of which amplifies the attitude it origins from. If epistemic virtues are construed along these lines, they can be considered constitutive elements in an account of knowledge.

What is the impact of all this on the topic at issue here, the topic of collective epistemic agency and the possibility of collective epistemic virtue? Remember Hookway's twofold claim that i) communities possess genuine (epistemic) virtues, and ii) vices in individual inquirers can be virtues when possessed by members of a team. In order to evaluate these claims let us first ask whether the features of epistemic virtues summed up so far can reasonably apply to groups or collective agents in general. The features identified were:

- Character trait – V is a virtue in the ethically relevant sense: showing a lack of V gives reason to be blamed;
- Complex dispositional property – V is a dynamic and self-amplifying complex of cognitive and emotional dispositions that motivates and is satisfied by behavior A_V;
- Gradation and polarity;
- Reliability: V regularly bottoms out in virtue adequate behavior A_V;
- Epistemic relevance – trait V and behavior A_V are salient features in the pursuit of knowledge.

Assuming that the *blame* for a lack of virtue first and foremost concerns the lack of virtuous behavior and not the lack of the virtue in its purely dispositional form allows to reasonably ascribing epistemic virtues to collectives. It is uncontested that collectives such as research groups do have specified epistemic goals and display specific behaviors in the pursuit of these goals. Hookway's assumption of collectives having genuine epistemic virtues is based on the fact that many epistemically relevant processes – *e.g.* discussion – even presuppose plural agency, and on the fact that epistemic communities have an overall influence on individual learning and belief processing. Such facts seem to entail the existence of genuine collective epistemic properties and traits, for example the virtuous trait of "facilitating debate". Given that debating is not an individual's property, we seem committed to ascribe the virtue of "facilitating debate" to some collective agent. It is certainly plausible to consider collectives as epistemic agents in their own right and, consequently, to evaluate their epistemically relevant behavior in terms of efficiency, seriousness, honesty, etc. It seems, then, that groups can be blamed for a lack of epistemically responsible (or virtuous) behavior, and that they can be praised for displaying an epistemically responsible behavior. Examples of collective epistemic character traits displayed in a trait specific behavior are given in the following terms: "The investigative committee was patient and tenacious. It followed up on all the potential leads"; "The review board was courageous in questioning what everyone took for granted".[37] These descriptions link statements of observed behavior with ascriptions of character traits such as courage, patience and tenacity. But unless we defend an exclusively behaviorist account of internal states, the descriptions still leave open the question of whether groups or collectives as such are the bearers of epistemic virtues in the full sense of the term, that is, whether they have internal character traits that qualify personhood. And unless we agree that ascriptions of internal character traits to collectives are somehow metaphorical, we must try to give an account of how individual personal character traits are to be integrated into collective traits and/or the behavior into which they bottom out.

3. Collective subjecthood

a) Margaret Gilbert's normative account

Margaret Gilbert and Deborah Tollefsen were the first to shape the label "Collective Epistemology"; they both defend the view that collectives as rational agents are genuinely *intentional* subjects. In his "Groups with Minds of their own" Philip Pettit augments the rationality and intentionality of "social integrates" explicitly to even institutional *personhood*, arguing that "rational unification is a project for which persons must be taken to assume responsibility" (Pettit 2003, 185). Since social integrates do display the behavior required for personhood – *i.e.* make avowals of intentional states and actions and acknowledge them as their own – Pettit concludes "that they are institutional persons, not just institutional subjects or agents" (*ibid.*). Tollefsen however argues on the basis of Strawson's account of "participant reactive attitudes" that ascribing responsibility does not neces-

---

[37] Lahroodi 2007, 282.

sarily imply personhood: "I do not think organizations are persons or could be persons. [...] I argue that, because organizations are interpretable, our assumption of rationality is justified, and hence organizations are rational agents with rational points of view" (Tollefsen 2002, 408, note 10). Whatever stance we might take toward the question of institutional or group personhood, it seems uncontroversial that Gilbert's strong "plural subject" account of collectives abets notions of group personality or group character. Gilbert's "plural subject" account is essentially normative, holding that a distribution of individuals will become a "plural subject" in virtue of a specific normative act of "joint commitment".[38] As the ruling principle of plural subjecthood, joint commitment requires that each member "must openly express his or her readiness to be jointly committed with the relevant others", and that all members "understand themselves to have a special standing in relation to one another" such that "no individual party [...] can rescind it unilaterally" (Gilbert 2002, 126f). The normative force of the "joint commitment" to behaving, believing or feeling "as a body" requires adopting a non-distributive "We-attitude", that is, a plural first person perspective that cannot be analyzed in terms of the individual members' I-perspectives. Gilbert claims, for example, that a group G in circumstances C can have a genuine belief that p, without any of G's individual members holding the belief that p.[39] The normative force of the "joint commitment", then, seems to cut off inferential relations between the group's We-belief and the individual members' I-beliefs. A group belief in this account resembles those classes of beliefs that are not rationally justified, but rather warranted by certain types of *prima facie* justification. If a group belief is considered a belief in the sense of being an intentional belief, *i.e.* is more than just a declarative speech act, then it seems to be a belief that is *prima facie* justified by the act of joint commitment, just as – according to certain

---

[38] "A and B (and...) (or those with feature F) constitute a plural subject [...] if and only if they are jointly committed to doing something as a body – in a broad sense of 'do'" (Gilbert 2006, 144f).

[39] "It is not a necessary condition of a group's belief that p that most members of the group believe that p. Indeed, [...] it seems that it is not necessary that any members of the group personally believe that p" (Gilbert 1987, 191).

views – perceptual beliefs are *prima facie* justified by perceptual experience or axiological beliefs by emotional experience. A group belief $'p_G'$ then is not an epistemological state in the sense of being the result of a reasoning process, but a state enacted by a normative act of jointly committing to believe p as a body, meaning roughly that the group members declare that p "at all public points of their lives" and behave at these points as if they were convinced of the truth of p (Gilbert 1987, 198).

Exploring the possibility of collective character traits such as epistemic virtues or vices we might ask whether these traits can be enacted in the same way as intentions and beliefs are supposed to be enacted. An account of virtues as complex properties involving thought, emotion, and action seems to entail this possibility, since virtues then could be enacted by ways of a joint commitment to displaying the right thought, the appropriate emotion and the right action. To a certain degree, such an approach is encapsulated in Gilbert's account of collective guilt feeling, which is given in terms of a joint commitment to appropriate judgments (acknowledging blameworthiness for one's acting) and reparative action. The account is based on a cognitivist theory of emotion according to which an emotion's essential component is an evaluative judgment and its essential function is to motivate action. The cognitivist theory allows accounting for emotions in terms of beliefs and intentions, which, in turn, allows applying the "joint commitment" approach of collective believing and collective intending to collective 'emoting'. Within this framework, the virtuous character trait of feeling guilt for having wronged someone is open to the normative constraints of enactment by joint commitment.[40]

Normative theories of collective properties emphasize that such properties are to be clearly distinguished from aggregates of individual properties. They usually hold that the binding unity of a collective state cannot result from "simple aggregation", but needs some additional under-

---

[40] For further details of Margaret Gilbert's account of collective guilt see Gilbert 2002.

pinning.[41] This is certainly right but not incompatible with aggregate accounts of collective properties that are not flatly summative but give due weight to the integration of individual into collective properties. Often, aggregate accounts are presented as merely 'flashing' on a momentary distribution of individual states, taking the collective state as the sheer sum of these momentary individual states. In such a static set-theoretical picture of an aggregate state no necessary relation between the individual states seems to hold. Therefore, so it is argued, an aggregate approach cannot account for the individuals' responsibility to comply with the collective state. Moreover, a mere summative account of a collective character property is of no help to our present purpose of evaluating Hookway's claim. Given that vices and virtues stand in polarity relations of gradual increase and decrease, the intuitively plausible second part of this claim – that individual shortcomings of epistemic virtues (or individual epistemic vices) can contribute to an increase in collective epistemic virtue – is at odds with the concept of a mere summative property. Within the frame of a summative property, low levels of an individual virtue or a 'negative' virtue value (vice) can only diminish the collective virtue value.

The claim of a value modification of individual traits by their integration into a collective trait obviously challenges the static character of a summative construal of aggregate properties and calls for a dynamic model of aggregation. Yet for the same reason the claim challenges the normative account of the properties of "plural persons". Even if we assume that individual properties and traits play a significant role in the process leading to the "joint commitment" that enacts a collective property, the normative account takes it that once the property is enacted it is not subject to further

---

[41] Margaret Gilbert distinguishes "groups" or "collectives" as genuine "plural subjects" from "populations" that are mere "aggregates" or feature-defined sets of individuals (Gilbert 2002, 134f.). "Aggregative accounts" of collective guilt in terms of "personal guilt" and "membership guilt" she takes to be wanting. Philip Pettit distinguishes "integrated collectivities" or "social integrates" as "institutional persons" from "aggregations of people", "aggregated collectivities" or just "aggregates" which "do not reason at all or that do not impose the discipline of reason at the collective level" (Pettit 2003, 178).

modification by individual properties. Since the collective property is not dependent on individual properties but solely on a normative act, it is a rigid property that remains unchanged until a modification is enacted by a new normative act of "joint commitment". The collective property, although engendered by a "joint commitment", is not a malleable joint or shared property. Given its characteristics, the normative account –just like the summative construal of aggregate properties – provides only static collective properties. Unless there is a "joint commitment" (with its features of explicitness and public expression) to modifying a collective property, say virtue V_C, the latter will not be modified. It is difficult to see how an account that cannot integrate the various shades and degrees of individual states deals with a claim such as Hookway's according to which individual traits are transformed by their integration into a collective trait.

The normative model with its conception of a disconnection of collective from individual states admittedly applies to contexts of corporate collectives, especially with regard to the maxims upon which they agree to act and their declared principles. With regard to evaluative states and attitudes, however, the conception is problematic, and even more so if the collective considered is not corporate-like. As psychological research suggests, the intuitive taxonomy used to comprehend collectives roughly comprises four types of groups: "intimacy groups (e.g. family), task groups (e.g. a work team, a jury), social categories (e.g. women, the upper middle class) and loose associations (baseball fans, people in line in a post office)" (Lahroodi 2007, 284). These categories are said to be distinct in their degree of "entitativity", that is the extent to which a collective "is perceived as being a coherent unit in which the members [...] are bonded and united together in some fashion" (*ibid.*).[42] Interestingly, it is not "task groups" or

---

[42] Apparently, the term "entitativity" here is used in the sense of "integrative tightness", and not in the sense of individuality or unity which cannot come in degrees. It is "the *integrity or wholeness* of something" that comes in degrees and in many varieties, depending on "certain specific relations among the parts of the object" (Simons 1987, 326). Differences in "integrative tightness" can cause, however, "degrees of warrant for accepting the existence of an individual composed of certain parts" (op. cit., 331).

corporate collectives that show the highest degree of entitativity, but "intimacy groups". And, as this research further suggests, entitativity is closely correlated not to normative acts of "joint commitment" but to the dynamics of perceived interaction between individual members (*ibid.*).

The normative account's problem of disconnection between collective states and individual states becomes conspicuous when the properties ascribed to collectives are virtuous traits. The account of virtues given in the first section takes virtues to be highly complex phenomena that involve thought, feeling and intending and are, furthermore, polar and gradual. The span of trusting, for example, ranges from the (epistemic) virtue of confidence to the vice of gullibility, or from confidence to systematic disbelief. Whether a token of trust in the truth of a given proposition p displays an epistemically virtuous or a vicious state depends on many situational parameters. This is similar to character polarities such as courage and recklessness, or courage and cowardice. An agent courageous in circumstances C is able to ideally combining different attitudes in view of the situation at hand. His overall way of acting may well include behavior susceptible to be interpreted as recklessness or cowardice. With regard to collective agency, the complexity of virtuous traits even increases if individual traits V_I are considered as ingredients of a collective trait V_C. If, on the other hand, due to its enactment by a "joint commitment" the collective virtue V_C does not comprise the individual traits V_I, it can scarcely cope with the complexity of V-states. Do individual members have to jointly commit to being reckless to a certain degree and to be coward to a certain degree in order to be jointly committed to being courageous as a body? Is it plausible to assume that the enactment of a collective virtue entails the commitment to being vicious to a certain degree?

b) The Lehrer-Wagner model of dynamic aggregation

As I suggested before, the challenge of attributing virtues to collectives cannot be met by static accounts of collective properties. This applies both to summative accounts which focus on a momentary distribution of individual properties, and to normative accounts that emphasize the enactment of collective properties by a "joint commitment" which bars the latter from integrating individual properties and from modification. Attributing complex properties such as virtues to collectives calls for a dynamic model of "collective persons". It is true that character traits such as virtues are considered relatively stable dispositions that are expected to bottom out in reliably predictable patterns of behavior. They are not, however, immune to change and modification. Personal character traits are subject to continual adjustments and the dynamics of self-reinforcement. If this is true with respect to natural individuals, it is even more so with respect to collective or plural persons. An account of collective character traits cannot neglect the traits of individuals involved, and it cannot neglect the dynamics of the relations and interactions between these individuals and their traits. It seems to me that the model of social aggregates and aggregation worked out by Keith Lehrer and Carl Wagner provides a powerful tool for the analysis of virtue ascriptions to collective persons. The Lehrer-Wagner model is a dynamic account of social aggregation that holds a good balance between ontological claims concerning collective persons and their traits on the one hand and the commitment to scientific theories about the psychic and neurophysiologic endowment of natural individuals on the other hand.

For the present purpose, I draw on a version of the Lehrer-Wagner model presented in Keith Lehrer's paper "Individualism, Communitarianism and Consensus" (Lehrer, 2001). There, Lehrer tackles the question of whether explanatory primacy for achieving a common goal – for example consensus with regard to A – should be assigned rather to individual or to collective contribution. The answer given is that an appropriate dynamic modeling of consensus creating processes makes either claim for primacy vanish in the "magic of mathematics". Why? Because the dynamic model of the process leading to the common achievement consists in an iteration matrix of mutual value attribution according to which each individual's allocations become continually "encumbered" with those of all other individuals involved (*op. cit.*, 115). Therefore, it is pointless to insist that a given state within this aggregation process is an individual or a collective state: "The individual allocations and the communal allocations are identical and symmetrical" (*ibid.*).

The core of the Lehrer-Wagner model is the mutual assignment of a certain value or weight with regard to a personal allocation. The example used to account for consensus is about two people who need to consent on the distribution of a given amount of money. Each of them assigns a certain weight of decision (value between 0 and 1) to herself and to the other person. These assignments determine the individual allocations converging in each loop of iteration. In Lehrer's wording: "Each person, *j*, would assign a weight , to each other person, *k*, at each state *s*. Thus the allocation for person *j* resulting from aggregating from state *s* to *s*+1 is as follows (*op. cit.*, 116):[43]

$$A_j^{s+1} = A_1^{s} w_{j1}^{s} + A_2^{s} w_{j2}^{s} + \ldots + A_n^{s} w_{jn}^{s}$$

The decisive idea is that in each loop of iteration (in each state *s*) the weights w_j^{s} assigned by each person, *j*, to each other person are factored into new aggregates of individual allocations A_j^{s+1}, so that the latter become more and more permeated ("encumbered") by a collective factor. These aggregates are not mere sums of individual states, but rather their "amalgams" (*ibid.*) and, hence, can count as both "individual allocations" and "communal norms".[44] Lehrer's approach is similar in some respect to Michael Bratman's account of "shared intentions" according to which shared intentions are explicable in terms of a web of interlocking individual intentions: "Shared intention ... is not an attitude in any mind. ... Rather it is a state of affairs that consists primarily in attitudes of the participants and

---

[43] 'A' stands for aggregate allocation; subscripts mark persons, superscripts mark iterative states 0, 1, 2 of aggregation (*op.cit.*, 113).
[44] For the example used – George and Mary and their allocating a certain sum of money to two different charities – Lehrer assumes that the weight assigned to the other is held constant, but that it is "for them to decide in each state" (*op.cit.*: 114).

interrelations between these attitudes" (Bratman 1993: 107f). According to Bratman, the state of shared intention is generated when individuals mutually aim "at the efficacy of the intention of the other" (*op. cit.*: 109) and hence "bring into the content" of their own intentions the efficacy of the other intentions (*op. cit.*: 104). This structure allows for a sort of mutually controlling one's intending and acting, so that it is plausibly called "we-intending" or "shared intending".[45]

In the Lehrer-Wagner model, however, the mutual "encumbering" takes a more global dimension than Bratman's mutual "bringing in" the intentions of others into the content of one's own intention. While Bratman's model of "shared intention" is framed by a belief-desire model of action, Lehrer's model of reaching collective states calls in addition for emotional acts and attitudes. Often, the required assignments of values are mainly emotional evaluations, and we can assume that the mutual touch of the feeling implied connects people more effectively into enduring personal aggregates than mere goal-driven intending. In an earlier version of the Lehrer-Wagner model, value assignment is explicitly related to the affective attitude of trust.[46]

4. Collective virtue and vice – intentional aggregation and non-intentional integration

The double complexity of collective character traits – the complexity of virtues and vices on the one hand and the complexity of collective properties on the other hand – calls for a dynamic model of shared personal states. A model that integrates affective acts and attitudes is promising when it comes to account for collective virtues in general. In order to answer the more specific question involved in Hookway's claim, *i.e.* how contributions of individual vice can increase collective virtue, the model seems in need of amendment by some account of a spontaneous ordering

---

[45] For further details see also Bratman (1997).
[46] See Lehrer 1997.

mechanism. I therefore suggest to first applying the Lehrer-Wagner model to the constitution of collective virtues in general and then to consider in a second step what else is needed to tackle the problem of modifying the values of individual contributions. With regard to the first part of the task, we can simply substitute "collective virtue" to the goal of "consensus" in the model, and "character weight" to the "weight of competence" which individuals mutually assign to each other in the process. The dynamic model then shows how the parties will approach the goal of a collective epistemic virtue V_E in repeated loops of converging aggregation, where iteration is both a function of each person's j "allocation" of V_E and a value of "character weight" which each individual j attributes to each other person k at each state s. For reasons of compatibility with ethical requirements it must be assumed, however, that in the process of character 'consensualization' the "weighing" of others' traits in relation to a given "allocation" is not intentional or conscious on all its levels. Why is that so?

A first step in answering this question is that no matter how we may think about the ontology of collective properties, it does not seem a good move to develop an account of collective (epistemic) virtue that cannot be reconciled with individual ethics. The dilemma is that, on the one hand, Hookway's claim has a strong intuitive plausibility, while, on the other hand, it seems to engender the implausible commitment to cultivate individual vice for the sake of an increase in collective virtue. For if collective virtues can be improved by some ingredient of individual vice, is it not an ethical duty to cultivate individual vice in order to comply with the collective aim of maximal collective virtue?

In Hookway's approach, individual epistemic vice appears like a spice which, as ingredient of common epistemic activity, improves the quality of the latter. Just as a good dish depends on good spicing – that is on proper amounts of constituents that improve its quality without being the stuff a substantial dish is made of – the good quality of epistemic activity depends on proper amounts of constituents that, by themselves, could not count as valuable. The problem for the collective virtue dish is that a commitment to contribute in the best possible way to achieve a maximal value of collective virtue seems to entail that individuals are able to ad-measure in a controlled way the right kind and amount of vice to be added. This in turn entails the ability to assess the value of all the individual traits involved in a given collective situation, including the assessment of the expected amount of vice that other participants intend to admeasure to their contribution. If such assessment is taken to be fully intentional, it cannot but lead into a regress of mutual evaluation that is formally similar to the regress of mutual belief. Additionally, if we assume that character assessments are fallible, a commitment to cultivate some amount of individual epistemic vice in order to achieve a high level of collective epistemic virtue is at constant risk of over- or underspicing. Since both these outcomes are rather vicious than virtuous, a commitment to cultivate epistemic vice hopelessly perverts the superior value of the optimal outcome.

Maintaining the claim of a beneficial integration of epistemic vice into collective epistemic virtue apparently calls for an additional ordering principle which supplements the dynamics of mutual character evaluation and virtue convergence. Often, ordering principles for such emerging phenomena with heterogeneous character cannot be stated in terms of law like procedures. Instead, it is useful to invoke spontaneous ordering mechanisms known under the label "invisible hands". According to Geoffrey Brennan and Philip Pettit who investigate spontaneous ordering in the sense of self-sustaining or self-regulating patterns in human affairs, the ordering of "invisible hands" is supported by "decentralised and contingently non-intentional" means of "behavioural control" (Brennan & Pettit 1993, 191f). "Invisible hands" produce aggregate effects that can be either intended – as in the case of driving conventions – or unforeseen – as in the case of the littered beach or the congested road (*op.cit.*, 201-205).

For our purpose, however, invisible hand mechanisms operating on the basis of intentional (*i.e.* contingently non-intentional) control are not the ideal type of supplementary ordering principle. We do not seek to explain how intentionally guided virtuous behaviour of individuals leads to collective vice, or how intentional vicious behaviour of individuals leads to collective virtue. Rather, we need to explain how essentially non-intentional vicious by-products of intentional virtuous behaviour can enhance the resulting aggregate virtue. Again, from an ethical point of view, the global aim of individual intentional endeavour must be maximal virtue – both under the collective and the individual perspective. The global aim of maximal virtue is formally similar to the global aim of maximal consensus with regard to a certain issue. Consensus, as we have seen, can be achieved when the parties involved approach this goal in repeated loops of continuous aggregation of their continuously encumbered allocations. The global aim of maximal virtue requires that individuals allocate virtues that they intentionally cultivate. Epistemically virtuous agents cannot plan to intentionally cultivate epistemic vices for the purpose of 'spicing' collective virtue. If they display some amount of epistemic vice – and they will – vice occurs as non-intentionally formed by-products of belief-producing processes and other epistemic activities.

From a virtue ethical point of view, this non-intentional character of the vice involved is an important feature. Beneficial integration of non-intentional vice into the intentionally pursued goal of virtue aggregation requires, I suggest, an account of a spontaneous ordering mechanism which mainly orders *non-intentional* attitudes. Brennan and Pettit actually develop such an account by distinguishing the regime of an "*intangible* hand" from the regime of an "*invisible* hand" defended in the established accounts. In distinction to the "invisible hand" that operates through means of intentional control, the "intangible hand" is a system "that exploits our natural, more or less approbative or disapprobative dispositions and puts them into effect in generating certain aggregative results" (Brennan & Pettit 1993, 206). Here, the operative means of behavioral control are supposed to be not only "decentralised" but also "essentially non-intentional", consisting in simply giving a degree of positive or negative regard to motives, traits or goals of others. The "intangible hand" account resorts to so called "regard-motivation" prompting the individual responses that are relevant for the aggregate effects. "Intangible hand" mechanisms are supposed to work on presumptive grounds, on the basis of the possibility of one's acting being assessed by (dis)approving observers.[47] Due to the attitudinal character of the individual responses that produce the associated results, devices of this kind are qualified as "intangible": "The attitudinal responses in play lack the palpable quality of actions and that is why we describe the devices as intangible" (*op.cit.*, 209). Brennan and Pettit hold that "intangible hand" devices are paradigmatically operative in the "committee arrangement" of a jury, where they make, for example, "conscientiousness more probable … among the members of a jury" (*op.cit.*, 213). Thereby, the committee arrangement "serves to activate the motivation in three steps: by making conscientiousness a salient good; by making it a presumptive dimension of assessment; and by making it a feasible dimension of assessment" (*ibid.*).

For our purpose this conception of an ordering "*intangible* hand" seems an appropriate means to supplement a Lehrer-Wagner style model in accounting for the dynamics of convergent aggregate character traits. The suggestion is that the regime of an "intangible hand" comes into play by spontaneously admeasuring non-intentional vicious by-products of intentionally formed virtuous attitudes, with the effect of either neutralizing them or integrating them beneficially into the intentionally pursued aim of a collective virtue. Ethics requires to intentionally cultivating virtues, but spontaneous mechanisms such as "intangible hands" are needed to balance the contributions of individual traits in aggregate processes. By absorbing the shortcomings of unintentional vice, they can ensure the coherence between collective virtue and individual virtue in spite of some individual deviant behavior.

Taking collective virtues as ethically relevant character traits excludes both explaining them by means of an enactment by "joint commitment" and accounting for them merely in terms of aggregates created by

---

[47] "People … may reward or penalise a sort of behaviour just by being in a position to observe, and be assumed to observe, it" (Brennan & Pettit 1993, 208).

the spontaneous mechanisms of "invisible hands". While the first account focuses on observable behavior at the expense of motivation, the second involves a haphazardness that allows recasting well intentioned individual attitudes into vicious aggregate attitudes and *vice versa*. Both accounts allow that a collective behaves in a 'virtuous' way while its individual members do not intentionally pursue the path of virtue. The problem with this approach is that measuring collective virtue in terms of mere factual behavior contradicts the rich concept of virtue which includes attunement to the good and a motivational force flowing from it. A sparse conception of virtue in purely behavioral terms cannot meet the requirements of personal character traits. If epistemic virtues shall count as character traits that dispose their bearers to pursue the epistemically good, and if they are traits for the absence of which one is to be blamed, it is impossible to ascribe them to collectives without demanding that they are coherent with individual attunement to the good and its corresponding motivation. Attributing ethically relevant character traits to collectives requires admitting intentional coherence, in the sense that individual intentions, beliefs and emotions must align with the collective character. Intentional coherence allows, however, for factual deflections from these ruling attitudes. Such deflections may result from individuals struggling with their weaknesses in pursuing the intended goal, from unfavorable situational parameters, or from the need to adapt to being continually "encumbered" with personal character traits of other participants. Factual deflections are neither intended nor used as means to modify the collective character. They 'happen' to be (essentially) non-intentional attitudes and/or behavioral patterns integrated by mechanisms of an "intangible hand" into the intentionally pursued aggregate effect. This construal aligns with claims to the effect that the sanctions involved in an "intangible hand" device "may be effective without serving as the actual reasons why members tend to be conscientious rather than not", and that they "may be effective through being stand-by supports" activating "regard-motivation without deactivating other, more powerful motives" (Brennan & Pettit 1993, 209).

Hookway exemplifies his claim that the vices of individual inquirers can be virtues when possessed by members of a team in the following words: "A research team may benefit from having some members who are dogmatic, and unwilling to take on board new possibilities, while others are much more ready to take seriously seemingly wild speculations" (Hookway 2003, 189). Here, the virtue of the research team – say its open-mindedness – appears as a sort of ideal distribution of the intentional virtues and non-intentional vices of the individual team members. Without some vicious traits of individual dogmatism, for example, the team's overall virtue of open-mindedness could tilt over into haphazard consideration of just anything. This could hardly count as epistemic virtuous behavior and might turn out very costly with regard to the team's efficiency. If, on the other hand, speculations were banished altogether from the team's activity, it could well happen that no innovative idea replenishes their research. It is true, however, that both dogmatism and wild speculation are attitudes that epistemically virtuous agents must not intentionally pursue.[48] They just are unavoidably given in our epistemic condition and, as such, they are admitted as factual deflections of more moderate intentional attitudes. Up to a certain degree, they can be integrated beneficially into a collective epistemic trait by the ordering mechanisms of an "intangible hand". Yet the "intangible hand" only does the 'spicing' of an aggregate which, in order to be essentially virtuous, must result from a process aggregating intentionally virtuous constituents.

---

[48] Hookway's use of the terms "unwilling" and being "ready to take seriously" something seems to suggest that his conception of a collective virtue does not require intentional coherence between individual and collective traits. If this is correct, the collective virtue is probably seen as result of the ruling of some "invisible hand" mechanism. As I argued before, I do not think that such an account can explain, say, open-mindedness of a research group as being a virtue in the ethically relevant sense of a character trait.

Bibliography

Axtell, G. (2000a), *Knowledge, Belief, and Character – Readings in Virtue Epistemology*. Lanham/Boulder/NY/Oxford: Rowman & Littlefield.

——(2000b), "Introduction". In: Axtell 2000a, xi-xxix.

Baehr, J. S. (2006), "Character, Reliability and Virtue Epistemology". *The Philosophical Quarterly* 56 (223), 193-212.

Bratman, M. (1997), "I intend that we *J*". In: R. Tuomela and G. Holmstrom-Hintikka (eds.), *Contemporary Action Theory*, vol. II: *Social Action*. Dordrecht: Kluwer, 49-63.

——— (1993), "Shared Intention". *Ethics* 104 (1), 97-113.

Brennan, G. and Pettit, P. (1993), "Hands Invisible and Intangible". *Synthese* 94 (2), 191-225.

Driver, J. (2000), "Moral and Epistemic Virtue". In: G. Axtell (ed.), *Knowledge, Belief, and Character – Readings in Virtue Epistemology*. Lanham/Boulder/NY/Oxford: Rowman & Littlefield, 123-134.

Gilbert, M. (2006), A Theory of Political Obligation: Membership, Commitment, and the Bonds of Society. Oxford: Clarendon.

——— (2002), "Collective Guilt and Collective Guilt Feelings". *The Journal of Ethics* 6/2, 115-143.

——— (1987), "Modelling Collective Belief". *Synthesis* 73, 185-204.

Greco, J. (2003), "Knowledge as Credit for True Belief". In: M. DePaul and L. Zagzebski (eds.), *Intellectual Virtue. Perspectives from Ethics and Epistemology*. Oxford: Clarendon Press, 111-134.

——— (1993), "Virtues and Vices of Virtue Epistemology". *Canadian Journal of Philosophy* 23 (3), 413-432.

Hookway, C. (2003), "How to be a Virtue Epistemologist". In: M. DePaul and L. Zagzebski, (eds.), *Intellectual Virtue. Perspectives from Ethics and Epistemology*. Oxford: Clarendon Press, 183-202.

Lahroodi, R. (2007), "Collective Epistemic Virtues". *Social Epistemology* 21 (3), 281 – 297.

Lehrer, K. (2001), "Individualism, Communitarianism and Consensus". *The Journal of Ethics* 5, 105–120.

——— (1997), Self-Trust – A Study of Reason, Knowledge, and Autonomy. Oxford: Oxford University Press.

Pettit, P. (2003), "Groups with Minds of Their Own". In: F. Schmitt (ed.), *Socializing Metaphysics*. New York: Rowman & Littlefield, 167-195.

Roberts, R.C. and Wood, W.J. (2007), *Intellectual Virtues: an Essay in Regulative Epistemology*, Oxford: Clarendon Press.

Schmid, H. B., Schulte-Ostermann, K., and Psarros, N. (eds.) (2008), *Concepts of Sharedness: Essays on Collective Intentionality*, Heusenstamm: Ontos.

Schmid, H. B. (2008), "Shared Feelings – Towards a Phenomenology of Collective Affective Intentionality". In: H. B. Schmid et al. (eds.), *Concepts of Sharedness: Essays on Collective Intentionality*. Heusenstamm: Ontos, 59-86.

Simons, P. (1987), *Parts: A Study In Ontology*, Oxford: Clarendon.

Tollefsen, D. (2004), "Collective Epistemic Agency". *Southwest Philosophy Review* 20 (1), 55-66.

——— (2002), "Organizations as True Believers". *Journal of Social Philosophy* 33 (3), 395-410.

Wood, W. J. (1998), Epistemology – Becoming Intellectually Virtuous, Leicester: Apollo.

Zagzebski, L. (1996), Virtues of the Mind – an Inquiry into the Nature of Virtue and the Ethical Foundations of Knowledge, Cambridge: Cambridge University Press.

PART II

An Account of Group Knowledge

RAIMO TUOMELA

1. Introduction

The main task of the present paper is to investigate the nature of collective knowledge and discuss what kinds of justificatory aspects are involved in it to distinguish it from collective belief.[49] The central kind of collective knowledge investigated in the paper is normatively binding group knowledge. A distinction is made between natural knowledge and constitutive institutional knowledge. In the case knowledge of the latter kind, in contrast to the former kind, justification and the criteria of justification are purely social. Knowledge is regarded as a primitive, irreducible notion that accordingly does not fall prey to Gettier-type paradoxes.

The paper also sketches a view of social epistemology that takes as its central notion impersonal knowledge which is independent of particular knowers but must still be based on the fact that some actual knowers have the knowledge. Epistemic justification relative to a group is first characterized for the strong, "we-mode" case that requires an epistemically justifying joint reason for the acceptance as true of a knowledge claim. Later a more general account applicable also to other kinds of groups is given. Based on the notion of epistemic justification, knowledge attributable to groups as well as knowledge attributable to individuals is accounted for.

One can speak of knowledge in an impersonal sense: It is accepted as knowledge that copper expands when heated, that Helsinki is the capital of

---

[1] Parts of this paper draw on Tuomela (2004) but the paper has been almost completely rewritten, and some of the analyses of the present paper do not fully agree with what was said in the earlier paper. As the paper attempts to deal with a relatively large problem area, proper in-depth argumentation concentrates on some key questions.

Finland, and that no one under 18 years of age is entitled to vote in national elections. Such knowledge of course is not an abstract entity floating around in some kind of Platonic "third world". Rather it is knowledge that some actual agent or agents actually have or have had as contents of their appropriate mental states (belief states) and that others on this basis can have as their knowledge. People find out things either by themselves or together, and often what they come to believe about the world is true and more or less well-grounded, thus knowledge much in the sense of traditional epistemology. We may say then that there is *collective knowledge* in groups or communities, e.g. in the scientific community, that such and such is the case. In some cases it can even be said that *groups as groups know*; and in all these cases there must be or have been actual individual knowers.

Section 2, *The We-mode Approach to Sociality*, and Section 3, *Group Knowledge: Some Central Ideas,* sets the stage for the epistemological discussion in the paper by introducing some central underlying notions. Section 4, *Theses on Group Knowledge*, gives the epistemological preliminaries of the paper. Section 5, *Epistemic Group Reasons and Joint Reasons*, gives an analysis of reasons attributed to group and joint reasons attributed jointly to group members. Section 6, *Achieving Group Knowledge*, discusses some aspects of rational group knowledge acquisition. Section 7, *A General Account of Group Knowledge*, analyzes group knowledge in more general terms. Section 8, *Group-Binding Group Knowledge* discusses both strongly and weakly binding group knowledge. Section 9 concludes the paper.

2. The We-mode Approach to Sociality

The notion of a group knowing as a group will be central for the purposes of this paper. To be able properly to discuss this matter, I will start by more general remarks on how to conceptualize social life in the most adequate way.

I distinguish between two kinds of "we-thinking" (forming thoughts and reasoning concerning group contents) and accordingly two kinds of collective intentionality: we-mode and I-mode collective intentionality. Here the I-mode involves individualistic "I-thinking) and "I-acting" primary to further one's own interests, which may involve thinking and acting for the benefit of the group and thus be in the "pro-group" I-mode. I have elsewhere argued that in many cases full-blown we-thinking is required on several grounds, including functional grounds.[50] We-thinking and collective intentionality in its full, "we-mode" sense (involving a "togetherness-we" as the subject of thoughts and actions) forms the core of human sociality. Below I will argue for its epistemic benefits.

The we-mode approach is based on the intuitive idea that the acting agent in central group contexts is the group viewed as an agent capable of action, and the individual agent conceptually is not the primary actor but rather a representative acting for the group. A group can thus be instrumentally viewed as a group agent in view of its members being capable of jointly and uniformly produce outcomes. While the we-mode group (an organized group capable of action) can be regarded as an agent from a conceptual and justificatory point of view, ontologically it exists only functionally as a social system capable of producing uniform action. It is an intentional agent only in the sense that mental attributes are extrinsically attributed to it, and it can only function through its members' functioning appropriately.[51] The group is here and in most contexts later in the paper assumed to be a "we-mode group" capable of functioning as a unit. A we-

---

[50] See Tuomela (1984; 1995; 2000), and especially (2007), for the we-mode approach.

[51] Such a social agent system, viewed as an entity, in general is not reducible to the individuals' monadic or (inter)relational properties. This holds true at least if no "positional" structural elements such as positions, offices, and roles are involved on the "jointness level" ("meso level" as distinguished from the proper "macro level" with group attributes and structures).

The social agent system is not literally a collective agent (person) because its lacks the ontological features of full-blown human agents—e.g. it does not have a body and cannot have "raw feels" and strictly speaking a mind. Thus it lacks the phenomenology of real agents. However, from a conceptual point of view we may speak of it as a quasi-agent.

mode group is accordingly assumed to commit itself to a group "ethos" (certain constitutive goals, beliefs, standards, norms, etc.) and to acting accordingly. It constructs itself as a group in a quasi-entifying sense.[52] This intuitive picture can be explicated for the group-member level and seen to involve three central ideas in analogy with a single intentional agent. When a single agent acts intentionally it acts on purpose, or for a reason intending and thus being committed to an end. It also acts in coordinated way as a unit. Corresponding to a single agent's reason, commitment, and coordinated part actions, we have in the group case an *authoritative group reason*, *collective commitment*, and the satisfaction of a *collectivity condition*. To wit, at the group-member level the group members function as group members largely as if they were intentionally functioning parts of an organism. The very idea of group membership in the case of an organized group such as a we-mode group entails that the members ought to act as proper group members and try to satisfy its ethos in a committed way as a group. Because of this, the ethos gives them their central reason for acting as group members. The reason is an authoritative one at least in cases in which the group members themselves have participated in the creation of the ethos by their collective acceptance and thus, so to speak, given up a relevant part of their "natural" authority to the group. Furthermore, qua members of a group agent, the group members will necessarily "be in the same boat" when acting as group members. This will be explicated by the

---

[52] Here is my account of we-mode groups in Tuomela (2007: 19):

A collective g consisting of some persons is a *(core) we-mode social group* if and only if

(1) g has accepted a certain ethos, E, as a group for itself and is committed to it. On the level of its members, this entails that at least a substantial number of the members of g have as group members (thus in a broad sense as position-holders in g) collectively accepted E as g's (namely, their group's, "our") ethos and hence are collectively committed to it, with the understanding that the ethos is to function as providing authoritative reasons for thinking and acting qua a group member;

(2) every member of g "group-socially" ought to accept E as a group member (and accordingly to be committed to it as a group member), at least in part because the group has accepted E as its ethos;

(3) it is a mutual belief in the group that (1) and (2).

collectivity condition, the satisfaction of which comes about through the members' collective commitment to the ethos and action on the basis of this commitment.

We can use group level language to illustrate the central conceptual idea of *collective acceptance* (as true of something). To recall, the group is assumed to accept an ethos with commitment to its satisfaction and maintenance.[53] On the group-member level, this amounts to the group members' performative collective acceptance (indeed, collective construction) of an ethos (e.g. a goal) as the group's ethos (goal) to which they collectively commit themselves, where collective commitment accordingly is "reasoned" by the group ethos and where collective commitment also involves the members' being directedly socially committed to each other to functioning as group members, typically to furthering and maintaining the ethos.[54] We-mode thinking, "emoting", and acting accordingly presuppose reflexive collective acceptance ("construction") of the group's ethos and often also of some other, nonconstitutive content as the object of the group's attitudes. The collectively accepted contents in general are for the use of the group and can be assumed to further its interests. In all, the members are assumed to view and construct their (we-mode) group as an entity guiding their lives when their group membership is salient, and it also requires them to function as ethos-obeying and ethos-furthering group members.

In contrast, an I-mode group is not in general based on the members' collective construction of their collective as their group but is rather based on the members' private acceptance of goals, beliefs, etc. and is made up of the members' interdependencies and interaction. As a detailed account

---

[53] Collective acceptance of the ethos can here be taken conceptually to be analogous to a performative (or "declarative") speech act that has the world-to-mind direction of fit of semantic satisfaction and thus makes the ethos goal-like. At the same time it will also have the mind-to-world direction of fit as giving and being—or being analogous to— an assertion.

[54] Cf. the somewhat different account and defense of the importance of joint commitment by Gilbert in her 1989 book and later works.

of I-mode groups will not be central below, I will not discuss them further here.

3. Group Knowledge: Some Central Ideas

Knowledge in the personal case involves abilities and skills at least in the case of ordinary knowledge. If a person knows that p she must have reasons for the truth of p and be able to use p in her reasoning and action—at least to some extent. I will below regard it as right to say, at least in the ideal case, that personal knowledge entails justified true belief, although this is not strictly a defining feature of knowledge and although the converse entailment is not claimed to hold and indeed can be assumed not to hold (as e.g. the Gettier paradoxes indicate).

I will require below that a *full-blown* knower has the concept of knowledge, viz. belief with good reason, although admittedly small children and higher animals may be taken to "know"—in a *shallow* sense that does not involve having the concepts of knowledge, belief, or good reason. The shallow sense must still involve some of the right overt behavioral and "reliability" aspects of knowing.

In the conceptual framework of this paper, there will be a putative knower and an evaluator of knowledge—indeed, in principle indefinite many evaluators. A knower, be it a social group or a single agent, will be considered mainly from the point of view of the epistemic criteria—or the epistemic "perspective"—it employs. We can speak of groups (qua quasi-agents) both as knowers and as attributors of knowledge; and we can take groups to represent epistemic perspectives (criteria and standards of epistemic justification) and be social "carriers" of epistemic perspectives. Arguably, justified knowledge about factual natural matters can only be obtained by the whole scientific community that accepts the basic methods and standards of scientific inquiry. Thus, in this case the group will consist of an ideal scientific community of researchers who all operate according to the best scientific standards.

As said, I will discuss knowledge from an external evaluator's point of view. Thus, I assume that there is an external evaluator that can make knowledge judgments or knowledge attributions of the kind "Agent g knows that p" (where g may stand for a single or collective agent) or "It is collective knowledge in group g that p". In the epistemology I am sketching the most central statements, basic knowledge *acceptances* (usually judgments), will have the form: A(g*, K(g,p)). This statement reads "evaluator g* accepts as true or judges that g knows that p", where g* in general stands for a social group, e.g. the scientific community at a certain time point, and g is a social group or, alternatively, a non-collective agent to which knowledge is being attributed. In the case of a reflective agent g, g* can be g (in such a case g judges that it itself knows that p). However, in this paper g* is typically assumed to stand for a more comprehensive (both concerning its size and its justificatory capacities) group than g. Thus we can say that in our treatment g* is "epistemically wiser" than g. (This assumption is not, however, needed for our most basic analyses.) The evaluator group g* need not be a socially existing group—it need only be a placeholder for an epistemic perspective that may be different from the one that g incorporates. On the other hand, g* can be a successor group (e.g. in scientific contexts the host of a new or different theory or theoretical approach). In such a case we may want to deal with a succession of groups g*, g**,…, which, however, need not yield "absolute" truth as its limit.

The above kinds of acceptance statements of the basic form A(g*, K(g,p)) are pragmatically central, for they serve to make epistemology practical and humanly accessible. To see why, we can assume that a basic acceptance claim entails justified true belief: A(g*, JB(g,p) & p is true), that is, g* claims that g justifiably correctly believes (viz. "acceptance believes") that p and that p is true. To have the converse statement conclusive knowledge-dependent justification will have to be involved, in part in order to block Gettier paradoxes.[55]

---

[55] Cf. Gettier (1963); Rosenberg (2002).

As to the truth requirement, it is a presupposition of all rational scientific thinking that there is an external world in which things are thus and so. Given this, the claim that a proposition p is true makes sense and can be instrumentally useful. However, all descriptive claims about the mind-independent world (in contrast to the institutionally created world) are fallible—they ultimately depend on some human beings' judgments. Thus a traditional knowledge ascription such as that g knows that p must always be viewpoint-dependent in the sense that p in a natural human language is never an isolated statement but part of an interconnected system of propositions, an epistemic perspective. There may thus also be an ascriber-evaluator with its background knowledge and evaluative capacities. Accordingly, "p is true" in the classical definition of knowledge is pragmatically feasible only when it appears (or at least can appear) in an intentional and intensional context such as "g* claims that JB(g,p) and that p is true".

We have now arrived at a kind of relational view of knowledge, as both g and g* relativize knowledge to epistemic perspectives, the attributee g generally less explicitly than the attributor g*. Because classical knowledge entails truth and justification it goes beyond mere mental states such as belief. Truth and justification are somewhat problematic notions. The problem is not so much the possible unclarity and relativity of the notions but rather their concrete application to central cases where we wish to speak of knowledge. Thus, most if not all past and extant scientific theories can be argued to be known to be false, yet we speak of scientific knowledge at least in the case of some current theories (which one day probably will be superseded). According to fallibilism claims about truth are in flux: it always factually—and not only logically or conceptually—possible that a claim saying that certain things about the external world are thus and so is false.

Given this view, the best way to deal with the meant kind of cases without giving up the strict, truth-entailing classical notion of knowledge may be to speak of knowledge in terms of justified acceptance claims such as "g has accepted theory p as true" (or "p is acceptable as true for g") on the ground that p has survived a reasonable amount of justification-giving scientific testing. (Acceptance here must minimally entail that g lacks the belief that –p is true.) One may debate about how to interpret the demand of justification here, but it is at least excluded here that the justification (viz. empirical evidence) entails the truth of the theory, because in general scientific theories are not deductively entailed by the empirical evidence (and other grounds) for them. Scientific serendipity – central for genuine innovation and progress in science—involves non-deductive leaps, leaps which violate the idea that the grounds of the truth of the theory establish its truth.

I will adopt the "acceptance language" to some extent below, even if I will also, compatibly, speak of knowledge and truth in a rather classical way—although always embedding knowledge in a social context, in a context involving an evaluator. This gives a unified way of dealing with knowledge and it seems also to capture explicitly some factors that in the present epistemological literature have been suggested as relevant and important. I will assume that knowledge is a conceptually irreducible notion—partly in view of the Gettier paradoxes and recent discussion in the literature. This makes it possible to argue that full-blown knowledge entails justified true belief (or acceptance). However, we need to deal with truth only in the context of claims about truth, as we view g's knowledge from the point of view of g* and discuss g*'s claims about g's knowledge. Furthermore, even within this setting, the truth requirement can be relaxed (e.g. in the above kind of scientific cases) or then a loose common sense notion of truth or assertability can be used. We may wish to make sense of statements like "At time t the scientific community g had arrived at the knowledge that p but at a later point of time, t', p was refuted and the knowledge claim did not any more hold true". The belief (or acceptance) requirement must also be relaxed to some extent (cf. e.g. the case of non-operative members when groups know as groups—Section 8 below).[56]

---

[56] I will not explicitly discuss the Gettier paradoxes in this paper, as these paradoxes are concerned with the reductive, classical definition of knowledge. My non-reductive

As argued, justification is dependent on the social group in question in the sense discussed above. Relative to one group, say the original attributee g, a claim may be justified while relative to the epistemic standards of an attributor group, g*, that might not the case. Above g* was taktaken to stand for an actual or potential social group with its background knowledge and epistemic perspective. There are epistemically better and worse perspectives (i.e.. attributor groups g* with differing background knowledge and assumptions, etc.). I will assume that the best perspective, as far as we presently know, is the perspective defined by the method of science.[57] This perspective is idealized and normative. It is strictly applicable only to fully rational inquirers, but approximately also typical reallife scientists can satisfy the canons of the method of science to an appropriate degree. In the case of epistemic inconsistencies and other new perspectives g*, g**, ... will develop and supersede old ones and this may lead to the replacement of a knowledge content p, say a theory, by a better theory p´, and the new epistemic perspective may also be epistemologically better in that it involves better cognitive and material resources for justification and perhaps also better criteria of justification. The present idea involves that the ultimate contingent criterion for truth about the world in general is scientific observation, and, indeed, such empirical information can also be an important criterion for choosing between different epistemic perspectives.[58]

The present somewhat relativistic epistemology is not relativistic all the way down, so to speak. On the *cognitive* and *personal* level there need

---

approach concurs with Gettier's (1963), own comments on his paradoxical examples: There is no knowledge in certain cases in which the three classical clauses are satisfied at least as long as non-circular justification is meant; and such non-circular justification must be meant if a reduction of knowledge is at stake.

[57] See my own account of it in Tuomela (1985).

[58] In Tuomela (1985: Chapter 9) I have provided my own account of the "comparative goodness" of theories, and that account is also applied to the comparison of conceptual frameworks in partial reliance of the notion of degrees of (nonconceptual) "picturing"; these Sellarsian, 1968, conceptual frameworks are closely related to the present kind of epistemic perspectives.

not be an end to the sequence of same-order or higher-order perspectives used to evaluate knowledge claims. Still, on the *functional* level of behavior and goal satisfaction relativism loses its grip. To make a programmatic claim, humans are by and large able to cope with reality and survive. This may involve both their cognitive capacities (innate capacities to think and reason epistemically) and their subpersonal capacities. Their basic needs thus tend to get satisfied in part due to the fact that they have knowledge about the world.[59]

One of my more specific concerns will be to give an account of group beliefs and knowledge in the sense that the group *a group* believes or knows something.[60] A central case here is group-socially normatively *binding* group belief and knowledge. In this normative case the group is at least weakly obligated to reason and act on the truth of the content of the belief in question on group-internal grounds. These grounds concern, more generally, the group's commitment—and thus its members' collective commitment—to achieve the group ethos (and possibly other goals or analogous ends involving the world-to-mind direction of fit of satisfaction). The members are then also obligated to each other to obey the group-socially normative obligations. (Morality in a strict sense need not always come into play here.)

Given that a group cannot function unless at least some of its members function qua members, I will assume that a group cannot know unless its members or at least some of them know the item in question. A group g's normatively binding belief concerning a topic, P, will accordingly depend on its members' beliefs—indeed "we-mode" beliefs that are basically

---

[59] Cf. the discussion of nonconceptual "picturing" in Tuomela (1985: Chapters 5 and 9).

[60] I will require below that the groups under discussion be autonomous both in an external and internal sense. Roughly speaking, external autonomy means that they (and their members) are not heavily coerced from outside (to the extent they would lose their autonomy as agents), and internal autonomy means that the group members do not strongly coerce each other but make their decisions and undertake their acceptances autonomously.

"acceptance" beliefs—about P and on their relevant intentional "interconnections" concerning P. As to what we-mode acceptance belief amounts to, it suffices here to say that it centrally involves the idea of functioning as a group member.[61] Thus, when g believes that p, the members of g, collectively considered, will be assumed to believe (accept) that p when functioning as group members and thus be collectively committed to p. Their private beliefs related to P (here covering p and –p) can be different from those they adopt as members of g.[62]

There are two kinds of beliefs that groups qua (somewhat metaphorical) believers can have: (1) group beliefs (viz. beliefs attributed to a group) concerning the mind-independent external world (e.g. grass is green)—and more generally facts that are not at least entirely artificial, and thus they depend at least in part "upon the way the external world is"; (2) group beliefs and we-mode beliefs about facts which are social and artificial in the sense that they are performatively created and are such that it basically is entirely up to the group members to decide about their truth or, rather, correctness.[63]

---

[61] See Tuomela (2007) for my recent analyses of the we-mode.

[62] Both the members' we-mode beliefs and the group's beliefs in the present case are "acceptance" beliefs but not necessarily also "experiential" beliefs (see Tuomela (1992; 2000) for discussion). Acceptance beliefs are simply what result from accepting the content in question. As acceptance belief is a dispositional state of an agent leading him to reason and act appropriately. In contrast, an experiential belief is a dispositional state which involves also the agent's mental experiences related to the content's being real or existent. However, a group cannot strictly speaking have mental experiences (as it has no mind in a literal sense). It can only have acceptance beliefs, to be analyzed in terms of its members' we-beliefs (we-acceptances), which of course can involve experiential features.

[63] Let me add two points. First, in some contexts, e.g. in the case of moral beliefs truth may not be an appropriate notion to use but rather correctness or correct assertability. For the sake of simplicity, I will in this paper generally use 'true' in a broad sense covering these cases. Second, some factual presuppositions must often be required to hold true even in the case of institutional and collectively constructed beliefs. To take a simple example: If a group is to decide about what its unit of money is going to be, suitable kinds of pieces of paper will qualify but the presuppositions prevent e.g. plan-

I will call group beliefs of kind (1) *natural*. As to (2), I will concentrate on its central subclass formed by (*constitutive*) *institutional beliefs* (e.g. squirrel pelt is money, to use a quasi-historical example).[64] A constitutive institutional belief here is one that is constitutive of the group's existence and its ethos. There are weaker kinds of institutional beliefs such as group stereotypes like the belief that the earth is flat, but I will not here discuss them in particular. Below I will understand institutionality in a broad sense involving normative "groupness" and "we-modeness" and concentrate on normatively binding group beliefs, where the normativity is based primarily on the fact that there are operative members for the group who have been authorized to make normatively binding decisions and agreements and/or to accept views for the group. The set of operative members may in some cases consist of all group members, in which case there need not be prior authorization. I will also comment on non-normative beliefs that groups qua believers can have. Furthermore, although this is not believing qua a group, we can speak of group beliefs even in a weaker sense in which the group does not believe qua a group. In this weaker case there are shared "we-beliefs" that something p in the group held by group members. Such shared "experiential" we-beliefs may accompany binding acceptance beliefs and then we have group beliefs in the strongest possible sense, viz. the sense involving both normativity and experiential beliefs (e.g. of the kind perceptions involve).[65]

Let me finally remark that the following basic general approaches to analyzing group knowledge have at least some initial feasibility, depending on what aspects of group knowledge are focused on:

(1) The group accepts an item of knowledge as true qua a group and is properly epistemically justified in its acceptance: *Acceptance belief approach.*

---

ets, angels, or Abelian groups from qualifying. By the word 'basically' in the text I refer to these kinds of presuppositions.

[64] See Tuomela (2007: Chapter 8) for institutional beliefs, both constitutive and non-constitutive.

[65] See Tuomela (1992).

(2) *Shared we-belief approach* based on aggregated experiential we-beliefs—either in the I-mode or in the we-mode, depending on which of the respective perspectives is salient in the agent's mind.

(3) Combination of (1) and (2).

Note here that in this broad outline (1) basically (but not invariably) requires *voluntary* activity but (2) is not. The present paper concentrates on clarifying (1), but my view is that (3) makes for the overall best approach to the problem of collective and group knowledge.[66] Some aspects related to (2)—the shared we-belief approach—will nevertheless be taken up below.

4. Theses on Group Knowledge

The following factors should be noted when discussing the justification of normatively (perhaps only instrumentally normative) group-binding group beliefs. First and foremost, the group is assumed to be a quasi-agent in the sense of being we-mode group—a group capable of intentional action and thus involving its members' we-thinking. Thus authoritative group reasons for member action and members' collective commitment to e.g. group beliefs (acceptances rather than experiential beliefs) will be central for the group's functioning as a unit. Beliefs are acceptances rather than experiential beliefs. We-mode beliefs about a topic P will have to accord with the "ethos" (viz. the *constitutive basic* goals, values, beliefs, standards, and norms) of the group and are in this sense *for* the group. In the epistemic case it is of course the epistemic part of the group's ethos (viz. its epistemic values, standards, and norms as well as prior knowledge) that matters. As said, in general for (factual) knowledge to be obtained the ethos must consist of, or at least contain, the central elements of the ethos of the scientific community, thus scientific standards and criteria, because the method

---

[66] See Tuomela (1992; 1995: Chapter 7) for a discussion of group belief.

of science is the best method for gathering knowledge.[67] Notice that group members' private (or "I-mode") beliefs and their justification is a separate matter. That question will not be properly discussed in the present paper.

In accordance with the discussion so far, I will in this paper defend in particular the following theses on group knowledge, being here concerned only with we-mode groups:

(T1) (a) A group's knowing that p qua a group entails that the group must have accepted that p as true and that the group is justified in accepting that p. Group acceptance entails that the group is committed to p as a group.[68] Group justification involves here that the group must have a good epistemic reason for its acceptance of p as true. (group level)

(T1) (b) On the level of group members, the group reason in T1(a) amounts to their joint reason for p, if the group is an egalitarian one in the sense of all members' actively, without delegation participating in group decisions and the like. The group members must in the we-mode case (involving group-binding collective commitment) share a justifying *joint* reason for the knowledge content p. (joint member level)

(T1) (c) An individual group member's knowledge that p in case T1(a) involves the justificatory aspect that she ought to be able to reason and act in the we-mode, in accordance with the fact that p has been justifiably accepted by the group. (individual member level)

---

[67] Think e.g. of the various kinds of controls the scientific method imposes. One ideal is *double-blind experimentation* that yields *testable* and *repeatable* results. As to other requirements, there is far-going agreement in the literature about them. For my own criteria, see Tuomela, 1985, Chapter 10. There I classify the criteria in general terms as follows: *objectivity*, *criticalness*, *autonomy*, and *progress*.

[68] Group commitment basically amounts to collective commitment by its members. See Tuomela (2007: Chapters 1, 6 and 8) for details.

(*T2*) In the case of *constitutive institutional knowledge* the criteria of epistemic justification are *social* (viz. based on group acceptance, hence collective member acceptance), whereas in the case of *natural knowledge non-social* elements of justification are normally crucial.

(*T3*) Knowledge is a social institution in the sense that the epistemic practices (gathering of knowledge, acceptance of something as the group's view, relevant inferences and action on its basis, and the justification of acceptances) in a group are governed by its ethos, thus by its normative epistemic standards; and, as opposed to mere reason-based belief, knowledge accordingly has a special institutional status.

My main concern below will be a group's knowing as a group that something is thus and so. There are weaker cases of group knowledge and I will make some comments concerning them, too. In those weaker cases we can speak of there being shared knowledge in the group that thus and so and take this to involve that some epistemic group standards still will be used to evaluate that knowledge.

I will below discuss (T1) and (T2). As to (T3), I will not properly argue for it in this paper. Let me just say briefly what I mean by the institutional status of knowledge. First, the acceptance by a group of p as true in a justified way must be required. This makes p group knowledge in a strong sense involving that the group members are to regard p as being something for group use. E.g. the kind of constitutive institutional knowledge that squirrel pelt is money has that kind of status due to group acceptance of squirrel pelt as money. Basically, squirrel pelt is money if and only if it is accepted as money in the group and for the group.[69] Also group stereotypes like "The star constellation at one's birth determines one's fate" (= p)—that are non-constitutively institutional knowledge in the group—have a somewhat similar institutional status, but in principle such stereotypes are

---

[69] See Tuomela (2002: Chapters 5-6) and, especially, Tuomela (2007: Chapter 8).

empirically falsifiable. We may think that in some group this latter piece of "knowledge" that p is accepted as true in and for the group and is thus "perspectivally" true. Thus p can be said to have a special, institutional status in the group: that p is the case is not just a private belief or piece of knowledge of group members but something that has obtained the status of group knowledge, and that status depends on group acceptance and the ensuing practices.[70]

5. Epistemic Group Reasons and Joint Reasons

Suppose that the group has as its task or problem to determine whether the ship far out in the sea is a schooner. While the group members' initial views may differ, group discussion may lead to an acceptable group view of the matter. Sometimes the group members' pieces of knowledge complement each other. For example, one member may know what kind of stern a schooner has, while another one knows how many masts it must have. Group discussion (argumentation, bargaining, voting, persuasion, and whatever is involved) may lead not only to an acceptable group view but also to a shared group reason for the view. Whatever the method that is initially used for arriving at a group view, collective acceptance of the reason as the group's reason must ultimately be required in the case of a we-mode group, a group that can act fully as a group on the basis of we-thinking.

A group can be taken to have the knowledge that p even in a case where it only accepts that p as true but where the members may all have private reasons for their knowledge claims. The members' reasons must still be compatible in this kind of I-mode case in order for there to be knowledge in the group, because inconsistent reasons could not all be conducive to the truth of p (inconsistency would entail conduciveness to p in the case of one member's reason but to –p in case of another member's

---

[70] See Kusch (2002) for a recent "communitarian" account of knowledge that resembles my account but makes knowledge even more social than mine does.

reason). But when the reasons are consistent and when there is mutual belief among the group members that their reasons put together form a consistent group reason, the group knows as a group and can act as a group on its knowledge—e.g. your reason R1 and my reason R2 together, e.g. conjunctively or disjunctively, form a mutually known dyad reason R. For instance your epistemic reason for believing that a heavy storm is imminent may be your own quasi-meteorological observations (e.g. that there are dark blue clouds on the horizon and that the wind is picking up, etc.) while my reason is the weather report that I have just heard on the radio—our reasons are consistent and may complement each other. So what can feasibly be required in the case of a group knowing as a group is that there be a factual group reason (a reason attributed to the group, g) or a *joint* we-mode reason (when speaking on the level of group members) for the *acceptance* and *truth* of p. We can thus in principle distinguish between a group reason for accepting (or, here equivalently, believing that) p and the joint reason for it, although at least in simple cases they extensionally coincide.[71]

In the fully general case we can think of a group as an entity and ascribe reasons for it to accept something. As in the case of an individual agent, this analogical way of thinking entails that knowledge that p in the case of the group agent requires that it accept (or "acceptance believe") p for a good epistemic reason. But a group cannot accept p for a good epistemic reason without its members, or at least the operative members of the group, having a good joint epistemic reason to accept p, because a group cannot function as a group without its members functioning appropriately as group members. Furthermore, a group knowing as a group must be functioning in the we-mode, because, in analogy with the individual case, the group must have bound itself at least to an extent to the content p and to its reason, R, for it. Viewed from the members' point of view this entails that they must be functioning for a group reason qua being "in the same boat"

---

[71] For simplicity, I will below often not make a point of distinguishing them from each other and will mostly concentrate on joint reasons (that must be there anyhow even when a separate group reason is present).

and being collectively committed to p and to R (this holds true strictly for non-structured, egalitarian groups where all members are operative ones). It follows that for a group to know as a group its members must know in the we-mode, i.e. they must know for a group reason and satisfy the collectivity condition and the requirement of collective commitment.

Let me still spell out in more detail why a joint reason is functionally needed when a group knows as a group. Most centrally, a joint epistemic reason is needed for the item's acceptance as true (and for a rational commitment to it) because it gives more *stability and persistence* to the group's consequent relevant epistemic activities. More specifically, we have the following arguments:

(a) Knowledge (justified true belief) is supposed to *guide action* and, what is central here, to do it better than mere belief and even true belief. As in the case of an individual's knowing something, also a group agent must have epistemic grounds for its beliefs in order to know. The justification tells why the belief is better than an accidentally true claim or mere true belief; and in the case of e.g. repeated action and changing circumstances, true belief with an informative truth-conducive reason will fare better in the stability and reliability sense than mere true belief.

As to the collective case, we noted that a group's reason entails a joint reason when viewed from its members' point of view. They may have different epistemic reasons for a claim but if the group is to achieve knowledge, their reasons must for the sake of group unity be combinable to a full joint reason, and this requires at least that the participants correctly believe that the others have parts that are parts of the joint reason (without perhaps knowing what exactly those part reasons are). Such a joint reason makes it possible for the group to act as a unit on the basis of its knowledge. For example a group's knowing in a particular case that the boat out there is a schooner may be based on one member knowing that the boat has the right number of masts, another one that it has the right kind of stern, etc., such that the combination of such reasons amounts to a fully acceptable epistemic group reason that makes the group's belief an item of knowledge. More generally, the group members have complementary justifications for the group belief p while the full justification in some cases cannot on theoretical or practical grounds be had by any single member. It must be emphasized that in order to yield knowledge the group reason must of course be a good epistemic reason and not only one offering social unity and homogeneity.

(b) Rational group discussion and the group's more comprehensive background knowledge (to which all the members contribute) generally tends to yield better epistemic reasons than provided by individual private reasons concerning truth-conduciveness and reliability (recall the schooner example and other similar cases). Such discussion may be able to combine the best of different kinds of individual views into a tenable comprehensive view. (On the other hand, as "groupthink" phenomena show, also poor results can be arrived in groups that do not function sufficiently rationally but may e.g. give a leader, such as President Kennedy in the Cuban crisis, too much influence.)

(c) At least in practice, a group functioning as a group often has better resources to test how good its justifications are and improve its reasons on the basis of such testing. This gives a dynamic perspective to knowledge gathering that may yield better results together with the employment of group discussion and evaluation than, for instance, individualistic aggregation of new information.

(d) In general, the group can act more successfully and reliably and also successfully take more risks (at least from its internal point of view) when acting for a good group reason (based on the result of group discussion from a "we-perspective") than in the case of aggregated individual I-mode reasons (e.g. given by majority voting). Thus there tends to be both more successful acting and acting of a different kind when the requirement of group justification is satisfied and taken by the group members to be satisfied.

(e) The group can better argue for, and explain, its view and publicly defend it when there is a good joint reason for it than when that is not the case. To be able to act as one agent the group members should be able to speak with one voice when arguing as group members for the group's view.[72]

Even with good joint reason and thus justification for the acceptance of p, the group might still collectively be in error concerning a natural belief that p—consider again phenomena of groupthink. Thus, rational group discussion and, indeed, any method of justification may fall short of yielding truth in this case: A joint reason in general does not entail truth in the case of natural beliefs and it need not even give the kind of justification that factual knowledge requires. Justification is relative to the knowers' background beliefs, and the requirement that the group members try to secure that they have good evidence is similarly a matter relative to background perspective and beliefs. For instance, distinguishing between "façade" and real schooners typically depends on those kinds of factors.[73] However, it is reasonable to require more epistemic group effort in these kinds of cases than in the case where normal conditions obtained and were known by the participants to obtain. Extraordinary knowledge claims such as claims about the existence of paranormal phenomena require better justifying reasons than do ordinary knowledge claims.[74]

A weaker approach would tentatively attribute group knowledge to a group when it claims to know and has not acted obviously irrationally in acquiring its "knowledge". If it appears later that the group members had been somehow deluded, the claim about the group's knowledge should be withdrawn—if there in fact was no schooner. On the other hand, if there

---

[72] There are various non-rational phenomena related to group processes, e.g. "groupthink", social loafing, and crowding phenomena. Here I am idealizingly dealing with collectively rational group activities and thus what groups can epistemically achieve.

[73] Cf. Rosenberg (2002: Chapter 4) for a recent discussion of this kind of cases.

[74] This solution—involving the defeasibility of knowledge attributions but not yet necessarily relativity to epistemic standards—of course relies on the availability of a non-tautological notion of normal conditions.

was one, part of their evidence might have been distorted without this affecting the truth of the claim that they knew that there was a schooner. As emphasized in Section 1, all knowledge claims are fallible and may later be shown to be based on incorrect or distorted evidence. The present weak approach seems viable, provided that the required minimal rationality in acquiring knowledge is taken to amount to the use of the method of science.

In contrast to natural knowledge, the *constitutive institutional case* is different in that in principle in this case the group is "always right", to use a slogan, because the truth of the item p of knowledge and the justification of the group's acceptance of p both (conceptually and metaphysically) necessarily are social and conceptually and metaphysically necessarily so. More precisely, the group is right in this case if it functions properly both in a factual and a normative sense (and this involves its complying with the presuppositions of the case as pointed out in note 16). Proper functioning here means that there is externally and internally autonomous collective acceptance that p and that the collective acceptance is genuine to the extent that the members also act in accordance with it, viz. use squirrel pelt as money, etc.[75] In the present, institutional case we can speak of performative truth. The conceptually central ground or conceptual model for institutional beliefs is *collective performative speech acts*. Suppose that we, the group members, jointly declare that squirrel pelt is to be our money by representing by our actual use of money that squirrel pelt is money. Then squirrel pelt *is* money in our group, and our group knows it is money and describes it as money. Squirrel pelt has acquired a special institutional status. Let me emphasize, however, that there also can be and is non-linguistic collective acceptance, although it must still have the required performative aspect.

---

[75] In Tuomela (2002: Chapter 5) I define collective acceptance as coming to hold and holding a relevant we-attitude. In Chapter 8 of my 2007 book I give another but basically equivalent explication in terms of collective commitment with the appropriate direction of fit.

In the case of natural belief there is in general mind-to-world direction of fit of satisfaction. This means in colloquial terms that the mind is required to fit the world. In contrast, in the case of constitutive institutional belief (e.g. squirrel pelt is money) the direction of fit is world-to-mind. That is, when viewed as constitutive the institutional belief in question (also) has the world-to-mind direction of fit (in contrast to the case when it is viewed merely as expressing what the world is like according to its subject). Thus, in the constitutive case the world is to be changed and kept changed by the participants so that it fits their mind, but—as the group is here also taken to have *asserted* the content in question—the belief thus also has the mind-to-world direction of fit.

The authorized operative members who have formed the piece of knowledge *actually* have the knowledge (at least at the time of making the decision or agreement in question). Non-operative members, in contrast, are only subject to the "ought", a "group-social" one, that they also should acquire the piece of knowledge in question.[76] This is still more than what we have in the case of a mere "visitor" to the group. She may learn about the piece of knowledge e.g. by testimony from someone (or from written text) and thus have the source in question as their justified source of knowledge (see below for more on this). The content in question, say that squirrel pelt is money in the group, is "quasi-objective" group-grounded knowledge. For external observers the piece of knowledge that squirrel pelt is money initially has only the mind-to-world and not the world-to-mind direction of fit of satisfaction (cf. above). Note, too, that group knowledge is in general (and unless otherwise decided by the group) public in the group, the group's property. But it need not be information similarly knowable to outsiders.

---

[76] See Tuomela (2007) for the notion of institutional (or group-social) "ought" that is not properly normative (viz. moral, legal) but is rational in a group-dependent, collective sense. The institutional "ought" is by itself non-normative and grounded by the group's committing (binding) itself to an item. It generates the discussed kind of "ought" for the members relative to the group ethos.

We have noted in this section that typical cases of group belief formation at least in small organized groups are based on group discussion (communication purporting to find out whether something p is true and what the reasons justifying it are if taken to be true).[77] The central thing is that the result of the discussion must be "collectivized" if a group-binding we-mode reason is to be acquired, and, on both conceptual and functional grounds, unity-creating collective commitment to p is needed here as a basic social "glue" to enable group action qua a group.[78] Thus p will have to be jointly accepted here in this strong sense, and for p to be an item of knowledge there must also be a group reason that justifies p in the group's view. On the level of the group members, the group reason involves the members' (or at least the operative members') joint reason to accept and, typically, to maintain the belief in question.[79] Such a joint reason need not be occurrent in the members' minds but may be only dispositionally had. Furthermore, the members need not accept (or be disposed to accept) the reason under the same description, so to speak. They may thus accept a reason in a *de re* rather than *de dicto* sense and be free to describe the reason in their own personal ways.

6. Achieving Group Knowledge

Operating with the intuitive model of a group agent being relevantly analogous to an individual agent, we will now consider some aspects of the achievement of group knowledge. This dynamic process contains as its central elements (1) the fact, say Z, supposed to represent the central epis-

---

[77] In large groups the communication may be more centralized and involve the employment or means of news papers and TV and other mass media. In some cases also aggregation methods can be used to find out what the group's view is.

[78] See Tuomela, Chapter 1, for arguments.

[79] In logical terms, a group reason, GR, is attributed to a group, g, relative to the acceptance of an attitude, ATT, yielding a statement $GR(g,ATT(p))$. In contrast, a joint reason, JR, is attributed to the group members (at least the operatives) $A_1,...,A_m$, yielding a statement $JR(A_1,...,A_m, ATT(p))$. $GR(g,ATT(p))$ entails $JR(A_1,...,A_m, ATT(p))$ at least in the case of operatives, the converse does not hold without qualifications.

temic reason (or "reason fact") for the group. Z is supposed be (2) conducive to the truth of p and indeed to be (3) a good epistemic reason for believing (accepting as true) that p. (Recall that in the constitutive institu-institutional case specifically performative acceptance is to be required.) The group, g, in question is supposed to (4) believe that (1), (2), and (3), and indeed to (5) believe that p is true on the basis of Z—and thus put together (1) – (4) in the epistemically right way. (5) of course amounts to (6) group knowledge that p.

Let me expand my account of the epistemic process in question that partly amounts to epistemic group reasoning. Here, Z can be a natural fact, e.g. an experimental fact or an everyday observational fact as in the schooner example (the case of natural belief). Alternatively, it can be a fact about collective construction, e.g. that g collectively constructs squirrel pelt as money by means of its performative collective acceptance (the case of constitutive institutional belief). Assumption (1) is obvious: the reason must exist in a suitable sense expressible by a that-clause. Similarly the general requirement of conduciveness to truth in (2) is required, although here I will leave its more exact content open. Let me nevertheless say that at least typically in the case of natural beliefs Z should entail that p is closer to the truth than without it, roughly that $P(p/Z) >> P(p)$, where P stands for probability and $>>$ for "much larger than". Note also that in the case of institutional belief Z will trivially be the very fact of joint acceptance (or, more generally, group acceptance partly analyzable in terms of joint acceptance), and this entails the truth of (2). (1) and (2) support (3). (4) is an assumption relying on the epistemic rationality of g. As a rather obvious rational consequence of (4) g indeed connects Z and the belief that p in (5) and also comes to regard Z as a sufficiently good reason for accepting p as true. How strong the support here needs to be depends on the reasoner's (the group's or an outside observer's) basic epistemological views—see the discussion in Section 5. Clause (6) just states the content of (5) in terms of knowledge. Because of (5), g is committed to acting appropriately on its knowledge that p.

Our next problem is how to cash out this group-level characterization for the member level. In the case of the members in relation to (3) – (5), we speak of their collectively accepting p as true and also say that Z counts as a good reason for believing that p. Group commitment in turn amounts to the group members' being collectively committed to (4), thus to acting on the truth of p and to defending Z as a good reason for p. In the case of the end point (5) of the epistemic process, we can speak of the group members' knowing as a group that p. Assuming that this is a case of spontaneous knowledge formation we can assume that the group reason simply amounts to a joint reason we can more explicitly write out the member-level process for inductive knowledge acquisition as follows:

(i)   Z is the case, where Z is either a natural or an institutional fact.

(ii)   Z is conducive to the truth of p.

(iii)   Z is a good epistemic reason for believing (accepting) that p.

(iv)   the members of g (or at least its operative members) collectively believe (accept) that (i), (ii), and (iii).

(v)   the members of g (or at least its authorized "operative" members or leaders) collectively believe (accept) that p is true (partly) for the reason that (i) – (iv*).

(vi)   the members of g (or at least its operative members) know that p as a group.

Let me note concerning (v) that the group members, when functioning as proper group members (in a sense involving collective commitment), collectively accept Z as a justifying (viz. epistemically good) reason for believing that p, and collective acceptance here makes it a joint reason for accepting that p. This joint reason has the world-to-mind direction of fit as is the case with proattitudes, but in distinction to mere want it has the normative feature of favoring the action that it is a reason for (viz. acceptance that p). In the case of natural belief the acceptance of Z as a joint reason must take place mainly because of (i) and (ii) while in the institutional case

(iv) is central. Here (iv) gives the central justificatory element, because it gives the social aspect of justification for the collective knowledge that p (for the "collective knowing" aspect rather than for the ground of the truth aspect of justification). A social reason will be at play also in the case of natural beliefs as we are dealing with a group context.[80]

As to the joint reason, in weakest cases of collective knowledge by joint reason a shared "we-reason" (e.g. belief content) can be meant. A we-reason in this case is an agent's personal (private) reason accompanied by his belief that also the others in the group (or most of them) have it and that this is mutually believed. This case is an I-mode one and expresses knowledge *in* a group rather than a group's having knowledge as a group. However, suppose next that the members collectively commit themselves to the content, say p, as their shared belief content. They are then qua group members committed to it and believe that others are similarly committed (and perhaps that they also believe that this is mutually believed). When the collective belief is thus accompanied by collective commitment we may arrive at a group-binding group belief that p (which need not yet quite be a we-mode one). In this case the group must of course be disposed to act on the truth of p. When it knows that p there must also be a good epistemic reason for the belief that p.[81]

As noted, my account is employs "acceptance beliefs" in the case of full group beliefs, for here the group members must be taken to form a jus-

---

[80] Here is a piece of simple practical reasoning that also illustrates the member-level side of a group's achieving a piece of knowledge but from a somewhat different angle:
(a) Group g intends to find out whether p is the case (e.g. whether a certain theory is true).
(b) We (the members of g) intend to find out if p is true.
(c) I, qua a member of g, will do my part of our finding out if p is true.
(d) My part being to do X (e.g. to perform calculations Y), I set myself doing it.
Here (a) group-socially "reasons" (justifies) (b), given that the bootstrapping problem possibly involved has been solved); (b) reasons (c)), and ((c) reasons (d)). The present illustration does not, however, take a stand on whether the group's epistemic investigation results in knowledge with a *good* epistemic reason.
[81] There are also other cases of group-binding beliefs falling between full-blown normatively binding we-mode group beliefs and aggregative cases (see Section 8).

tified view (judgment) from the group's perspective and not only from their own personal perspective. Thus e.g. "experiential", private beliefs play no central roles here (they are not even required). A group belief needs that a suitable group judgment such as "We believe as a group that p" is required to get the whole group fully involved. Furthermore, to have a case of the group knowing as a group it must be committed to the reason Z, and thus the group members must be collectively committed to Z, in which case we have we-mode knowledge. It cannot then be a mere accident that the agents share the we-belief that p or that they know that p.

When a group knows that p as a group, an individual member, who does not yet have the knowledge in question, can "pick it up" at least when it is public knowledge in the group. If the individual believes that it is knowledge in the group that p, then, being committed to what the group knows, he will take himself to know that p, although his believed knowledge and understanding of p may be so shallow as not to allow him to appropriately use it as a premise in his inferences and as a ground for his action. This is knowledge by *testimony*. Accordingly, a group member can here be assumed to believe with good reason that p, for this is what the belief that he knows that p amounts to.

Let me end by commenting on joint reasons that are *compound* ones, e.g. *conjunctive* or *disjunctive* reasons. They are typically connected to the *division of labor* in the group. To comment on the conjunctive case, the agents here might be researchers in a project aiming to find out whether p or –p. Testing the hypothesis that p is taken to require complex collaborative research. As a result of the process each participant A_i comes up with a partial justifying reason Z_i such that $Z = Z_1 \& ... \& Z_i \& ... \& Z_m$. Thus the conjunctive compound reason Z is a conjunctive combination of each of the partial reasons, but each participant is assumed to accept Z as a justifying reason for believing that p. In the we-mode case the participants are indeed assumed to be collectively committed to taking Z as a justifying epistemic reason for p. They need not be required to be able to describe each

Z_i in the "right" way. It suffices that they trust that each A_i has done an acceptable job in securing that Z_i is an acceptable partial reason. [82]

Social reasons might be even more complex than above. One might occasionally require that an agent's reason be not only what was just said but also that the others have the mentioned kind of social reason for their belief that p (viz. his partial reason for his belief that p would be not only that Z is the case and that the others take Z to be their reason but that the others also have as their partial reason not only Z but also the social reason that all the others take Z as their reason and take this to be mutually believed in the group). In principle, these reason loops can be iterated.

Our discussion so far supports the view that at least in some central cases social groups can better acquire natural knowledge than individuals acting separately and even individuals acting in groups that are not capable of effective action, thus gathering of information and justifying potential items of knowledge. My claim has been that we-mode groups are (or probably are) overall best for this task. What I have not above considered is the

---

[82] In some cases it seems essential that the participants' individual idiosyncratic reasons are taken into account. Thus e.g. Surowiecki (2005) in his semipopular book argues for the wisdom of crowds. For instance, "market knowledge" is a case in point. Markets may "know" in which direction a company share is moving when no single specialist has a good guess about the matter, although it must be said that at least economic markets often are volatile and, as it were, emotionally exaggerate the case at hand. Surowiecki requires (a) diversity of opinion, (b) independence of judgments, (c) decentralization, and (d) aggregation. These conditions (that can be applied both to I-mode and we-mode cases) hardly justify beliefs but may correlate with reliable group-level predictions in the crowd case, given a suitable regular distribution of individual beliefs (either I-mode or we-mode ones). While conditions (a)-(d) may happen to be satisfied in the case of crowds but they may of course also become intentionally satisfied by design in organized groups such as we-mode groups. Much more investigation is of course needed to be able to form a justified view of "market knowledge" and the "wisdom of crowds".
For a recent discussion that also comments on the above type of crowd wisdom cases, see List (2005) and List and Pettit (2011: esp. Chapter 4). It is shown especially in the latter work that and how a group may benefit from *democratization*, from *decomposition*, and from *decentralization*.

dynamic situation involving several competing information-seeking groups, but here I cannot discuss this problem area.[83]

7. Toward a General Account of Group Knowledge

I will next elucidate still other epistemic concepts for the social case.[84] The basic problem that I will try to deal with is what group knowledge (in a sense entailing justified true group belief) amounts to. Accordingly, it is important to give an account of justification, and this account will be a social account claiming that justification is dependent on a group's epistemic standards. Generally speaking, my account of justification assumes, compatible with my paradigm case of the method of science, that justification in the case of natural belief should be conducive to truth. Thus one central distinction between justified and unjustified belief is that the former—under the present "veritistic" idea—would be more likely to be true than the latter. Belief aims at truth: to believe something p is to believe it to be *true*. However, almost in any process of epistemic justification specific contextual and background information needs to be involved, and this fact in part explains why my account below is perhaps somewhat sketchier than one might initially have desired.

I take the scientific method in general to be the best method of justifying *natural* beliefs. It is conducive to truth, i.e. *informative* truth, as tautologies are of no interest to us in this context. I will below (in (*EJ*)) refer to laws and principles acquired by, and/or belonging to, the scientific method. A central feature of the scientific method is requirement of testability concerning the hypotheses and theories of science. Testability is ac-

---

[83] I have discussed cultural change and evolution, partly in terms of dynamic replicatory system, in my earlier work. See Tuomela (2002: Chapter 7), and especially Tuomela (2007: Chapter 9).
[84] My discussion below has benefited from Longino's (2002) related account, even if my analyses are based on somewhat different ideas. Among other things, she gives a social analysis about epistemic justification. However, space does not allow a comparison here.

companied by a self-correction procedure: if testing a natural-factual claim shows it to be false it is to be rejected or modified. What the epistemology of the scientific method—here taken as a normative doctrine deriving its instrumental norms from the epistemic values of information and truth—precisely taken is cannot be properly discussed in this context.[85]

Here is a summary of my general account of epistemic justification applicable especially to scientific contexts:

> (*EJ*) A proposition p is (rationally) *epistemically justified* for group g (in a situation C) if and only if (in C) g accepts p in virtue of p fitting and being supported by (a) the relevant data available to the members of g and (b) the laws and general principles accepted by g that pertain to data of these kinds.

For an egalitarian we-mode group g, it holds that g accepts p in situation C if and only if in C, the members of g, when functioning as group members respecting the ethos of g, rationally collectively accept p as true in C on the basis of the joint reason that (a) and (b) in that situation constitute for them. Thus, they acquire the shared we-belief (viz. we-acceptance) that p on the basis of a joint reason. In the more general case, at least the operative members in the group are required to share the joint reason and belief while the others group-socially ought to be in that "same epistemic boat". Collective acceptance requires obedience to the objective *truth-conducive* factors (a) and (b) (although the required minimal strength of conduciveness may be debated about). C can be taken to consist of the right normative and social circumstances.[86] The nature of p and the context of its collective acceptance will determine the direction of fit of its satisfaction conditions (recall Section 1).

The account (*EJ*) can also be applied to the case of I-mode groups in addition to we-mode groups. In the I-mode case acceptance and clauses (a)

---

[85] For my own, Sellars-flavored account, see Tuomela (1985: esp. Chapter 9).

[86] See my account in Tuomela (1995: Chapter 5).

and (b) are to be understood in a weak sense only. A joint reason for p is not required in this case.

The analysis *(EJ)* can be rendered in the form of an epistemic judgment made by an informed third party, e.g. the community of (ideal) social scientists (recall Section 1). In other words, we have the judgment or acceptance statement A(g*(EJ(g,p))), where EJ means "epistemically justified". This statement indicates that justification is dependent on both group g's and the external party g*'s epistemic standards. Group g regards p as epistemically justified, if it has reflected on the matter, and g* adds its own judgment of the truth of the resulting statement EJ(g,p). As the formulation of the account *(EJ)* without mention of g* suggests, epistemic acceptability is here regarded as an objectively (viz. not group-dependently) true matter. This, however, is an idealization and requires that g*, roughly speaking, consists of the community of all rational agents judging the matter in the "ideally right way" based on, say the best scientific standards optimally applied to the present case. (This is vaguely put, but conveys the general idea.) My account *(EJ)* then is seen to be implicitly doubly dependent on group standards, viz. on those of both g (explicit although underlying dependence) and g* (implicit dependence). In the case of non-reflective groups or cases where the group has not reflected on the epistemic status of the propositions its members have collectively or separately accepted, the statement EJ(g,p) is due to the activity of g*.

What do (a) and (b) involve in more detail? Briefly, (a) may involve observational data obtained by means of rational methods of observation—such as scientific field observation or experimentation. Note that in the case of constitutive institutional group beliefs (e.g. when p = squirrel pelt is money), as contrasted with natural beliefs, the data part (a) drops out or at least does not contain observational evidence in the same sense as in the case of natural beliefs. As to (b), it may be proposed that the Sellarsian conception of the scientific method be used here.[87] Thus we would include in the laws and general principles the so-called "semantical rules" (to use

---

[87] See e.g. Sellars (1968) and the interpretation of it in Tuomela (1985).

Sellars's somewhat misleading terminology) of group g. Such semantical rules would fill part of the bill and particular scientific theories (also inference rules, for Sellars) the rest. These rules are world-language, language-language, or language-world rules (laws).

In Sellars's system there are ought-to-be rules and ought-to-do rules in the case of all the three kinds of rules. The rules say, respectively, what a rationally functioning group ought to be like functionally and what its members ought to do (in terms of their inferences and overt actions) for the satisfaction of the ought-to-be rule in question. Clauses (a) and (b) are here assumed to incorporate the central elements of the scientific method (concerning acceptable problems and knowledge claim formation as well as testing and evaluating those claims) and thus to be conducive to truth (which is going to be viewpoint-dependent or "perspectival" truth).[88] While there will be a common framework of semantical rules for all groups expressing what is to be demanded of rational agents, there will be underdetermination of epistemic justification relative to (a) and (b) at least as long as particular features of the group—background views such as expressed by the ethos of the group in question—are *not* taken into account.

The overall account of justification in Sellars is an interesting combination of both foundationalist and coherentist ideas. The account of the structure of knowledge we get in broad outline is this: Given our ordinary framework, there are basic beliefs both of a perceptual and of an introspective kind that are noninferential and that are justified in specific concrete circumstances. Although noninferential, they are not self-justifying, for their justification is approximately a matter of their being licensed by certain constitutive principles of our conceptual framework, including domain-specific theories, and ultimately a matter of the acceptability of the framework as a whole. Let me emphasize that the acceptance of a conceptual framework is a *social* matter, it is the members of a community who accept and use it. Thus Sellars's theory of epistemology clearly is social. However, as my present account does not really depend on the Sellarsian

---

[88] See Tuomela (1985: Chapter 6).

108

view I will not here go into more detail.[89] Nor will I discuss the problem of the right mix between coherentism and foundationalism.

The notion of epistemic justification defined above is a social and even an *institutionalized* notion in a broad sense. This is because it deals with the group members acting in their various positions as members of g, which requires that they obey the ethos of g or at least do not intentionally violate it. Thus all epistemic notions which involve the present notion of epistemic justification are institutionalized in the mentioned wide sense (cf. below). This holds both for natural and institutional beliefs in our earlier sense dealing with the content rather than the source of beliefs.

Consider a proposition (content) p which is collectively or individually accepted by the members of a group g. Then we arrive at the following

---

[89] Let me comment on Sellars' theory of knowledge in some more detail, as I propose to take it as a background theory for the account of this paper (see Sellars 1956; 1968; 1975; Delaney 1977, for exposition and defense of the theory). According to Sellars, all knowledge is more or less heavily laden with background assumptions and knowledge. In particular, as to observational knowledge, there are no self-authenticating, nonverbal episodes, and those reports that do qualify as observation statements derive their epistemic authority from the knowledge of other related facts. In the case of scientific knowledge there will be scientific domain-specific theories which in addition to the mentioned kinds of general semantical rules of language will provide justification.

As to the problem of the structure and justification of knowledge, the central debate has been taking place between foundationalists and coherentists. Foundationalists assume that there are basic, justificationally privileged items of knowledge (e.g. observation statements of certain kinds) and assume that other kinds of knowledge be justified on the basis of them, while coherentists argue holistically and take justification to depend on the whole system of knowledge in principle, without there being privileged items of justified knowledge. One can claim, however, that in running together the notions of inference and presupposition, both the foundationalists and the coherentists link together the notions of *non-inferential* and *self-justifying* knowledge (cf. Delaney 1977). The foundationalist emphasizes the fact that (i) not all knowledge can be inferential and concludes from this that (ii) there must be some self-justifying instances of knowledge. Sellars accepts (i) but argues does (ii) does not follow from it. In contrast, the coherentists focus on the fact that (1) no knowledge is self-justifying and concludes from this that (2) all knowledge is inferential. Sellars accepts (1) and argues that (2) does not follow from it.

account of knowledge in a group, which account applies both to I-mode and we-mode groups:

> (*K*) p is *knowledge in* g in a situation C if and only if in C,
> (a) p is true and (b) epistemically justified in g.

This is compatible with regarding the notion of knowledge as primitive, as I do not claim that justification can be analyzed without reference to knowledge of some kind. Thus the if-part requires for its truth that the notion of knowledge is employed when spelling out clause (b). I also claim in accordance with this and my the earlier discussion in this paper that attribution of knowledge also depends on cultural and other factors. Gettier-type paradoxes are relevant in the sense that they seem to show that there in those paradoxical cases is no knowledge (sufficient justification) while the knower itself believes that it knows. In my previous symbolism, we have a case with A(g, EJ(g,p)) & A(g*, –EJ(g,p)). That is, the justification claim EJ(g,p) is acceptable to g, while it is not acceptable to the "epistemically wiser" perspective manifested by group g*. A rational group g should in this case, with A(g*, –EJ(g,p)) being true and this information being available to g, retract the original justification claim and arrive at –A(g, EJ(g,p) and, upon rational reflection, also to the stronger judgment A(g, –EJ(g,p)).

Let me finally note that there clearly is room for degrees of justification. There are thus degrees of goodness in relation to the grounds for the truth of p, to the knower's relevant reasoning and acting abilities and thus her understanding concerning p, and to the social bond between the group members. So an agent can have knowledge (or know) that p in stronger and weaker senses. Thus, a person may know that $E=mc^2$ but he may not have deep knowledge about it.

8. Group-Binding Group Knowledge

What can we now say of group-binding knowledge based on institutional (or group-social) normativity? I will explain the idea by discussing my earlier "positional" account of group beliefs (and other group attitudes). The positional account is concerned with normatively group-binding group beliefs and concentrates on normatively structured groups with positions and a distinction between operative members (e.g. a governing board in a corporation) and non-operative members, the operatives being suitably authorized for decision making and/or acting for the group.[90] Structure requires the mentioned kind of authority system and possibly normatively specified positions or roles in addition.[91] The task of the (internally or externally) authorized operative members is to create group-binding, indeed normatively and objectively (indeed, publicly) binding decisions (intentions, plans, etc.) for the group by means of their collective acceptance. Furthermore, the operative members are assumed to act correctly as members of the group and for the group, being normatively collectively committed to what they accept for the group. Thus, what they do is in the we-mode.

The operative members' collective acceptance in this account is "thick", group-obligation-involving collective acceptance of a view for the group. This is basically because the operative members have been authorized to collectively accept—e.g. by making agreements—normatively binding views and goals for the group. This collective acceptance may take into account division of labor, and as a consequence even a single position holder may in some cases be the sole acceptor. In some cases the operative members can be replaced by a collectively accepted codified device, such as a voting mechanism.

Accordingly, a group is taken to believe ("acceptance believe") something p if it accepts p as its view and if this is based on the operative

---

[90] For the positional account see e.g. Tuomela (1992; 1995; 2007). Positions in structured groups are defined by "task-right systems" (Tuomela 1995: Chapter 1). As to the operative/nonoperative distinction, in small groups often all the members are operatives—based on their acknowledged "natural" authority to function as group members.
[91] In the broadest sense positional functioning amounts to functioning as a group member who respects the ethos of the group (this is we-mode functioning basically). This broad sense is independent of whether the group is normatively structured into positions and roles.

members' mentioned kind of collective acceptance (agreement or other obligating acceptance) of p for the group. The non-operative members of the group ought to accept (explicitly or tacitly), or at least go along with, what the operative members accept as the group's views. They need not even have detailed knowledge about what is so being accepted. But they are still collectively committed to the accepted items in cases where they have authorized the operative members to form views for the group, or at least they ought to be so committed.

As to group knowledge, in accordance with what has already been said, the basic idea is that a group knows—relative to its own standards—that something p precisely when it believes it with good group-grounded reason (or, equivalently, believes it knows that p) and the group-grounded good reasons are good also from a more rational (and objective) point of view, and p is true. Notice that my earlier analysis of epistemic justification in g may still not fully transcend g (viz. there may be an "epistemically wiser" group g^* which makes the contrary judgment $A(g^*, E(g,p))$ or the stronger $A(g^*, -E(g,p))$). The requirement of rationality may anyhow be taken to make the justification "sufficiently" objective. I must here leave the problem somewhat open and say only that my paradigm is the method of science; and as long as my criterion of epistemic justification is understood along those, truth-conducive lines, it will amount to objective, albeit still group-relative justification.

Spelt out in full, here is my elucidation of epistemically justified normatively group-binding group belief, viz. of the notion of the group's believing that it knows that p whereby the group employs its own epistemic standards of justification:[92]

(*JBG*) Group g is *justified in believing* that p in the normative group-binding sense in the social and normative circumstances C if and only if in C there are operative members $A_1,...,A_m$ of g such that

---

[92] See Tuomela (1992; 1995; 2007) for my analysis of "positional" group belief.

(1) $A_1,...,A_m$, when acting as group members in the we-mode sense (and accordingly performing their positional tasks and due to their exercising the relevant joint-decision-making system of g) intentionally jointly accept p, as a group, for g as the group's view and because of this exercise of the decision-making system they ought to continue to accept and positionally believe it (and thus accept it in the we-mode);

(2) p relates appropriately to the realm of concern of the group and is epistemically justified for g (recall (EJ));

(3) there is mutual belief (possibly only I-mode belief) among the operative members $A_1,...,A_m$ to the effect that (1) and (2);

(4) because of (1) and (2), the (full-fledged and adequately informed) nonoperative members of g generally tacitly accept, or at least ought to accept, p as members of g;

(5) there is mutual belief in g to the effect that (4).

Let us recall our previous distinction between natural and institutional belief (and knowledge). Suppose g believes that p in the normative, group-binding sense and p is a true proposition. Then we can speak of the group's group-binding "quasi-knowledge", which still may lack justification and thus may not satisfy (BG). When it is up to the group-external world to determine whether p is true (the case with mind-to-world direction of fit), we are dealing with knowledge in a sense different from the case in which it is up to the group to determine what is correct or true. For instance, if p = Grass is green, we are dealing with the mind-to-world direction of fit type of situation. But if p = Squirrel pelt is money and the group is medieval Finns, we have knowledge, i.e. constitutive institutional knowledge, which is collectively self-made and has the world-to-mind direction fit (in addition to also having the mind-to-world direction of fit). In both cases there can be group knowledge, but in the second case the knowledge, being collectively self-created, is tautologically warranted (and self-validating): The justification is fully social (and independent of the way the group-external world is) in the latter but not in the former case. What is also important to notice is that in both cases there is in a sense truth of the matter, for it is an objective fact that grass is green and we can assume that it is also an objective sociological fact that medieval Finns collectively accepted and used squirrel pelt as money (even if the fact that squirrel fur is money is merely a group-grounded institutional fact).

To arrive at an elucidation of group knowledge that p, I propose that the truth of p (or, more generally, correct assertability, to cover moral cases) also needs to be required, for the group might be wrong no matter how good reasons it takes itself to have.[93]

> (*KG*) g *knows* that p *as a group* and thus in the *normative group-binding* sense in the social and normative circumstances C if and only if in C (i) g believes that p in the normatively group-binding sense and p is epistemically justified (in g), (ii) p is true (for g).

Here the phrase 'as a group' entails that the group members are collectively committed to p for the group in a sense entailing that they at least instrumentally ought to accept ("acceptance believe") that p. The criteria of justification here are those of g, and thus the knowledge dealt with here is group-dependent knowledge—defeatable by the existence of an "epistemically wiser" group g* for which it holds that $-A(g^*, EJ(g,p))$.

It follows from (*KG*))—given the entailed clause (1)(b) of (*BG*)—that the operative members must know that p and indeed generally mutually we-know that p in the we-mode (but they need not know it *also* in the I-mode). However, the non-operative members might not know that p, despite being obligated to knowing. Mutual or shared we-knowledge here amounts to this: the members all know that p and believe that the others know p and also that this is mutual knowledge in g.

I have been assuming above that knowledge is propositional and linguistically expressible; and when linguistically expressed it is social be-

---

[93] This contrasts with Longino (2002).

cause of being dependent on a linguistic community. What about know-how, viz. skills? Skills involve a propositional knowledge component which fits my analysis, but they also concern action—i.e. disposition to the kind of action that the skill concerns. That part I do not attempt to analyze here.

My present analysis of group knowledge is compatible with the possibility that a group member may be justified in the I-mode without the group being justified on the same basis: A joint reason might be missing. For instance, the constitutive goals and standards (etc.) of the group might simply prohibit the kind of I-mode or private justification that the group member has for his belief that p. (Even all group members might be justified without the group rationally having a joint reason—cf. cases requiring compromises.) Conversely, the group might be justified in its acceptance that p even if some members (e.g. non-operative members) are not, and might privately have good reasons against the truth of the content in question, but just go along with what the operative members have accepted.

Let me finally note that not all group beliefs are normatively group-binding in the above sense. Thus there can be (1) normatively group-binding (and possibly supported by I-mode beliefs by the group members), (2) normatively group-binding but not backed by personal, I-mode beliefs, (3) weakly normatively group-binding as the leaders have led the others to believe that they ought to believe in a certain way, which resulted in collective commitment; (4) non-normative but still group-binding because of based on a joint plan which is accepted in a non-normative, thin sense by the participants and which involves collective commitment but no group-obligation; or finally (5) non-normative and non-binding.[94]

The most typical group beliefs seem to be the normatively group-binding group beliefs in the sense of (1) and (2) and the non-normative beliefs in the sense of (4). We have:

---

[94] See Tuomela (2007: Chapter 6) for discussion and examples.

(*KGG*) g *knows* that p *as a group* in C if and only if in C (a) g believes that p in one of the senses (1)-(3); (b) p is epistemically justified (for g), and (c) p is true (for g).

As before, the knowledge is based on justification on the basis of the standards of g. If the relativization "for g" can be omitted we can speak of knowledge in an objective sense.[95] This would amount to making the analysans of (*KGG*) acceptable to the group g* consisting of all rational inquirers, resulting in A(g*(EJ(g,p)).

9. Conclusion

The central topic of this paper has been group knowledge, mainly knowledge attributable to a group. In the first section I listed the following theses to be investigated and defended in this paper:

(*T1*) (*a*) A group's knowing that p qua a group entails that the group must have accepted that p as true and that the group is justified in accepting that p. Group acceptance entails that the group is committed to p (analogously with the case of an individual agent). Group justification involves here that the group must have a good epistemic reason for its acceptance of p as true. (*group level*)

(*T1*) (*b*) On the level of group members, the group reason in T1(a) amounts to their joint reason for p, if the group is an egalitarian one in the sense of all members' actively, without delegation participating in group decisions and the like. The group members must in the we-mode case (involving group-binding collective commitment) share a justifying *joint* reason for the knowledge content p. (*joint member level*)

(*T1*) (*c*) An individual group member's knowledge that p in case T1(a) involves the justificatory aspect that she ought to be able to reason

---

[95] However, it seems that case (3) can also be satisfied on the basis of I-mode activities that are group-based (I have called such cases pro-group I-mode ones).

and act in the we-mode, thus in accordance with the fact that p has been justifiably accepted by the group. (*individual member level*)

(*T2*) In the case of *constitutive institutional knowledge* the criteria of epistemic justification are *social* (viz. based on group acceptance, hence collective member acceptance), whereas in the case of *natural knowledge non-social* elements of justification are normally crucial.

(*T3*) Knowledge is a social institution in the sense that the epistemic practices (gathering of knowledge, acceptance of something as the group's view, relevant inferences and action on its basis, and the justification of acceptances) in a group are governed by its ethos, thus by its normative epistemic standards; and, as opposed to mere reason-based belief, knowledge accordingly has a special institutional status.

As to the defense of (*T1*), the most central question dealt with in the paper was to analyze group reasons (reasons that group agents have) and joint reasons (reasons that group members jointly have) and to argue that they are to be required in cases of a group's knowing qua a group, viz. when the analysans of (*KGG*) in Section 8 is satisfied. (*T2*) was discussed in terms of institutional beliefs like "Squirrel pelt is money" which are completely socially created (in contrast to "natural" group beliefs like "There are neutrinos"). Thesis (*T3*) was not discussed at depth, but its truth naturally follows from the general social view of epistemology adopted in the paper.

Bibliography

Delaney, C. (1977), "Theory of Knowledge". In: C. Delaney et al. (eds.), *The Synoptic Vision: Essays on the Philosophy of Wilfrid Sellars*. Notre Dame: University of Notre Dame Press, 1-42.

Gettier, E. (1963), "Is Justified True Belief Knowledge?" *Analysis 23,* 121-123.

Kusch, M. (2002), *Knowledge by Agreement*. Oxford: Oxford University Press.

List, C. (2005), "Group Knowledge and Group Rationality: A Judgment Aggregation Perspective." *Episteme 2,* 25-38.

List, C. and Pettit, P. (2011), *Group Agency: The Possibility and Status of Corporate Agents*. New York: Oxford University Press.

Longino, H. (2002), *The Fate of Knowledge*. Princeton and Oxford: Princeton University Press.

Rosenberg, J. (2002), *Thinking About Knowing*. Oxford: Oxford University Press.

Schmitt, F. (1994), "The Justification of Group Beliefs". In: *Socializing Epistemology*. Lanham/MD: Rowman and Littlefield, 257-287.

Sellars, W. (1968), *Science and Metaphysics*, London: Routledge and Kegan Paul.

————— (1975), "The Structure of Knowledge". In: H.-N. Castaneda (ed.), *Action, Knowledge, and Reality: Studies in Honor of Wilfrid Sellars*. Indianapolis: The Bobbs-Merrill Company, Inc., 295-347.

Surowiecki, J. (2005), *The Wisdom of Crowds*. New York: Anchor Books.

Tuomela, R. (1985), *Science, Action, and Reality*. Dordrecht: Reidel.

————— (1992), "Group Beliefs". *Synthese 91*, 285-318.

————— (1995), The Importance of Us: A Philosophical Study of Basic Social Notions. Stanford: Stanford University Press.

————— (2000), "Belief versus Acceptance". *Philosophical Explorations 2*, 122-137.

————— (2002), The Philosophy of Social Practices: A Collective Acceptance View. Cambridge: Cambridge University Press.

————— (2004), "Group Knowledge Analyzed". *Episteme 1*, 109-127.

————— (2007), The Philosophy of Sociality: The Shared Point of View. New York: Oxford University Press.

On Dialectical Justification of Group Beliefs

RAUL HAKLI

Abstract

Epistemic justification of non-summative group beliefs is studied in this paper. Such group beliefs are understood to be voluntary acceptances, the justification of which differs from that of involuntary beliefs. It is argued that whereas epistemic evaluation of involuntary beliefs can be seen not to require reasons, justification of voluntary acceptance of a proposition as true requires that the agent, a group or an individual, can provide reasons for the accepted view. This basic idea is studied in relation to theories of dialectical justification in which justification is taken to require ability to justify. Since the reasons offered can in principle always be challenged, there is no ultimate end to the dialectical chain of justification. This makes justification of acceptance, and thus group belief, social and, in a way, contextual, but this does not seem to entail strong forms of epistemic relativism.

1. Introduction

Beliefs and other propositional attitudes are commonly attributed to groups and collectives. I once saw a news article with the title "Farmers believe cows 'moo' with an accent" (Reuters, Aug. 23, 2006). My first guess was that this was a conclusion of an opinion poll conducted among farmers the results of which indicated that most farmers share the belief that cows moo with an accent. In such cases what the term "group belief" refers to is actually a combination of beliefs or opinions of the individuals within the collective in question. Such group beliefs are often called *summative* group beliefs, because of the idea that a group belief is, in some sense, just a "sum" of the beliefs of the group members.

As I read the news article further, it turned out that this was not a case of a summative group belief after all. The article said that it was actually a group called "West Country Farmhouse Cheesemakers" that proclaimed the view that cows moo with an accent. Some of the farmers had noticed the phenomenon and informed the others, they had discussed it within their group, and had found out that other group members had recognised same kind of development in their herds. They had then contacted scientists who had studied similar phenomena among birds. Finally, the group had made this view public through their web page, and a spokesman of the group had been interviewed by Reuters. This is not a case of simple summative group belief but what, since Gilbert (1987), has been called non-summative group belief, a view that a group has deliberately adopted as the view of their group. Non-summative group beliefs are genuinely addressed to the group and they are not reducible to individual beliefs. In general, it is not necessary that any individual group member believes the content of a non-summative group belief correctly addressed to the group (Gilbert 1987). A typical example occurs when a committee in which the committee members' views are polarized decides to adopt a view that no individual committee member endorses but is willing to accept as a compromise. A shared belief among the group members does not suffice for a group belief either since the group members must have some kind of an agreement over the acceptability of the view as the group's view (Gilbert 1987).

It seems that such non-summative group beliefs can be epistemically justified and that their justification is not necessarily based on the justification of the group members' beliefs. For instance, by collecting the evidence available to group members or by combining the special expertise of individual group members, the group may be epistemically in a better position than any of its group members individually are. It may even be the case that a group manages to aggregate the views of the individuals in a way that the product is a justified view that none of the individual group members have. As an example, consider Goldman's (1999: 81) example of a weather forecast agency that bases its official weather forecast on the predictions of individual forecasters by giving more weight to the predictions of the experts with the most accurate prediction histories. Assume that the forecasts concerning the temperature at a certain time diverge so that the official forecast is a weighted average of the individual forecasts. Assume further that the individuals personally rely on their own views over the official view. In such a situation, the official group view can be considered justified even though none of the group members personally hold that view.

The question posed in this paper is under which conditions such non-summative group beliefs are epistemically justified. The type of justification under concern here is epistemic justification of the accepted view, not justification of the decision to accept a particular view. Such group decisions are often made for pragmatic reasons, but here our focus is on epistemic reasons. In order to answer the question, we have to consider different theories of epistemic justification of beliefs and see whether they will apply in the case of non-summative group beliefs. First, however, we need to consider what is the nature of such group beliefs, because it has been suggested that they should not be conceived as beliefs but rather as *acceptances* (Cohen 1992: 53–60; Wray 2001; Meijers 2002). If this is the case, it may have implications for epistemic justification. Thus, we have to consider what distinguishes beliefs and acceptances from each other and how their differences affect their epistemic evaluation.

The article is structured as follows: In Section 2, I discuss the nature of group beliefs in light of the distinction between belief and acceptance. In Section 3, I consider theories of epistemic justification and study, given the distinction above, which sorts of theories would be apt for epistemic evaluation of beliefs and which for epistemic evaluation of acceptances. In Section 4, I discuss dialectical theories of justification and study whether the justification of group beliefs could be conceived dialectically. In Section 5, I review criticism presented against dialectical views. Conclusions are drawn in Section 6.

2. The nature of group beliefs

In order to answer the question whether group beliefs are beliefs as ordinarily understood, we must consider what beliefs are as they are ordinarily understood. Here we need not give a full account of what beliefs are, but we adopt a realist stance on folk-psychological notions. They are some kind of intentional states or attitudes, possibly dispositional, and something that the agents can, at least to some extent, be reflectively aware of. Beliefs are intimately connected to perceiving, thinking, and acting. Being situated in the world, we automatically form beliefs about it. We process these beliefs when we think; a person may realize what she believes by becoming aware of her thoughts and convictions. Her thinking the matter further will then lead her to form new beliefs and revise old ones. We use our beliefs as reasons for action, and other people can infer our beliefs from perceiving our actions. There are thus several roles commonly attributed to beliefs: Beliefs provide us information about the world, they facilitate our thinking, and they guide our action.

As is well known, thinking and acting may not always accord. We may believe one thing and say another, which makes it problematic to identify belief with dispositions to think or act in a way presupposing the truth of the alleged belief. Consider, for instance, community norms that require people to behave as if they believed what everyone is expected to believe. It is conceivable that people in such situations can, on the one hand, have beliefs that are not manifested in action, and, on the other hand, have acting dispositions that are not based on beliefs but perhaps on cultural habits or desires to believe. It is not possible to identify beliefs in a straightforward fashion with dispositions to act in certain ways because people may sometimes believe differently from what could ever be revealed by observing their behaviour.

This is not to say that we are always introspectively aware of what we believe. Consider colour illusions, or the Müller–Lyer illusion: Although I am familiar with the illusion and know that the lines should be of equal length, it still very much seems to me that the other one is longer, and I wonder whether this time it actually was drawn slightly longer by mistake. It is not clear even to myself whether I believe that the lines are of equal length or not. Also we are not always right about why we do what we do. In cases of self-deception, for instance, I may have radically false beliefs about my motives. Sometimes the situation may be such that we do not realize what we think until we say or do something; acting sometimes comes first and thinking later. Even then we may be wrong about the beliefs and desires that actually prompted our actions, but only cite beliefs and desires that render our actions rational in retrospective. Various types of biases in human judgement and decision-making have been documented in psychological studies (see e.g. the review article by Pronin 2007, and its references).

It thus seems that thinking and acting may sometimes come apart. Folk-psychological explanations of our own actions and actions of other people are couched in terms of beliefs and desires, but these terms sometimes refer to subconscious states that prompt our actions and sometimes to our conscious judgements and higher-order preferences. This suggests that words like "belief" and "desire" are ambiguous. For instance, we seem to attribute beliefs to all kinds of entities (like animals, children, computers, thermometers, companies, countries etc.), but it is not at all clear that we always mean the same thing. This suggests that there may be more than one type of thing, more than one type of doxastic state that we refer to when we talk about beliefs. The possibility I am entertaining is that there are two interesting types of doxastic attitudes as suggested by such philosophers as K. Lehrer (1979), R. Stalnaker (1984), and L. J. Cohen (1992), namely beliefs and acceptances.

However, these notions have been characterized in different ways by these authors and their followers. Often the notion of belief is left intuitively understood, but when a characterization has been attempted, it is typically given in dispositional terms. According to Stalnaker (1984: 15), to believe a proposition, say *p*, is, roughly, to be disposed to act in ways that would tend to be successful in a world in which *p* were true. Cohen (1992) speaks of beliefs as dispositions to feel that things are thus-and-so. He does not specify what such a feeling is exactly, but I assume that a feeling of conviction or persuasion when one thinks about the truth of a proposition would count as one typical example.

The notion of acceptance has been characterized in different ways as well. The broadest definition comes from Stalnaker (1984: 79–80), according to whom to accept a proposition is to treat it as a true proposition in one way or another. This notion includes believing, presupposing, postulating, and other such attitudes. Cohen's formulation of acceptance is narrower, and acceptance is contrasted with belief. According to Cohen, acceptance that *p* means adoption of a policy of treating *p* as true in theoretical and practical reasoning. There is some ambiguity in this characterization since it can refer either to the act of adoption, or the resulting state and the commitments that follow from adopting such a policy, but the ambiguity is taken to be relatively harmless. In Cohen's theory, one can accept what one does not believe, and one can believe what one does not accept. The latter would not be possible in Stalnaker's terminology. Lehrer's (1979) characterization of acceptance is the strictest of these three. For him, the acceptance of a proposition (in a particular context) means assenting to the proposition when one's only purpose is to assent to what is true and to refuse to assent to what is false.

In spite of the different characterizations given to these terms by these authors, I consider their views largely compatible once the terminological differences are sorted out. I will adopt the terminology used by Cohen: I will take beliefs and acceptances to be distinct attitudes. When I need to refer to a broader class that includes them both, I will use the term "doxastic attitude". This notion I take to be equivalent with Stalnaker's notion of acceptance. Moreover, I will follow Tuomela (2000), who distinguishes between *pragmatic acceptance* and *acceptance as true*. The former is at least partially motivated by interests whereas the latter is only concerned with truth. I take the latter to be equivalent with Lehrer's notion of acceptance, and I will also sometimes call it *epistemic acceptance* because that term reflects better the difference between the two notions of acceptance: In both, the content is accepted as true, but for different kinds of reasons.

Doxastic attitudes of these two types have been attributed different properties. It seems that we automatically form beliefs when we interact with our environment independently of our goals, our beliefs vary in strength, and they need not be explicitly linguistically formulated. Acceptances, on the other hand, seem to be under voluntary control, goal-dependent, categorical, and linguistically formulated. Acceptances function as premisses guiding our intentional action, whereas beliefs presumably affect also our unintentional actions. I assume it is correct to attribute both beliefs and acceptances to human adults and children whereas very small children and animals are only capable of beliefs since acceptance requires linguistic ability and ability of reasoning.

Arguably (see Hakli 2006), the voluntariness of acceptance should be understood as the decisive feature distinguishing it from belief. Others have emphasized the importance of goal-dependence as characterizing acceptance. The main argument for taking voluntariness to be the distinguishing feature instead is that goal-dependence does not properly distinguish acceptance from belief. Beliefs too can be biased and pragmatically motivated, and acceptances need not be. For instance, my beliefs concerning my personal qualities may be more positive than evidence warrants, but I may realize this and decide to accept a more neutral self-image. This acceptance will result in more modest judgements about myself, although my belief can still remain and unconsciously affect my behaviour in relations with others. If the argument is correct, the doxastic states that are voluntary should rather be classified as acceptances whereas the remaining, involuntary doxastic states can be called beliefs. For example, we cannot really help but believe that there are no goblins, but we can certainly decide to act as if there were, that is, we can accept it as true that there are goblins when we are acting in a particular context, like in a children's play, for instance. What we accept as true need not be believed, it can be just "make-belief", and it need not be based on evidence but some pragmatic purpose. In some cases this acceptance may be based on evidence only and not be directed by any pragmatic concerns.[96]

---

[96] This suggestion is somewhat controversial, since not all philosophers endorse the distinction and those who do draw the lines in a different fashion. I will briefly consider an objection by Fabio Paglieri (2006: 28–35), who is sympathetic to the distinction and to the idea of finding one decisive difference between belief and acceptance. However, he seems to be committed to the idea that acceptance is necessarily tied to pragmatic goals, since he suggests that the defining feature of acceptance is its pragmatic value. He attempts to show that voluntariness cannot be the distinctive feature of acceptance by arguing that we cannot always voluntarily accept whatever proposition we like. He invites the reader to consider the following scenario: Imagine you are standing on the edge of a deep chasm, "[...] your feet are just on the brink of the ravine, the wind coming from below is howling all around you, shuffling your clothes and disarranging your hair, while the other side of the cleft is many meters away from you, completely out of reach. You certainly believe there is an abyss opening in front of you, and you also believe that another step in that direction would plunge you into it beyond recovery. Now, would you be capable to accept the contrary proposition at will, i.e. taking it as a ground [...] for your next step? I think not – and I also think we would all agree to consider a madman whoever is capable of accepting such a proposition against all evidence, as lacking some basic 'safety device' in his mind."
I admit that for me at least it would probably be extremely difficult to accept it as true that there is no abyss and take it as a premiss in my action and take a further step. However, I do not see this as a principled difficulty showing that I lack control of my thoughts or of my steps. Rather the difficulty stems from insufficient motivation because I am not suicidal. So the "can" that Paglieri has in mind is clearly different from the intended one. They both concern human psychology rather than metaphysics but Paglieri conceives a situation in which the agent cannot do something because she is not sufficiently motivated. However, the intended notion of "can" has to do with situations in which the agent cannot do something even though she is motivated and tries to do it. Were I sufficiently motivated to commit a suicide, I consider it possible that I could decide to think that there is no abyss and that I can therefore safely walk further, and by focussing on this thought step ahead. Other people have done it, and we do not consider them mad but desperate. In fact, plausibly they have entertained thoughts like this in order to encourage themselves to take the crucial step.
However, even if Paglieri's thought experiment were successful, it would not show that my suggestion of defining acceptance as voluntarily treating a proposition as true is problematic. If it were true that in some cases I would not be able to voluntarily take a proposition to be true, it would just show that acceptance is not always possible.

In any case, my proposal of defining acceptance as a voluntary doxastic state is a terminological suggestion and should be understood as a refinement of the ordinary language conception of belief that seems to be ambiguous. If there really are two kinds of doxastic states with radically different properties and functional roles it makes better sense to have different labels to them. In that way we may get a better understanding of several epistemological puzzles. As argued in Hakli (2006), non-summative group beliefs are voluntarily formed views, and as such they are acceptances, not beliefs in the above strict sense (even if they were beliefs understood in the broad everyday sense). Similarly, groups are often attributed pro-attitudes like wants and desires but they should similarly be understood rather as voluntarily adopted goals, following Cohen (1992: 40–67). This allows us to make sense of the everyday language that ascribes folk-psychological states to collectives: We can predict and explain actions of collectives and still maintain that the agency of collectives depends on the agency of individuals who accept views and goals for the collectives.

Note that this sort of "rejectionism" that denies that groups can have beliefs in the same sense that individuals do does not force us to reject the possibility of group knowledge based on non-summative group beliefs. For elaboration on this, see Hakli (2007) or Wray (2007). The argument is based on Cohen's (1992: 86–100) view according to which knowledge may not require belief but may rest on acceptance as well. Lehrer (2000: 12–14), in fact, suggests that it is acceptance—not belief—that is necessary for knowledge. The specific type of acceptance here is the epistemic acceptance of a proposition for the purpose of attaining truth and avoiding error. Bypassing questions concerning knowledge, let us now consider epistemic evaluation of beliefs and acceptances.

Walking is voluntary action as well, but sometimes it is not possible to walk because the way is blocked.

3. Epistemic evaluation of doxastic attitudes

One of the main concerns in epistemology in recent decades has been to give an account of justification of beliefs. Perhaps the main reason for this has been that justification has traditionally been conceived as a necessary condition of knowledge, the central notion in epistemology. Indeed, sometimes the notion "epistemic justification" is taken to mean justification required for knowledge (see e.g. Greco 2005). Independently of whether justification is required for knowledge or not, justification is of interest since there is something normatively better in justified belief as opposed to unjustified belief. Also a belief's being justified seems, at least according to some theories, to be a property that we can be aware of more easily than a belief's amounting to knowledge: We may be able to recognize justified beliefs and be guided by this normative notion. It is not as easy to recognize instances of knowledge because of the truth condition that is external to us; think of sceptical scenarios, for example.

Theories of epistemic justification are often divided into two classes: internalist and externalist theories. According to internalist theories, whatever the justification of an agent's beliefs consists of must be internal to the agent, that is, other beliefs or other mental states of the agent. In addition, it is often thought that the agent has access to these other beliefs or mental states so that she is, at least in principle, capable of providing reasons for her beliefs or cite evidence in favour of her beliefs. One form of internalism is evidentialism according to which an agent's possession of sufficient evidence and access to it guarantees justification.

Externalist theories deny such internalist claims and allow that justification of an agent's beliefs may, at least partially, depend on factors that are external to the agent and possibly something that the agent herself is not aware of. For instance, justification of a belief may depend on the properties of the causal processes that produced the belief. Reliabilism that requires that in order to be justified a belief has to be a product of a reliable belief-forming process is one commonly endorsed form of externalism. Also theories that invoke modal conditions like sensitivity or safety principles are considered externalist since the modal conditions specify how the agent's beliefs should behave in other possible worlds, and the agent may not have access to such modal data.

Both kinds of theories are supported by certain intuitions invoked by paradigmatic example cases. For instance, a commonly shared intuition supporting internalist views is that in demon worlds in which our senses are systematically deceived we would still somehow be justified in our beliefs, because no matter what we do, there is no way we could arrive at a better judgement. Then again there are often told cases about subjects who have some sort of an ability to reliably form correct beliefs, for instance, about the sex of a chicken, but they cannot explain how they get these beliefs nor can they give any reasons for them. It seems that their beliefs should still get some kind of positive evaluation because they have been seen to be reliably true. On the other hand, in both types of cases, it seems that something valuable is missing too: in cases like the demon world the reliable connection to truth is missing and in cases like the chicken sexers the ability to provide reasons is missing.

This has led several epistemologists to suggest various combinations of internal and external conditions. Many current accounts of epistemic justification try to preserve the attractive features of internalist and externalist theories (and simultaneously avoid their problems) by somehow combining the requirement for reasons or evidence to that of the reliability of the process. Some philosophers suspect the viability of such "compatibilist" approaches and instead settle for one or the other (see e.g. Bernecker 2006). Others have altogether abandoned the whole quest for a unified and absolute notion of justification as hopeless and instead turned to a kind of pluralism according to which there are many epistemically good properties but no unified notion of justification (Alston 2005).

If we assume that there are actually two types of doxastic states as suggested in the previous section, this has consequences concerning the epistemic assessment of such states, normally conflated under the term "belief". My claim here is that the problem with compatibilist approaches is that they are trying to give an account that covers two separate kinds of phenomena precisely because they do not distinguish belief and acceptance, and this has led to the frustration that has motivated abandoning the search for a notion of justification. Our everyday conception of belief seems to cover everything from an automatically formed perceptual belief that it is raining to the careful judgement that Fermat's last theorem is true, or, indeed, from a dog's awareness of a rabbit to the scientific community's acceptance of an extensively tested theory. These phenomena are so different that it seems implausible that they should all be assessed according to the same criteria. Justification of belief and justification of acceptance are two different things. Seeing the difference between two kinds of doxastic states explains our mixed intuitions.

We can see this more clearly by considering standard example cases presented in the literature to support one or another type of theory: Externalist theories have been supported by examples that invoke externalist intuitions that concern e.g. the importance of reliability of the processes of belief formation. Such cases are, for instance, cases of chicken sexers or cases with perceptual beliefs of animals or little children. Even if one's own intuitions did not always accord with the authors', it is crucial to notice a common feature of these cases: The example cases in which the subjects are presented as knowing without being able to cite any reasons are all cases involving beliefs in our refined terminology. The beliefs in these examples are results of reliable processes, but they require no decision or agency on the part of the believer, and the believer is not in a position to explain how she got these beliefs nor can she give reasons for them. It is important to note this because had these cases involved a conscious decision to form a view by considering the evidence pro and contra, the intuition that these are cases of knowledge seems to disappear.[97]

---

[97] Of course, a chicken sexer can voluntarily decide to accept that a certain chick is a hen based on her strong feeling that the chick is a hen but then she has at least some

On the other hand, the typical cases that seem to intuitively support internalist views that require reasons or evidence are such that the agent has formed a view by doing everything in her power to form an epistemically responsible judgement on the matter at hand (such as performing thorough inquiry, carefully weighing evidence, considering reasons pro and contra, etc.), but has still, due to an epistemically hostile environment such as the demon world, come to a false conclusion. The intuitive epistemically good feature in these cases is to be found in the agent's active inquiry and acceptance of a view on the basis of evidence. Considering just a simple perceptual false belief in a demon world would not invoke similar intuitions.

More generally, it seems plausible that if an act or an attitude is voluntary for an agent, its evaluation requires considering the reasons for the act or the attitude. On the other hand, if something is involuntary, we cannot in general require the agent to provide reasons for it. However, we may evaluate it by considering the properties of the causal mechanisms that produced it, and this leads us to externalism. Certainly, if there is a choice point for the agent either to adopt an attitude or not then we are entitled to expect that the agent has reasons for making the choice. And if it is epistemic justification we are interested in, also the reasons that are of interest must be epistemic. On the other hand, if there is no choice point for the agent, the agent is not directly responsible for the attitude and the agent's reasons are not similarly relevant for its evaluation (although there is always the indirect responsibility for our beliefs due to the earlier choice points concerning our actions). Thus, I would like to suggest that involuntary beliefs should be assessed according to externalist criteria, e.g. reliability, whereas voluntary acceptances should be assessed according to criteria that internalists have considered important, like possession of evidence or reasons.

---

reason for this view, namely her feeling of confidence that the chick is a hen. In Cohen's (1992: 17–18) theory, this would count as a belief being a reason for acceptance.

If we take non-summative group beliefs to be voluntarily formed acceptances, as I have suggested, reliabilist accounts of justification of group beliefs that do not require reasons are inadequate. Even if a group of people could reliably form true views by some method, e.g. weighted voting schemes discussed by Goldman (1999: 81–82), these views would not seem to be justified unless the group were able to provide reasons for them, or at least for using these voting schemes that they have decided to use. Epistemic justification requires epistemic reasons for accepting a certain view or for using a certain procedure to determine a group view. An epistemic reason for using a certain voting scheme could be that the scheme has been found reliable in forming true group views or, better yet, that it can be proved optimal in yielding true views under some reasonable assumptions.

Several theories of epistemic justification require reasons and might thus suit for justification of acceptance and, in particular, non-summative group beliefs. These include such internalist theories as traditional foundationalism, coherentism, evidentialism, and internalist virtue theories like responsibilism. These theories have been extensively discussed and criticized in the literature concerning epistemic justification in general, and some criticisms have been presented specifically in the context of group beliefs (Schmitt 1994, Corlett 2007). In what follows, I will not consider all these theories but concentrate on one family of theories that I find promising as a candidate for a theory of justification of group beliefs, namely *dialectical* theories of justification as presented in particular by Annis (1978) and Williams (1999a; 2001).

According to these theories, what determines the justificatory status of an agent's belief is whether she can respond to the challenges posed by the members of her community. As I understand responding to mean providing reasons or evidence, these theories seem to be motivated by internalist intuitions. They try to avoid the problems faced by traditional internalist theories, foundationalism and coherentism. They differ from foundationalism in the sense that there is no fixed set of basic beliefs that would be intrinsically justified. Rather, the default status for all beliefs is that they are justified unless they are challenged. This is sometimes called the default–challenge model of justification. Any beliefs can be challenged in principle so there are no indefeasible basic beliefs as in foundationalism, but the challenges must be motivated as well: They have to be based on real doubt (Annis 1978), or they must be reasonable (Williams 2001: 145–172). Which beliefs enjoy the default status and which challenges count as reasonable may depend on the social context of inquiry.[98]

---

[98] Because of this link to the social context, these theories do not seem to be purely internalist. I have suggested earlier (Hakli 2007) that justification of belief should be understood in externalist terms and justification of acceptance in internalist terms, but this may be incorrect if justification of acceptance is understood to be dialectical. According to Hilary Kornblith (2008), dialectical theories are externalist because justification depends not only on matters internal to the agent but also her society, the challenges that it may present and the default entitlements that it may permit. The agent may be unaware of them, at least prior to the dialectical process. Dialectical theories are internalist only if they are restricted to the community of the agent herself. That is, in Kornblith's view, traditional internalist theories that require reasons for beliefs, can be seen as dialectical theories in which the agent is only required to answer to the possible objections that she herself can think of.
One could try to argue that dialectical theories should be conceived as internalist theories because in them justification depends on the agent's reasons and her access to these reasons. The society only determines the limit how far the agent must go in giving these reasons in order to count as justified. In Williams' (1999a) presentation, this is the main difference between the dialectical theory and traditional foundationalism that requires that the agent have access to reasons all the way to basic beliefs. According to Williams, reasons are not needed if the agent's view enjoys a default status, but also that seems similar to foundationalism in which an agent is not required to have reasons for her basic beliefs.
Pritchard (2009b: 17–18) distinguishes between internal and external conditions. An internal condition is such that the facts that determine whether the agent has satisfied the condition are accessible to the agent by reflection alone. According to Pritchard, any theory of knowledge that incorporates at least one necessary epistemic condition is an internalist theory of knowledge. In this sense, the dialectical justification condition is not an internal but an external one since one does not know by reflection alone whether it will be challenged or not. However, a condition that requires only that an agent have internally accessible grounds for her beliefs is such an internal condition. That condition seems to be entailed by the dialectical condition. In order to be able to satisfy the dialectical condition one must have at least some grounds for her views so that she can defend the view for possible challenges. Thus it seems that the require-

134

4. Dialectical conception of epistemic justification

Several authors have suggested that justification could be conceived dialectically (see e.g. Annis 1978; Brandom 1983; Williams 1999a; Kusch 2002; Lammenranta 2004; Rolin 2008, influential ideas were presented earlier by Sellars 1963, and Wittgenstein 1974). They have not distinguished between belief and acceptance but mainly talked about justification of belief in general. I will here restrict to the case of acceptance and allow the possibility that involuntary beliefs should be assessed by different criteria. According to dialectical views, justification is contextual in the sense that epistemic assessment of judgements depends on the norms that govern the discursive practices in which these judgements are made. Justification is linked to the practice of justifying, the practice of giving and asking for reasons.

The basic idea of a dialectical theory of justification can be put roughly as follows: An agent is justified in accepting a proposition *p* if and only if she can successfully defend *p* against reasonable challenges; In the absence of reasonable challenges against *p*, the defence is vacuously successful, and *p* is justified by default. This basic characterization leaves several issues open and requires further specification. At least the following questions should be addressed: What is a reasonable challenge? Does it require a positive reason to doubt *p*, that is, evidence against *p*? Must the challenge be voiced, or is it enough that somebody could pose one? What does it mean to successfully defend a proposition? Must the defence be

ment of dialectical justification entails a requirement for the satisfaction of an internal condition. An account that incorporates the dialectical condition thus implicitly insists on the satisfaction of an internal condition. Thus it seems that any theory of knowledge that requires the satisfaction of the external condition of dialectical justification is necessarily an internalist theory of knowledge.

At this point one is tempted to ask whether the internalism/externalism terminology serves any useful purpose. It does not seem to be very illuminating anymore. Perhaps in the end it is not important whether a theory is classified as internalist or externalist. Maybe we can just consent to the general idea that justification of acceptance requires reasons whereas justification of belief does not.

voiced, or is it enough that the agent could defend it? What counts as a successful defence: Must one convince her opponent, or does it suffice to face the challenge e.g. by giving more evidence for the view or a non-question-begging argument undermining the challenge? Even if one does convince her opponents, does it necessarily suffice for epistemic justification? Who is entitled to challenge the view: The agent's fellow group members, the whole society, representatives of other societies, or even future epistemic communities? In the case of group views, who is entitled to defend the view and on which grounds? In particular, is it required that the agent is entitled to speak as a proxy for the whole group, and must the grounds be collectively accepted? I can only try some tentative answers to these questions here. I will proceed, in the next section, by looking at some criticisms targeted against the dialectical conception in order to see which answers to the above questions would help in meeting the criticisms. First, let us discuss some features and benefits of the dialectical conception of justification in the context of group views.

The dialectical conception makes explicit the social nature of justification. An agent's justification does not depend only on evidence she possesses or the causal relationships between the world and her beliefs. Also the social context, the evidence available to the agents' community as well as the epistemic practices of the community, are relevant in assessing one's views. A person's acceptance of a proposition may be a purely private mental act or it may be a public assertion in which she commits herself to the truth of that proposition.[99] Similarly, a group may, at least in principle, accept something only for the purposes of the group or it may present it to the outsiders as the view of the group. The target audiences in these cases are different, and it seems to make a difference to the justificatory status of the accepted view because it specifies the social context in which the view can be challenged. A person may be justified in her private acceptance of a

---

[99] See Walton and Krabbe (1995: 23) for explication of such propositional commitment.

view if she can respond to all possible counterarguments that she considers plausible in light of evidence available to her. However, should she go and assert that view to someone else, she takes the responsibility to respond to challenges made by others who may have further relevant evidence (Brandom 1983; Cohen 1986: 94). Only if she can meet the objections of others, does her view still count as justified in the broader social context.

Similarly, in order for a group to form an epistemically justified view it should first collect all the evidence available to the group members and openly discuss the arguments for and against the candidate views before voting or otherwise making the decision concerning the group view. It may even be considered a responsibility of the group members to criticize the candidate views and communicate their doubts and possible counterarguments in order to make an informed decision about the matter. This is important especially if the group members are under obligation to suppress differences in opinion and conform to the group view once it is formed.[100] Sometimes a group view may be accepted on the basis of a majority vote in spite of voiced criticism from the minority. Intuitively, it might seem that a group view should be dialectically justified among the group members in order to count as justified in a broader social context. However, this is not necessarily the case. For instance, the outside community may possess evidence that renders the minority view implausible, so the criticism does not arise in a larger context. Of course, the outside community may also possess evidence that renders a unanimous view implausible, so dialectical justification within a group does not guarantee dialectical justification in the context of a larger community.

There may be a special case in which dialectical justification within a group is sufficient for epistemic justification in a broader context as well. I mean cases of collectively constructed social facts emphasized by John Searle (1995) and Raimo Tuomela (2007), like what counts as money with-

---

[100] As noted by Mathiesen (2006), this aspect seems to be somewhat problematic for theories that require such obligations, such as that of Gilbert (1987).

in a community. In such cases, the accepted propositions become true in virtue of the very act of collective acceptance, so it seems impossible that they could be reasonably challenged from outside of the community in question. However, such collective acceptance is typically not epistemic acceptance but pragmatic since it is not based on evidence concerning existing social reality but on the group's goals to change that social reality.

Raimo Tuomela (2004) has argued that justification of collectively accepted group views requires collectively accepted reasons. This idea seems to cohere with the dialectical conception in the sense that a group is clearly in a better position to defend its view in public if its members have a shared understanding of the reasons for the view. Such a shared understanding often results from a successful dialectical process of argumentation in which all challenges to the view are resolved.[101] However, sometimes there is no unanimity concerning the reasons that support a view due to the division of epistemic labour or different epistemic principles used by different group members (see e.g. Staley 2007). It thus seems that sometimes a group view might be dialectically justified even if the group has not explicitly agreed on which reasons support the collectively accepted view. However, in such cases, there should at least be agreement on who can speak on behalf of the group and what kind of reasons would be acceptable for the group in order for the defence to count as the group's defence.

---

[101] Often, however, a group view is formed using some other process than dialectical argumentation, but even then collectively accepted reasons may result from the decision-making mechanism adopted. Philip Pettit (2003) has compared two procedures for aggregating individual judgements into a collective one: the *premiss-driven approach* in which the group votes on each premiss separately and then use logic to decide on the conclusion. The other option is to use the *conclusion-driven approach* in which the group members reason on the individual level and only vote on the conclusion. If the group uses the premiss-driven approach, the accepted premisses provide a collectively accepted reason for the collectively accepted conclusion and the group is in a better position to defend its view if it adopts the premiss-driven procedure. However, this procedure may lead the group to adopt a view that majority rejects or a view that no group member endorses.

Such agreement is needed also in cases in which there are collectively accepted reasons, because also the reasons may be challenged. Also in such cases, it may be up to an individual group member to defend the group view on the basis of her special expertise. In scientific research, for instance, it is typical that the evidence is distributed knowledge among the group members, that is, something derivable from the combined knowledge of individual group members. This can happen also in everyday situations in which a group view is formed partially on the basis of testimony of certain group members. As an example, consider the cow accent case presented in Section 1. Here there is distributed knowledge within the group that cows moo with accent, since the local farmers each know how cows moo in their area, although they may be unaware of how cows moo in other regions. As they meet and combine their evidence (e.g. by imitation or recordings), they will be able to infer the conclusion. Since the evidence may be based on testimony, responding to a challenge may require that the group resort to the expertise of individual agents.

In general, challenges may require an individual agent to go beyond her previously made acceptances in search for reasons for the accepted view. A dialectical process may thus open new directions of inquiry in order to find new evidence for one's view. Of course, it may also result in revision of the view in case its predictions turn out false.[102] In giving fur-

---

[102] By linking justification intimately to inquiry the dialectical conception can to some extent alleviate worries expressed by Jaakko Hintikka (2007: 1–2) according to whom epistemology is too concerned with securing current knowledge that it neglects the more important task of finding new knowledge. In order to find out whether our currently accepted hypotheses are justified in light of possible challenges we need to do inquiry. We can either try to establish the truth of the premises that entail our hypotheses or we can use our hypotheses as premises to infer consequences and then test them experimentally. Justification is intimately connected to interrogative inquiry as Hintikka (2007: 21–22) suggests, and this is easily seen if justification is conceived as dialectical. Dialectical inquiry is needed not only to find out which judgements are justified but also to find out relative to which premises and inferential principles they are justified. Moreover, since it recognizes that justification is relative to background commitments and principles, it can tolerate developing competing hypotheses that are based on different epistemic principles, which may be beneficial for collective inquiry (see also Kitcher 1990).

ther reasons for our acceptances we may eventually have to rely on our ordinary beliefs and find reasons for accepting their contents, thus transforming belief into acceptance (Cohen 1986: 91–97). At some point we may do no more than cite such ordinary beliefs for which we cannot give any further reasons and hope that our interlocutors share these beliefs. According to Cohen (1986: 93), such beliefs (or perhaps their existence) can still count as reason for acceptance. These beliefs can be evaluated in terms of externalist criteria like truth, reliability, or safety. Some of these beliefs might be called Wittgensteinian certainties or hinge propositions.[103]

Such beliefs include not only ordinary perceptual beliefs that I see a table in front of me, but also such epistemic principles that are taken to be so obvious that it is difficult to find other even more obvious principles that could justify them. Such principles could be, for instance, the principle of contradiction, the inference rule Modus Ponens, or a principle according to which if a person is in good lighting conditions and it appears to her that there is a table in front of her, she is *prima facie* justified in accepting that there is a table in front of her. It could be said that such epistemic norms and principles are collectively accepted by the epistemic communities, although the nature of such collective acceptance may differ from the collective acceptance typical in cases of groups that make explicit decisions using collectively accepted procedures. Here it is not the case that the members first make a decision concerning the epistemic norms to be used and then the practice follows. Rather the collective acceptance follows the practice developed over a long period of time. Collective participation to the practice and compliance to the norms constitute collective acceptance of the practice and the norms.

---

[103] When shared by other members of our epistemic community, such certainties also block Pyrrhonian scepticism: If legitimate challenges are to be based on real doubt, these beliefs cannot be legitimately challenged. A Pyrrhonian sceptic may suspend judgement—which is a voluntary acceptance—but she cannot help in believing, and this can be revealed in her actions (see also Lammenranta 2008). Thus there is no room for real doubt, thereby not for legitimate challenge either, and acceptances based on such beliefs enjoy the default status of justification.

5. Criticism against the dialectical conception

The dialectical conception of justification has been criticized by saying that being justified and being able to justify are two different things, and they should not be conflated (see e.g. Alston 2005: 18; also Rescorla 2009). As noted by Lammenranta (2004), this need not involve confusion. One may say that although such a distinction can be made, upon analysis they amount to the same thing: The state of being justified should be understood in terms of the process of justifying. At least this is a possibility that should not be dismissed too quickly but should be investigated.

The dialectical view could be challenged also by saying that it conflates the epistemic justification of a doxastic attitude to the justification required for asserting a view. Remember, however, that we are now considering voluntary acceptances. Since they are voluntary, they are more like actions than attitudes: An act of acceptance is very much like an assertion. According to Cohen (1992: 71–72), an assertion expresses acceptance, not belief, and also a mere mental act of acceptance can be understood as a silent assertion of a proposition to oneself. The only difference is that the audience is restricted to the agent herself.[104] Of course, a

---

[104] The dialectical view thus leads to one sort of contextualism concerning justification: Justification depends on the agent's social context and her capability to defend her view. Annis (1978) explicitly calls his theory contextualism and so does Williams (2007). It is not obvious whether a dialectical theory leads to the view now called semantic contextualism or ascriber contextualism (see e.g. Cohen 2008), however. These theories are semantic views concerning the meaning of the word "know" and its cognates. According to semantic contextualists, expressions of the form "*a* knows at *t* that *p*", for instance, "John knows, at noon February 3, 2009, that Barack Obama is the president of USA" may express different propositions depending on the context of the utterance of the expression. One of these propositions may be true whereas another one is false.

Despite superficial similarity it seems that the dialectical view and semantic contextualism are clearly distinct views and a proponent of a dialectical view need not endorse semantic contextualism. Three immediate differences must be noted: 1) Ascriber contextualism is a semantic thesis whereas the dialectical theory is an epistemic thesis. The dialectical theory concerns epistemic properties of subjects, not linguistic expres-

public assertion is an acceptance in Stalnaker's (1984: 79) broad sense of treating a proposition as true in one way or another.

There are two general kinds of criticism against dialectical conception of justification: Either the requirement of dialectical justification is too strong or it is too weak. Let us start with the former. Alvin Goldman (1994) agrees that there is a sense of social justification that depends on an agent's ability to justify it to others, but he considers it mistake to think that it is required for epistemic justification. Robert Audi (1993: 145–147) and William Alston (2005) have expressed similar views. Several counterexamples have been proposed against the view that ability to justify is a necessary requirement for epistemic justification. For instance, a sceptical audience might refuse to accept the agent's arguments no matter how good they are (Goldman 1994; Audi 1993). An agent may live in a deviant epistemic community in which readings of astrological charts count as reasonable challenges to one's views (Kornblith 2008). An agent might have for-forgotten her good reasons for her view but still be justified (Goldman 1994; Rescorla 2009). Young children or animals seem to have justified beliefs even though they cannot defend them (Audi 1993: 145–147; Rescorla 2009). Finally, it has been said that simple perceptual beliefs or background presuppositions of ordinary conversation can be justified even if they cannot be supported by any further reasons (Rescorla 2009).

---

sions that are about epistemic properties of subjects. 2) Ascriber contextualism concerns knowledge (or "knowledge") whereas dialectical theory concerns justification. 3) Ascriber contextualism focusses on the context of the agent making the knowledge ascription whereas dialectical theory focusses on the context of the epistemic subject. According to one version of contextualism, justification is contextual and since it is required for knowledge, also knowledge is contextual (Cohen 2008). A proponent of the dialectical view can agree that justification is contextual and required for knowledge but since, for her, context is determined by the subject and not the ascriber of knowledge, the knowledge claims do not change truth value in different contexts of ascription. For a more extensive comparison between the dialectical view and semantic contextualism, see Pritchard (2002).

Let us consider these criticisms and see whether it would be possible to respond to them. As a result we may get some answers to the questions posed earlier concerning the details of an account of dialectical justification. As the focus is on acceptance, I will bypass criticisms that seem to concern beliefs. The cases of simple perceptual beliefs and beliefs of young children and animals are all cases of involuntary beliefs, and I am not here proposing that they should be evaluated in dialectical terms.[105] They can even amount to knowledge in the sense of Cohen's (1992) belief-based knowledge or Sosa's (1991) animal knowledge. Note, however, that claims to the effect that particular instances of such beliefs are true or amount to knowledge do require reasons, because such claims are acceptances. These reasons that may concern e.g. the reliability of such beliefs are not required of the putative knowers but the ascribers of knowledge.

Some of the above counterexamples are clearly problematic for consensus views according to which one is justified in accepting that p if and only if one's community accepts that p. We avoid the criticism by defining the dialectical view in a way that does not require consensus: In responding to challenges against p one is not required to be able to convince the opponent in the sense that the opponent must accept p. It suffices that one can respond to the challenge, e.g. by providing another argument or more evidence for p or against the opponent's attack. The defence need not convince the opponent of the truth of p but it must be such that the opponent, given that she shares the epistemic norms of the community, can recognize it as a reason for accepting p in light of the arguments presented during the dialogue. If there is a role for consensus, it is in the collective acceptance of the epistemic norms that govern dialogues and the reason-giving practices in the epistemic community. Consensus should not be required of individual claims made within the community. As noted by Gutting (2003), it is possible to be the only person who conforms to the epistemic norms of

---

[105] Even if they should be evaluated in dialectical terms, it can be claimed that they should be granted the default status of justification (Lammenranta, forthcoming).

the community and thus one may be justified in her view even if nobody agrees. If everybody else has forgotten the epistemic norms of the community, their challenges may not be reasonable.[106]

Let us consider how a proponent of such a dialectical view could respond to above criticisms. Consider the example case of Heather provided by Goldman (1999: 29–30) as a counterexample to consensus views: Heather used to persistently lie about her health in the past and, as a consequence, she cannot convince anyone about her having headache, but, according to Goldman, she can still be justified in thinking that she has headache. The case of Heather shows that agreement cannot be a necessary condition for justification. In comparison to consensus views, the dialectical view gives different results in this case. First, note that the dialectical view of justification of *acceptance* does not prevent Heather from being justified in her *belief* that she has headache. Second, Heather can also be justified in accepting that she has a headache because she does not need to convince others, it is enough for her to adequately respond to the challenges. Suppose someone challenged Heather's report by claiming that she is lying as she has done before. She could defend herself by pointing out that there are no conclusive grounds to say that she is lying now because the reasoning from past cases is only inductive, and that she is the only one who has direct access to the evidence, that is, her subjective mental state of feeling pain. Presumption would again be in favour of Heather's claim, and the challenger would need to cite some further evidence in order to be justified in claiming that Heather is lying in this particular occasion.

Similar considerations apply in the other putative counterexamples: A sceptical audience need not be convinced, only reasonable challenges made by the audience need to be answered. What is reasonable is to be determined by the epistemic community, but it should not allow the sceptical audience the possibility to endlessly keep on asking for further reasons.

---

[106] Of course, the claim itself must not violate the epistemic norms of the community, because otherwise it cannot enjoy the default status of justification.

One possibility is to demand that the challenges require some evidence against the proposed view, not merely a mention of a logical possibility, as suggested by Willaschek (2007). Then mere bringing out the possibility of sceptical hypotheses cannot constitute a reasonable challenge because there cannot be any evidence for or against them. They are consistent with all the evidence we might possibly have.

The case of deviant epistemic communities is related to the previous case since a sceptical community is one example of a deviant epistemic community. There are at least two possible reactions to the case: Either it can be taken to show that the criteria for default status and reasonable challenge cannot be entirely up to the communities to decide, but some criteria should be required for all epistemic communities in order for them to count as epistemic communities. For instance, if the astrological charts are consulted not in order to reach the truth but in order to please a ruler fond of astrology, the practice is not recognizably epistemic, and the justificatory practices do not count as epistemic practices. Another way to respond is to recall that, according to the dialectical view, justification is relative to epistemic standards. If a view is accepted within a community that conforms to deviant epistemic standards, it can only show that the view is justified with respect to deviant epistemic standards. It does not say anything about the justificatory status of the view in light of normal epistemic standards. Of course, talk of "normal" and "deviant" standards already presupposes an evaluative epistemic position, e.g. "our" standards or viewpoint from which comparison can be made. I will return to these issues below in discussing epistemic relativism.

In the case of forgotten evidence for a proposition, the agent may again be justified in believing the proposition, but its acceptance requires that something can be said to support it if the claim is challenged. If the agent cannot provide any acceptable reasons for it, then the proponent of the dialectical view can bite the bullet and say that the agent is not justified in her acceptance. However, sometimes it may count as an acceptable reason that the agent remembers that she had a good reason for her view even though she has now forgotten *what* the reason was. In particular, if the agent can defend her view by saying that in previous cases in which she has forgotten the reasons for her views, these views have turned out to be true, presumption seems to be in her favour again.

Let us now move to the other type of criticism that claims that the ability to respond to challenges is not sufficient for epistemic justification. Counterexamples to this effect involve either deviant epistemic communities (for instance, in which readings of astrological charts count as acceptable reasons for a view) or people with special abilities to persuade audiences. Consider the case, presented by Goldman (1999: 30), of Karen who is very charismatic and can persuade anyone to believe what she says by her strong personality instead of a rational argument, so no challenges will arise. This kind of ability should not make her beliefs justified, so agreement cannot be sufficient for justification. More generally, as Goldman (2004) notes, we hold views that are not verbally expressed, and even those that are verbally expressed may face no explicit objections from people who disagree. The dialectical view seems to grant justification to such views because challenges to them are not actually raised.

One possible reaction would be to go along with the critic and admit that knowledge requires both being justified and ability to justify. Williams (2001) follows this strategy. He says that knowledge requires both personal justification (which is dialectical) and evidential justification (which requires reliability). In this way one can block knowledge also in the context of epistemically deviant societies that have intuitively too loose criteria for justification. However, in my opinion, reliability should not be taken as a necessary requirement for justification of acceptance. If there is a role for reliability in epistemic assessment of our doxastic states, it is in the assessment of involuntary beliefs. Their evaluation does not depend on reasons that can be given for them; it can be based on their causal ancestry instead, but their factual reliability can indirectly contribute to the justification of acceptances.

It might be possible to stick within the dialectical framework by allowing that the challenges need not be actually raised. Maybe it is enough that the audience possesses contrary evidence irrespectively of whether it is brought out and formulated into a counterargument for there to be a challenge to a proposed view. Goldman (2004) considers this possibility but notes that then the view makes justification too difficult, because it requires an agent to be able to resolve all objections that could possibly be raised against her view. However, we can recall the idea that objections must be reasonable: It is not necessary to resolve all possible objections, only those that are reasonable. Of course, the justificatory status now hinges on what counts as reasonable. Along with other epistemic norms such as what counts as reason or evidence, this is something to be determined by the epistemic community in question.

An alternative way to deal with these cases is to resist the temptation to go all the way in relativizing epistemological criteria to societies. This would allow the proponent of the dialectical view to say that not any kind of societal acceptance, like those based on charisma of the proponent, intellectual laziness of the audience, or deviant epistemic standards, suffices for epistemic justification, but a defence must satisfy some universal epistemic standards. Such an approach could also provide a response to charges according to which endorsing a dialectical view of justification leads to relativism or subjectivism. Let us finally consider this question. It is clear that there is no commitment to relativism concerning truth, but the idea of justification being relative to a social context seems to entail a kind of *epistemic relativism*, according to which there are no absolute criteria of justification. Both Annis (1978) and Williams (1999b; 2007) have denied that dialectical conception of justification leads to epistemic relativism.

Epistemic relativism can take weaker or stronger forms. According to weak epistemic relativism, the justificatory status of a view is always relative to an epistemic system, that is, the principles or practices used in a given culture for determining the justificatory status of a view. Such moderate epistemic relativism seems quite unproblematic and it seems to be entailed by the dialectical view.[107] However, it could be seen as leading to a strong form of epistemic relativism according to which no epistemic system is superior to another and there is no basis for rational or objective comparison or evaluation of epistemic systems (because such evaluation must also be relative to an epistemic system). Such strong epistemic relativism is something that both Annis and Williams want to deny.

According to Annis (1978), the view that epistemic justification is relative to social practices and norms of a group does not entail that there is no basis for rational criticism of these practices, because as epistemic practices these must have as their goals truth and avoidance of error. They can thus be compared and evaluated on the basis of how well these epistemic goals are achieved.[108] Annis thus seems to require that at least some criteria be universally accepted by all epistemic cultures. As mentioned, Williams (1999b: 54–55), on the other hand, adds a reliabilist component to his dialectical view: A successful defence of a view is not sufficient, but the belief it is based on must also be reliably formed in order to be fully justified. This requirement seems to be partly motivated by concern of relativism because justification now depends on additional objective criteria.

Kusch (2002: 134) has objected that Annis' insistence on intercultural epistemic criteria like the goal of truth is mistaken. Kusch considers it *ad hoc* to say that it is up to the particular culture to determine whether the epistemic criteria are satisfied but insist that the epistemic criteria are the same for all cultures. In Kusch's *communitarian* view (see Kusch 2002: 140–168) both the selection of epistemic criteria and the determination of whether the criteria are met depend on the social context. However, Annis' concern for truth appears motivated because the goal of truth seems to be a

---

[107] Although it does not necessarily mean that there is no room for a notion of justification that is not relativized to an epistemic system: An absolute notion of justification can be defined, e.g. by quantifying over all epistemic systems or by giving some system a privileged status.

[108] As argued by Fallis (2007), forming such epistemic goals seems to be possible also for groups.

necessary requirement for a practice to count as epistemic. We may certainly imagine societies in which there are various acceptable reasons that can be offered as arguments for one's opinions, but if they are not concerned with truth at all, these reason-giving practices are not recognizably epistemic practices.

Kusch (2002: 137) also objects to Williams' reliability requirement on the grounds that justification of judgements about reliability is contextual and has a default–challenge structure as well as any other judgement. However, Williams is clearly speaking about factual reliability instead of making judgements about reliability. Since dialectical view has nothing to do with relativism about truth, Williams' addition of a reliability requirement seems to be one possible way of blocking epistemic relativism. Even if our *judgements* concerning the epistemic standing of a view always depend on our culturally based epistemic framework, the *actual* epistemic standing of a view depends on, not only on our framework-relative judgements, but also on external matters like whether the view is true or false (Pritchard 2009a).

Although such external matters do not determine the justificatory status of group beliefs, they serve as objective criteria that can be used, at least in principle, to compare different epistemic systems. Some criteria can be used in practice, for instance, coherence that Boghossian (2006: 96–97) has suggested as a requirement that any epistemic system should satisfy. Some others, such as *veritistic value* that attempts to measure the success of the epistemic practices in producing true doxastic states and avoiding false ones (Goldman, 1999: 87–94) can at least in principle serve as an objective criterion: Given the denial of truth relativism, epistemic practices that succeed in classifying true views as justified and false views as unjustified can be taken to be objectively better than those practices that do not. It thus seems that endorsing the idea of dialectical justification does not force one to accept strong forms of epistemic relativism that make it impossible to evaluate epistemic criteria. Certainly, also evaluations of epistemic criteria are always made from the perspective of some epistemic culture, for instance, ours. As emphasised by Williams (2007), their criteria too are defeasible and can be challenged, but this does not necessarily mean that they are not objectively better criteria than the criteria in some other culture.

Yet another attempt to avoid relativism comes from Marcus Willaschek (2007) who tries to fill in some details to Williams' theory, in particular with respect to when a claim has the default status of being justified and how the standards of different epistemic practices can be compared. According to Willaschek, there is in every field a standard-setting context that determines the correct standards for epistemic evaluation of claims in that field. The standard-setting contexts are the contexts characterized by "expert practices", that is, epistemic practices employed by the people who know best about the subject matter in question.

Thus it seems that there are several possible ways in which one can endorse a dialectical conception of epistemic justification that makes epistemic justification dependent on epistemic systems and still reject strong epistemic relativism according to which there is no rational basis for evaluation of different epistemic systems. The claim that justification is always relative to some epistemic standards does not entail that all standards are equally good or bad.

6. Conclusions

I considered epistemic justification of non-summative group beliefs in light of the distinction between belief and acceptance. Since these group beliefs are voluntarily formed acceptances, it is reasonable to require that the group have reasons or evidence for the accepted view in order for the view to count as justified. Moreover, since group beliefs are public in nature and thus similar to claims or assertions, they are open to criticism and challenges, and their justification requires that reasonable challenges have been properly responded to by providing supporting reasons or evidence. These reasons may be challenged further, but the chain of justification cannot be infinite. At some point either a challenge cannot be met, and the view is not justified, or challenges are no longer made or they are no longer reasonable, and the view is justified. Where this happens depends on the social context, and the justificatory status is not absolute but relative to the epistemic practices applied and accepted in the epistemic community. Further inquiry may give reason to challenge a view once settled. Also the epistemic practices themselves may be challenged.

A preliminary formulation that emerged from the discussion takes a collectively accepted group view that p to be justified if and only if the group can successfully defend p against reasonable challenges by providing reasons or evidence that are collectively acceptable to the group and that support p according to the epistemic principles collectively accepted in the epistemic community of the group. The epistemic community determines what counts as a successful defence and as a reasonable challenge. However, this basic idea of a dialectical conception needs to be developed into a precise account in light of the challenges raised. Only some possible directions were tentatively addressed in this article and it is the job of the dialectic to push the inquiry forward.

Acknowledgements

I would like to thank the audience of the Workshop on Collective Epistemology (Basel, October 3–5, 2008) for their comments during the discussion. I am grateful to Markus Lammenranta for making several important suggestions to earlier drafts of this paper, and to Olli Niinivaara and Kaarlo Miller for their useful comments and helpful discussion. This research has been supported by Academy of Finland.

Bibliogpraphy

Alston, W. P. (2005), *Beyond "Justification"*: Dimensions of Epistemic Evaluation. Cornell University Press.

Annis, D. B. (1978), "A contextualist theory of epistemic justification". *American Philosophical Quarterly* 15 (3), 213–219.

Audi, R. (1993), *The Structure of Justification*. Cambridge University Press, Cambridge.

Bernecker, S. (2006), "Prospects for epistemic compatibilism". *Philosophical Studies* 130, 81–104.

Boghossian, P. (2006), *Fear of Knowledge*. Oxford University Press, Oxford.

Brandom, R. (1983), "Assertion". *Noûs* 17 (4), 637–650.

Cohen, L. J. (1986), The Dialogue of Reason: An Analysis of Analytical Philosophy. Clarendon Press, Oxford.

Cohen, L. J. (1992), *An Essay on Belief & Acceptance*. Oxford University Press, New York, USA.

Cohen, S. (2008), "Ascriber contextualism". In: J. Greco (ed.), *Oxford Handbook of Skepticism*. Oxford University Press, 417–436.

Corlett, J. A. (2007), "Analyzing social knowledge". *Social Epistemology* 21, 231–247.

Fallis, D. (2007), "Collective epistemic goals". *Social Epistemology* 21, 267–280.

Gilbert, M. (1987), "Modelling collective belief". *Synthese* 73, 185–204.

Goldman, A. I. (1994), "Argumentation and social epistemology". *Journal of Philosophy* 91, 27- 49.

——— (1999), *Knowledge in a Social World*. Clarendon Press, Oxford.

——— (2004), "The need for social epistemology". In: B. Leiter (ed.), *The Future for Philosophy*. Clarendon Press, Oxford, 182–207.

Greco, J. (2005), "Justification is not internal". In: M. Steup and E. Sosa (eds.), *Contemporary Debates in Epistemology*. Blackwell Publishing, 257–270.

Gutting, G. (2003), "Rorty's critique of epistemology". In: C. Guignon, and D. R. Hiley (eds), *Richard Rorty*. Cambridge University Press, 41–60.

Hakli, R. (2006), "Group beliefs and the distinction between belief and acceptance". *Cognitive Systems Research* 7, 286–297.

Hakli, R. (2007), "On the possibility of group knowledge without belief". *Social Epistemology* 21, 249–266.

Hintikka, J. (2007), Socratic Epistemology: Explorations of Knowledge-Seeking by Questioning. Cambridge University Press, Cambridge.

Kitcher, P. (1990), "The division of cognitive labor". *The Journal of Philosophy* LXXXVII, 5–22.

Kornblith, H. (2008), "Knowledge needs no justification". In: Q. Smith (ed.), *Epistemology: New Essays*. Oxford University Press, Oxford, 5–23.

Kusch, M. (2002), *Knowledge by Agreement*. Oxford University Press, Oxford.

Lammenranta, M. (2004), "Theories of justification". In: I. Niiniluoto, M. Sintonen, and J. Woleński (eds), *Handbook of Epistemology*. Kluwer Academic Publishers, Dordrecht, 467–495.

——— (2008), The Pyrrhonian problematic. In: J. Greco (ed.), *The Oxford Handbook of Skepticism*. Oxford: Oxford University Press, 9–31.

——— (forthcoming), "Disagreement, skepticism and the dialectical conception of Justification". *International Journal for the Study of Skepticism*.

Lehrer, K. (1979), "The Gettier problem and the analysis of knowledge". In: G. S. Pappas (ed.), *Justification and Knowledge*. D. Reidel Publishing Company, Dordrecht, Holland, 65–78.

——— (2000), *Theory of Knowledge, second edition*. Westview Press, Boulder, Colorado, USA.

Mathiesen, K. (2006), "The epistemic features of group belief". *Episteme* 2, 161–175.

Meijers, A. (2002), "Collective agents and cognitive attitudes". *Protosociology* 16, 70–85.

Paglieri, F. (2006), "Belief Dynamics: From Formal Models to Cognitive Architectures, and Back Again". PhD thesis, Universitá degli Studi di Siena.

Pettit, P. (2003), "Groups with minds of their own". In: F. F. Schmitt (ed.), *Socializing Metaphysics: The Nature of Social Reality*. Rowman & Littlefield Publishers, Lanham, Md, 167–193.

Pritchard, D. (2002), "Two forms of epistemological contextualism". *Grazer Philosophische Studien* 64, 19–55.

——— (2009a), "Defusing epistemic relativism". *Synthese* 166, 397–412.

——— (2009b), *Knowledge*. Palgrave Macmillan, Houndmills, Basingstoke, Hampshire, England.

Pronin, E. (2007), "Perception and misperception of bias in human judgment". *Trends in Cognitive Sciences* 11, 37–43.

Rescorla, M. (2009), "Epistemic and dialectical regress". *Australasian Journal of Philosophy* 87, 43–60.

Rolin, K. (2008), "Science as collective knowledge". *Cognitive Systems Research* 9, 115–124.

Schmitt, F. F. (1994), "The justification of group beliefs". In: F. F. Schmitt (ed.), *Socializing Epistemology: The Social Dimensions of Knowledge*. Rowman & Littlefield Publishers, Lanham, Md, 257–287.

Searle, J. R. (1995), *The Construction of Social Reality*. The Free Press, New York.

Sellars, W. (1963), "Empiricism and the philosophy of mind". In: *Science, Perception and Reality*. Routledge & Kegan Paul, London, 127–196.

Sosa, E. (1991), "Intellectual virtue in perspective". In: *Knowledge in Perspective: Selected Essays in Epistemology*. Cambridge University Press, 270–293.

Staley, K. W. (2007), "Evidential collaborations: epistemic and pragmatic considerations in 'group belief'". *Social Epistemology* 21, 3, 321–335.

Stalnaker, R. C. (1984), *Inquiry*. The MIT Press, Cambridge, Massachusetts, USA.

Tuomela, R. (2000), "Belief versus acceptance". *Philosophical Explorations* 2, 122–137.

——— (2004), "Group knowledge analyzed". *Episteme* 1, 109–127.

——— (2007), The Philosophy of Sociality: The Shared Point of View. Oxford University Press.

Walton, D. N. and Krabbe, E. C. W. (1995), *Commitment in Dialogue: Basic Concepts of Interpersonal Reasoning*. State University of New York Press, Albany, NY, 1995.

Willaschek, M. (2007), "Contextualism about knowledge and justification by default". *Grazer Philosophische Studien* 74, 251–272.

Williams, M. (1999a), *Groundless Belief: An Essay on the Possibility of Epistemology*. Princeton University Press, Princeton, New Jersey, 2nd edition.

——— (1999b), "Skepticism". In: *Blackwell Guide to Epistemology*. Blackwell Publishers, 35–69.

——— (2001), Problems of Knowledge: A Critical Introduction to Epistemology. Oxford University Press, Oxford.

——— (2007), "Why (Wittgensteinian) contextualism is not relativism". *Episteme* 4, 93–114.

Wittgenstein, L. (1974), *On Certainty*. Basil Blackwell, Oxford.

Wray, K. B. (2001), "Collective belief and acceptance". *Synthese* 129, 319–333.

——— (2007), "Who has scientific knowledge?" *Social Epistemology* 21, 337–347.

PART III

Probabilistic Proofs and the Collective Epistemic Goals of Mathematicians

DON FALLIS

Abstract

Mathematicians only use *deductive proofs* to establish that mathematical claims are true. They never use *inductive evidence*, such as *probabilistic proofs*, for this task. I have previously argued (Fallis 1997 and 2002) that mathematicians do not have good epistemic grounds for this complete rejection of probabilistic proofs. But Kenny Easwaran (2009) points out that there is a gap in my argument. In my earlier work, I only considered how mathematical proofs serve the epistemic goals of *individual* mathematicians. Easwaran suggests that deductive proofs might be epistemically superior to probabilistic proofs because they are *transferable*. That is, one mathematician can give such a proof to another mathematician who can then verify for herself that the mathematical claim in question is true without having to rely at all on the testimony of the first mathematician. In this paper, I argue that *collective epistemic goals* are critical to understanding the methodological choices of mathematicians. But I argue that the collective epistemic goals promoted by transferability do not explain the complete rejection of probabilistic proofs.

1. Introduction

In order to explain why people engage in the activities that they do, we often attribute goals and desires to them. For example, we hypothesize that a student wants to pass an exam in order to explain why she is studying so hard. And this technique can be used to explain the behavior of groups as well as individuals. For example, philosophers (e.g., Maddy 1997, Gold-

158

man 1999: 221-271) have tried to identify the goals of scientists and mathematicians that will explain their methodological choices.[109]

In this paper, I use this technique to try to understand one particular methodological choice of mathematicians. Namely, mathematicians will only use deductive proofs to establish that mathematical claims are true. Mathematicians will not use inductive evidence, such as *probabilistic proofs*, for this task (cf. Detlefsen and Luker 1980: 818-819; Fallis 2002: 374-376, Peressini 2003). The project here is to see if we can find a goal that will explain the complete rejection of probabilistic proofs.

Understanding why mathematicians only use deductive proofs to establish that mathematical claims are true is clearly critical for the philosophy of mathematics. But it is also an important issue in the philosophy of science more generally and even in epistemology. Philosophers (e.g., Descartes) as well as mathematicians clearly think that deductive evidence is epistemically superior to inductive evidence (cf. Couvalis 2004: 28-29). But this is largely an unexamined article of faith. Thus, it would be useful to explicitly identify the goals that deductive evidence, but not inductive evidence, allows us to achieve.

But before we get started, there are a few important points about this project that should be clarified at the outset. First, the methodological choices of scientists and mathematicians can potentially be explained by pragmatic goals as well as by epistemic goals. For instance, it may be that mathematicians who use probabilistic proofs cannot get their papers published or get funding from the NSF. However, following most other philosophers of science and mathematics, the project here is to identify *epistemic* goals (e.g., the goals of acquiring true beliefs, avoiding false beliefs, gaining understanding) that explain the complete rejection of probabilistic proofs.

---

[109] See Fallis (2002: 384-385) for a defense of using this technique to explain the methodological choices of mathematicians.

Second, there are actually many epistemic goals that deductive proofs *often* serve, but that probabilistic proofs *almost never* serve (e.g., as I discuss below, the goal of gaining understanding). However, a deductive proof can *always* be used to establish that a mathematical claim is true. Thus, in order to explain the *complete* rejection of probabilistic proofs, we need to find an epistemic goal that deductive proofs *always* serve, but that probabilistic proofs *never* serve.

Third, methodological choices can potentially be explained by the goals that individuals have in virtue of being members of a scientific community or by the goals that the scientific community itself has. For example, just as individual mathematicians only want to accept mathematical claims that are true, the mathematical community as a whole only wants to accept mathematical claims that are true. In trying to explain the complete rejection of probabilistic proofs, I will consider both types of *collective epistemic goals* (cf. Fallis 2007).

Finally, it should be noted that mathematicians often do make use of inductive evidence (cf. Corfield 2003: 103-129; Avigad 2008: 308-312; Bledin 2008: 497-498; Baker 2009). For example, it is an important part of why mathematicians believe that certain axioms are true (cf. Whitehead and Russell 1962 [1910]: 59; Maddy 1997: 36-62). Also, it can help to identify plausible conjectures that it might be worth trying to prove (cf. Brown 1999: 158-171). But the project here is to explain why inductive evidence is never used in place of deductive proofs to establish that mathematical claims are true.[110]

---

[110] Mathematicians do not always prove mathematical claims in order to establish that they are true (cf. Dawson 2006: 275-281). For example, mathematicians commonly search for simpler and more elegant proofs of results that have already been established. In fact, they prove results that are much more certain than the axioms from which they are derived, as when Whitehead and Russell (1962 [1910]) took several hundred pages to formally prove that 1 plus 1 equals 2. But the issue here is whether deductive proofs are superior with respect to establishing that mathematical claims are true.

2. Two Proofs of Primality

For the sake of concreteness, I will focus my discussion on two specific methods that mathematicians might use to establish that some number n is prime. A very simple (although time consuming) way to prove *deductively* that n is prime is to try dividing n by each of the numbers less than n. If none of these numbers divide into n without a remainder, we conclude that n *is* prime. Mathematicians are perfectly happy to use this *trial division test* to establish that a number is prime.

A very efficient way to prove *probabilistically* that n is prime has been suggested by Michael Rabin (1980). Rabin proved (deductively) that, if a number n is *not* prime, then most (over 75%) of the numbers less than n are "witnesses" to this fact. That is, if n is not prime, then most smaller numbers have a special property X that can be checked for very quickly and that implies that n is not prime.[111] So, if we want to establish that n is prime, we pick a whole bunch of numbers less than n at random and check to see if any of them have property X. If none of these numbers "testify" that n is not prime, we conclude that n *is* prime. Unlike the trial division test, the *Rabin test* has to make use of a randomization device (such as a coin flip) to determine exactly which calculations to perform. Although the Rabin test is extremely reliable, mathematicians will not use it to establish that a number is prime.

3. Explaining the Complete Rejection of Probabilistic Proofs

Several people (e.g., Peressini 2003; Avigad 2008) have pointed out that there is a clear distinction between deductive proofs and probabilistic proofs. *In principle*, a deductive proof provides a *guarantee* that a mathematical claim is true. That is, if no mistakes are made in the construction of a deductive proof, then there must be a valid derivation of the mathemati-

---

[111] See Rabin (1980, 130) for a precise mathematical statement of what property X is.

cal claim in question. By contrast, even if all of the calculations in a probabilistic proof are performed correctly, the mathematical claim in question might turn out to be false (e.g., because we got unlucky and missed all of the witnesses when we picked numbers at random).

However, mathematicians live in the real world of fallibility rather than the ideal world of infallibility (cf. Devlin 2004). As David Hume (1967 [1739], book I, part IV, section I) famously noted, "in all demonstrative sciences the rules are certain and infallible; but when we apply them, our fallible and uncertain faculties are very apt to depart from them, and fall into error." In fact, there are plenty of examples where mathematicians falsely believed (for quite a long time) that they had found a correct deductive proof of an important mathematical result (cf. Brown 1999: 156). Thus, deductive proofs in general do not actually provide mathematicians with certainty that mathematical claims are true.[112]

In order to explain the methodological choice of mathematicians, we need to find an *actual* epistemic benefit that deductive proofs provide and that probabilistic proofs do not (cf. Fallis 2002: 383).[113] However, I have

---

[112] Interestingly, George Couvalis (2004) argues that we can only know that we have deductively proved a mathematical claim by appealing to inductive evidence. In particular, our confidence that we have not made a mistake in this instance is based on the fact that we have rarely made mistakes in the past.

[113] It has been suggested that mathematics is *by definition* a deductive science. As Jeremy Avigad (2008: 307) puts it, "inductive evidence is not the right sort of thing to provide mathematical knowledge, as it is commonly understood." If this is correct, then someone who used a probabilistic proof to establish the truth of a mathematical claim would not acquire *mathematical* knowledge. But even if this is correct, it still begs the question of whether there is a good epistemic reason to define mathematics in this way. Indeed, some mathematicians (e.g., Zeilberger 1993, Wolfram 2002: 792-795) claim that this is not a good way to define mathematics. It might also be suggested that *deductive* proofs are simply intrinsically valuable to mathematicians. If this is correct, then deductivity itself is an actual epistemic benefit that deductive proofs provide and that probabilistic proofs do not. However, deductive proof being an end in itself is a somewhat unsatisfying explanation of the complete rejection of probabilistic proofs. We might have hoped that mathematicians only use deductive proof because it is the most effective means to achieving some further epistemic goal (such as avoiding errors or finding errors that have already been made). Along similar lines, Alvin

argued previously (in Fallis 1997 and Fallis 2002) that there are no such epistemic benefits. For example, while deductive proofs may not provide absolute certainty that mathematical claims are true, it might be suggested that probabilistic proofs do not provide us with *enough* certainty. However, the Rabin test can provide as much certainty as might be required (cf. Fallis 2002: 380; Easwaran 2009). We just need to pick enough numbers at random and check to see if any of them have property X. Moreover, the Rabin test can provide more certainty than many deductive proofs, such as the trial division test. Because the trial division test requires more calculations than the Rabin test, there is a greater chance of calculation errors and, thus, a greater chance overall that n is not actually prime even if the test says that it is.

It might also be suggested that probabilistic proofs do not allow us to *understand* why a mathematical claim is true. Understanding is certainly an important epistemic value in mathematics (cf. Avigad 2008: 312-314, Bledin 2008: 498). We do not just want to know *that* something is true; we also want to know *why* it is true (cf. Wolfram 2002: 1156; Baker 2009: section 3.4). And, unlike probabilistic proofs, deductive proofs often do provide such understanding. However, whether we use a deductive proof or a probabilistic proof, there is not much understanding to be had when proving that a number is prime. With both methods, we simply understand that the number cannot be divided evenly by any smaller number.

In Fallis 1997 and Fallis 2002, I consider several further epistemic goals that mathematicians have. In each case, I argue that probabilistic proofs promote these goals as well as deductive proofs in at least some circumstances (e.g., when proving primality). Thus, none of these epistemic goals explain the complete rejection of probabilistic proofs. However, we do not have an exhaustive list of the epistemic goals of mathematicians to

---

Goldman (1999: 78) has criticized Helen Longino for assigning "fundamental epistemic value to impartiality and nonarbitrariness" in science when we would have thought that they were valuable only because they "foster accuracy and truth."

work with.[114] Thus, my argument that there is no important epistemic distinction between deductive proofs and probabilistic proofs is not conclusive.

4. Easwaran on Transferability

Kenny Easwaran (2009) identifies an important gap in my argument. Like most other philosopher of mathematics, I focused exclusively on the epistemic goals of mathematicians as *solitary inquirers*. However, as Easwaran points out, there is an important *social* element to scientific and mathematical practice (cf. Kitcher 1993: 303-389, Goldman 1999: 221-71).[115] In particular, collective epistemic goals are arguably critical to understanding the methodological choices of mathematicians. Indeed, such a goal might explain the complete rejection of probabilistic proofs.

By paying attention to the social element of mathematical practice, Easwaran thinks that he has been able to identify the critical distinction between deductive proofs and probabilistic proofs. Easwaran points out that deductive proofs, but not probabilistic proofs, are *transferable*. A proof is transferable if one mathematician can give the proof to another mathematician who can then verify for herself that the mathematical claim in question is true without having to rely at all on the testimony of the first mathematician. In other words, a transferable proof "needs nothing outside itself to be convincing" (Tymoczko 1979: 59).

It is clear that deductive proofs are transferable. In order to convince herself that the mathematical claim in question is true without any reliance on the testimony, the receiving mathematician just has to check that each step in the proof is valid.[116] For example, in the case of the trial division

---

[114] W. S. Anglin (1997: 85-127) does provide a fairly comprehensive list of the things that mathematicians value.

[115] Heretofore, philosophers of science have paid much more attention to this social element than have philosophers of mathematics.

[116] In order to do this, the receiving mathematician must have sufficient mathematical expertise.

test, the receiving mathematician simply has to check that each calculation has been performed correctly to convince herself that n is prime.

Probabilistic proofs, however, are not transferable. For example, in the case of the Rabin test, even if the receiving mathematician checks that each calculation has been performed correctly, she might still worry that n is not prime. The Rabin test is only convincing evidence that n is prime if the receiving mathematician knows that the smaller numbers checked for property X were chosen at random. Now, any particular set of numbers *might* have been picked at random. However, the set of numbers might instead have been *deliberately* chosen from those few numbers that lack property X when n is not prime. And it is difficult to see how the receiving mathematician can know that this did not happen without relying on the word of the original mathematician.

The original mathematician could certainly establish that the numbers checked for property X were chosen as random in much the same way that other scientists establish that their data has not been faked (cf. Fallis 2000: 269). In fact, Easwaran considers several ways in which the original mathematician might do so. But he concludes (correctly I think) that there is always a possibility of deception. In order to convince yourself that the numbers were picked at random, you ultimately have to rely on the testimony of the original mathematician (or on the testimony of someone else who can vouch for the original mathematician).

Admittedly, you could avoid relying on testimony by picking your own numbers at random and checking to see if any of them have property X. This would provide you with excellent, and completely non-testimonial, evidence that n is prime. But you would (almost certainly) not end up choosing exactly the same numbers as the original mathematician. Thus, your belief that n is prime would not be justified by exactly the same proof that justified the original mathematician's belief.

Thus, with transferability, Easwaran has identified a distinction between deductive proofs and probabilistic proofs. But we could already draw a distinction between these two types of proofs. For example, probabilistic proofs make use of a randomization device whereas deductive proofs do not. What we want is to identify an *epistemically important* distinction. That is, we want to find a property of deductive proofs that always allows such proofs to promote an epistemic goal of mathematicians better than probabilistic proofs. In particular, this is what Easwaran needs in order to "defend the practice" of rejecting of probabilistic proofs. In the remainder of this paper, I argue that transferability is not such a property.[117]

The transferability of a proof allows a mathematician to check the proof for herself rather than having to rely on the testimony of another mathematician. Thus, the obvious suggestion is that transferability is valuable because it allows an individual to be *epistemically autonomous*. In general terms, someone is epistemically autonomous if she believes on the basis of reasons that she herself has considered (cf. Fricker 2006). Claims of the value of epistemic autonomy go back to Descartes and Locke (cf. Fricker 2006: 225). In fact, standard advice in critical thinking courses is not to rely on authority (cf. Huemer 2005: 523).

There are at least two ways in which the epistemic autonomy provided by transferable proofs can be epistemically beneficial to mathematicians. First, it can be beneficial to the individual mathematician who is epistemically autonomous. (Transferability is defined in terms of more than one individual. But it might be that this property is primarily valuable to the individual who receives the transferable proof from another mathematician.) Second, it can be beneficial to the mathematical community whose members are epistemically autonomous. In the following two sections, I discuss these two ways in which transferable proofs can promote the collective epistemic goals of mathematicians. However, I argue that the same benefits can be achieved with probabilistic proofs. Thus, transferability does not explain the complete rejection of probabilistic proofs.

---

[117] Jeffrey C. Jackson (2009) also argues that Easwaran has failed to identify an epistemically important distinction between deductive proofs and probabilistic proofs.

5. The Value of Transferability for Individuals

An individual who is epistemically autonomous is potentially less prone to error (cf. Fricker 2006: 242). If a mathematician asserts that she has proven that a particular mathematical claim is true and you just have to take her word for it, you are open to several potential sources of error. For example, this mathematician may have made a mistake in carrying out the proof. In addition, this mathematician may even be trying to deceive you (e.g., in order to get unwarranted credit for having proven this claim). For example, in the case of the Rabin test, no matter how many numbers she claims to have chosen at random and checked to see if they have property X, you have to worry about honest mistakes and deception. However, if a mathematician provides you with a transferable proof of a claim, you can reduce (if not entirely eliminate) such worries by checking the proof for yourself (assuming that you have sufficient mathematical expertise to do so).

As several philosophers (e.g., Huemer 2005; Fricker 2006) have pointed out, while it may sound good in the abstract, epistemic autonomy in general is not all that it is cracked up to be. If you had to consider the (non-testimonial) reasons for every proposition before believing it, you would not end up believing very much. We just do not have the time and expertise to do this for every proposition that we need to know (cf. Hardwig 1991: 693-694). In addition, unless you happen to have a great deal of expertise in a particular area, you are probably better off (in terms of reducing the probability of error) consulting experts and relying on their testimony (cf. Mathiesen 2006: 143).[118]

But if you restrict your epistemic autonomy to a limited domain, such as an area of mathematics in which you have great expertise, it may

---

[118] In general, people certainly value autonomy. But it is not clear that it is always rational for them to do so. For instance, people often prefer to drive themselves rather than fly even though it puts them at greater risk of injury and death (cf. Myers 2001). Similarly, it is not clear that epistemic autonomy is rational if it puts you at greater epistemic risk.

not be such a bad thing. You will not be epistemically impoverished in general. And you will not be epistemically impoverished in this area of mathematics because you have sufficient expertise to check the proofs in this area for yourself. You might miss out on a few true beliefs that you could have acquired through the testimony of other mathematicians in this area (e.g., because you do not have time to check all of the proofs in this area for yourself). But this may not be such a great epistemic cost since mathematicians tend to be extremely epistemically risk averse. Mathematicians are happy to forgo additional knowledge if that is what it takes to avoid falling into error. In other words, they are willing to trade off what Alvin Goldman (1987) calls *power* for greater *reliability*.

Even so, the benefits of epistemic autonomy for individual mathematicians do not explain the complete rejection of probabilistic proofs. First of all, an individual does not have to be epistemic autonomous in order to have mathematical knowledge. In particular, a mathematician can know that a mathematical claim is true even if she has not surveyed the entire proof for herself. There are deductive proofs that are so long that no individual mathematician has surveyed, or could survey, the whole thing. The standard example is the "10,000 page proof" of the classification of finite simple groups (cf. Brown 1999: 158).[119] In such cases, the justification that a mathematician has for believing that the mathematical claim in question is true is partially based on the testimony of other mathematicians (cf. Hardwig 1991: 695-696).[120] In particular, she has to trust that these other mathematicians correctly verified the parts of the proof that they were responsible for.

---

[119] Admittedly, in principle, with unlimited time and expertise, one person could survey the entire proof of the classification of finite simple groups. But, as noted above, our concern here is with the *actual* practices of mathematicians and the epistemic goals that these practices promote.

[120] In mathematics, there is a huge amount of collaboration in terms of discovering mathematical results (cf. Fallis 2006: 204). But there is also sometimes collaboration in terms of justifying mathematical results.

All that seems to be required for mathematical knowledge is that, for each piece of a proof, *somebody* has surveyed it (cf. Azzouni 1994: 166). In fact, the somebody who has surveyed some of the pieces might even be a computer. For example, in the case of the Four-Color Theorem, mathematicians used a computer to check the proof because there were too many cases for humans to check by hand (cf. Tymoczko 1979). Relying on a computer in this way to check a deductive proof is essentially like relying on testimony (cf. McEvoy 2008: 383).[121]

Another reason why the benefits of epistemic autonomy for individual mathematicians do not explain the complete rejection of probabilistic proofs is that probabilistic proofs actually allow mathematicians to be epistemically autonomous. While probabilistic proofs are not transferable, they are *reproducible*. For example, if someone claims to have proven that *n* is prime using the Rabin test, you can avoid relying on testimony by performing the Rabin test again for yourself. That is, you can pick your own numbers at random and check to see if any of them have property *X*. Although it will (almost certainly) not be exactly the same evidence that the original mathematician had, you will have excellent, and completely non-testimonial, evidence that *n* is prime. Admittedly, having to perform the Rabin test for yourself will require some effort on your part. But even if you are given a transferable proof of a mathematical claim, checking this proof is going to take some effort.[122,123]

---

[121] Jody Azzouni (1994: 169-171) argues, to the contrary, that, unlike testimony, reliance on a computer involves an appeal to empirical science. But see McEvoy (2008: 383-386).

[122] In addition, some steps will typically be left out of a published proof and the reader will have to figure out how to fill them in (cf. Fallis 2003).

[123] Epistemic autonomy can also allow mathematicians to be more *sensitive* to undercutting evidence. For example, if you know that the proof of theorem A relies on lemma B and you discover that lemma B is actually false, you will no longer be confident that theorem A is true. And such sensitivity may have epistemic value beyond simply enhancing your reliability. As Elizabeth Fricker (2006: 242) puts it, "sensitivity to defeating evidence ... is usually taken to be the hallmark of belief which amounts to knowledge." However, since mathematicians do not have to be epistemically autonomous in order to have mathematical knowledge, they do not have to be sensitive to all

6. The Value of Transferability for the Group

It often makes sense to attribute beliefs and knowledge to groups, such as the Supreme Court, the FBI, or the scientific community (cf. Hakli 2006). In particular, we frequently talk about whether particular mathematical claims (e.g., the Four-Color Theorem, Fermat's Last Theorem, the Poincaré Conjecture) are known by the mathematical community to be true. In addition, just as individual mathematicians do not want to accept mathematical claims that are false, the mathematical community as a whole does not want to accept false claims. In fact, philosophers of science (e.g., Kitcher 1993; Goldman 1999: 221-271) have tried to identify practices that allow the scientific community as a whole to accept fewer false claims (or more true claims). In particular, using transferable proofs arguably allows the mathematical community to accept fewer false claims.

If individual mathematicians are epistemically autonomous, the mathematical community as a whole is less prone to error. If a mathematician asserts that she has proven that a particular mathematical claim is true and everyone just has to take her word for it, the mathematical community has to worry about honest mistakes and deception. However, if a mathematician provides the community with a transferable proof of the claim, such worries can be reduced (if not entirely eliminated) by having several other mathematicians check the proof.

---

possible defeating evidence either. In fact, even if a mathematician does not rely on the testimony of other mathematicians, she will not be sensitive to certain sorts of potential defeaters. For example, mathematicians rely on pencils and chalkboards (as well as their own memory) without having a complete understanding of how these mechanisms work (cf. Azzouni 1994: 160). In addition, if you perform the Rabin test for yourself, you will be sensitive to many sorts of potential defeaters. For example, you will know to be worried if your set of randomly chosen numbers has some unexpected property (e.g., if you happened to pick 1, 2, 3, ..., $x-1$, x). Admittedly, any mechanism for randomly choosing numbers may leave us insensitive to certain sorts of potential defeaters. But mathematicians were presumably not worried about probabilistic proofs because they were unsure of their ability to pick numbers at random.

Since mathematicians are fallible, we do not want to have proofs checked by just one individual. Mathematics would be too insecure. As David Hume (1967 [1739], book I, part IV, section I) put it, "there is no Algebraist nor Mathematician so expert in his science, as to place entire confidence in any truth immediately upon his discovery of it, or regard it as any thing, but a mere probability. Every time he runs over his proofs, his confidence encreases; but still more by the approbation of his friends; and is rais'd to its utmost perfection by the universal assent and applauses of the, learned world." In addition, this sort of practice does not have the aforementioned drawbacks that epistemic autonomy can have for individuals. For example, the mathematical community usually has the *collective* time and expertise to do this for any important mathematical claim.

However, the goal of the mathematical community to avoid error does not explain the complete rejection of probabilistic proofs. For example, if someone claims to have proven that n is prime using the Rabin test, worries about honest mistakes and deception can be reduced by having several other mathematicians perform the test for themselves. These other mathematicians will (almost certainly) not end up picking the same numbers at random as the original mathematician. But this does not adversely affect the reliability of the practice.

Indeed, this is essentially the same sort of practice that takes place in science in general. The scientific community as a whole is more reliable because scientists are able to *replicate* experiments in order to confirm scientific results.[124,125] And it is more reliable even though scientists do not

---

[124] As Philip Kitcher (1993: 336) puts it, "attempts at replication are frequently (though not always) a good thing for the *community*." Kitcher even considers exactly how many scientists should try to replicate experiments in order to confirm new results. His model does this by factoring in the initial probability that the new result is correct, the benefit of building on the new result if it is correct, the cost of building on the new result if it is incorrect, the cost of the time spent trying to replicate the new result, and the reliability of the scientists who are trying to replicate the new result.

[125] Actually having someone else replicate an experiment can enhance reliability by catching mistakes and deception. But in addition, the mere possibility of someone else replicating an experiment can enhance reliability by deterring negligence and decep-

replicate experiments using the very same random sample of atoms, subjects, etc. that the original scientist used. Scientists take a new random sample and then perform the experiment again.[126]

But just as with individuals, simply being right that a claim is true is not the only important concern for groups which have epistemic goals. In particular, such groups typically want to have a shared understanding of *why* that claim is true. For example, it is problematic if the scientific experts on a particular topic (e.g., climate change) agree that a claim is true, but are not able to agree on why that claim is true.[127] But if a mathematician has to provide the mathematical community with a transferable proof of a claim, other mathematicians can easily acquire the very same reasons for believing that the claim is true.[128]

Admittedly, mathematicians (even experts in the same area) do not always take advantage of transferability to check a proof for themselves.[129] Thus, transferability only insures that they *would* have the same reasons if they did check. In other words, even if different mathematicians have dif-

---

tion in the first place (cf. Hardwig 1991: 706). Admittedly, it is not always feasible to replicate scientific experiments (cf. Hardwig 1991: 705-706). Even so, important results which other results build upon are tested indirectly. And this can also occur in mathematics regardless of whether a result was established using a deductive proof or a probabilistic proof.

[126] Probabilistic proofs in mathematics and (at least some forms of) induction in science both involve inferring that a full population has certain properties based on the fact that a much smaller, randomly chosen, sample of that population has those properties. But it should be noted that there are also important differences between the two techniques. For example, scientific induction typically involves inferring that the future will be like the past in certain ways, whereas any mathematical argument is presumably timeless.

[127] Similarly, when a court with several members (e.g., the Supreme Court) agrees on a decision, but not on why that decision is the correct one, the decision does not have as much legal force (cf. Warnken and Samuels 1997).

[128] As proofs are getting longer and more complicated, there can be disputes that are not all that easy to resolve (cf. De Millo et al. 1979: 272; Devlin 2004). As a result, using a deductive proof does not *guarantee* that mathematicians will end up with the very same reasons.

[129] As the example of the 10,000 page proof shows, it is not always even possible for them to do so.

ferent (often testimonial) reasons for believing that a claim is true, transferability insures that the non-testimonial reasons that ground their belief is the same.

However, the goal of the mathematical community to have shared reasons (even of this counterfactual sort) does not explain the complete rejection of probabilistic proofs. If several mathematicians perform the Rabin test for themselves, their belief that n is prime will not be justified by exactly the same (non-testimonial) evidence. In particular, they each know, of a *different* set of numbers, that those numbers do not have property X. However, what ultimately justifies their belief that n is prime is that several numbers have been chosen *at random* and those numbers (whatever they happen to be) do not have property X. Thus, they have the same reasons for believing that n is prime in the very same sense that different scientists who have replicated an experiment have the same non-testimonial reasons for believing a scientific result.

While Easwaran is certainly correct that different mathematicians who independently perform the Rabin test will not have *exactly* the same evidence, it is not clear why this is epistemically important.[130] In addition, it is not even clear that transferable proofs always guarantee that different mathematicians will end up being justified by exactly the same evidence. According to Easwaran, *proof sketches* count as transferable proofs. In other words, a rough outline of a proof can give a mathematician enough information to verify for herself that a claim is true without relying on the testimony of the mathematician who came up with the proof. However, it is acceptable for mathematicians to leave very large gaps in such proof sketches (cf. Fallis 2003). Thus, there is no guarantee that different mathematicians, when they check the proof, will fill in these gaps in exactly the same way.

---

[130] It is actually rather difficult to say when two proofs are exactly the same (cf. Dawson 2006: 272-275). It may be necessary to do so in order to settle priority disputes, such as determining who deserves credit for proving the Poincaré Conjecture (cf. Nasar and Gruber 2006). But settling priority disputes does not improve our *mathematical* knowledge.

7. Conclusion

Easwaran has identified a distinction between deductive proofs and probabilistic proofs. Namely, deductive proofs are transferable, but probabilistic proofs are not. However, this distinction does not explain the complete rejection of probabilistic proofs. It is not the case that transferable proofs always promote a collective epistemic goal of mathematicians better than non-transferable proofs. That being said, it is important to consider the collective epistemic goals of mathematicians when trying to explain their methodological choices. And it may still turn out to be the case that such a goal will ultimately provide an explanation for the complete rejection of probabilistic proofs.[131]

Bibliography

Anglin, W. S. (1997), *The Philosophy of Mathematics*. Lewiston, New York: Edwin Mellen Press.

Avigad, J. (2008), "Computers in Mathematical Inquiry". In: P. Mancosu (ed.), *The Philosophy of Mathematical Practice.* Oxford: Oxford, 302-16.

Azzouni, J. (1994), *Metaphysical Myths, Mathematical Practice*. New York: Cambridge.

Baker, A. (2009), "Non-Deductive Methods in Mathematics". *Stanford Encyclopedia of Philosophy*. http://plato.stanford.edu/entries/mathematics-nondeductive/

Bledin, J. (2008), "Challenging Epistemology: Interactive Proofs and Zero Knowledge". *Journal of Applied Logic* 6, 490-501.

Brown, J. R. (1999), *Philosophy of Mathematics*. New York: Routledge.

Corfield, D. (2003), *Towards a Philosophy of Real Mathematics*. Cambridge: Cambridge.

---

[131] I would especially like to thank Kenny Easwaran and Kay Mathiesen for many helpful discussions on this topic. I would also like to thank Jeff Jackson for his comments on a draft of this paper. Finally, I would like to thank the organizers (Hans Bernard Schmid, Marcel Weber, and Daniel Sirtes) and the participants at the *Workshop on Collective Epistemology*, Universität Basel, 2008 for their feedback.

174

Couvalis, G. (2004), "Is Induction Epistemologically Prior to Deduction?" *Ratio* 17, 28-44.

Dawson, J. W. (2006), "Why Do Mathematicians Re-Prove Theorems?" *Philosophia Mathematica* 14, 269-86.

De Millo, R., Lipton, R., and Perlis, A. (1979), "Social Processes and Proofs of Theorems and Programs". *Communications of the Association for Computing Machinery* 22, 271-80.

Detlefsen, M. and Luker, M. (1980), "The Four-Color Theorem and Mathematical Proof". *Journal of Philosophy* 76, 803-20.

Devlin, K. (2004), "Mathematicians Face Uncertainty". *Discover* 25 (1), 36.

Easwaran, K. (2009), "Probabilistic Proofs and Transferability". *Philosophia Mathematica* 17, 341-62.

Fallis, D. (1997), "The Epistemic Status of Probabilistic Proof". *Journal of Philosophy* 94, 165-86.

————— (2000), "The Reliability of Randomized Algorithms". *British Journal for the Philosophy of Science* 51, 255-71.

————— (2002), "What Do Mathematicians Want?: Probabilistic Proofs and the Epistemic Goals of Mathematicians". *Logique et Analyse* 45, 373-88.

————— (2003), "Intentional Gaps in Mathematical Proofs". *Synthese* 134, 45-69.

————— (2006), "The Epistemic Costs and Benefits of Collaboration". *Southern Journal of Philosophy* 44 (Supplement), 197-208.

————— (2007), "Collective Epistemic Goals". *Social Epistemology* 21, 267-80.

Fricker, E. (2006), "Testimony and Epistemic Autonomy". In: J. Lackey and E. Sosa (eds.), *The Epistemology of Testimony*. Oxford: Oxford, 225-50.

Goldman, A. (1987), "Foundations of Social Epistemics". *Synthese* 73, 109-44.

————— (1999), *Knowledge in a Social World*. New York: Oxford.

Hakli, R. (2006), "Group Beliefs and the Distinction Between Belief and Acceptance". *Cognitive Systems Research* 7, 286-97.

Hardwig, J. (1991), "The Role of Trust in Knowledge". *Journal of Philosophy* 88, 693-708.

Huemer, M. (2005), "Is Critical Thinking Epistemically Responsible?" *Metaphilosophy* 36, 522-31.

Hume, D. (1967 [1739]), *A Treatise of Human Nature*. ed. L. A. Selby-Bigge. London: Oxford.

Jackson, J. C. (2009), "Randomized Arguments are Transferable". *Philosophia Mathematica* 17, 363-68.

Kitcher, P. (1993), *The Advancement of Science*. New York: Oxford.

Maddy, P. (1997), *Naturalism in Mathematics*. New York: Oxford.

Mathiesen, K. (2006), "Epistemic Risk and Community Policing". *Southern Journal of Philosophy* 44 (Supplement), 139-50.

McEvoy, M. (2008), "The Epistemological Status of Computer-Assisted Proofs". *Philosophia Mathematica* 16, 374-87.

Myers, D. G. (2001), "Do We Fear the Right Things?" *American Psychological Society Observer*. http://www.davidmyers.org/fears/

Nasar, S. and Gruber, D. (2006), "Manifold Destiny". *New Yorker*. http://www.newyorker.com/archive/2006/08/28/060828fa_fact2

Peressini, A. (2003), "Proof, Reliability, and Mathematical Knowledge". *Theoria* 69, 211-32.

Rabin, M. O. (1980), "Probabilistic Algorithm for Testing Primality". *Journal of Number Theory* 12, 128-38.

Tymoczko, T. (1979), "The Four-Color Problem and Its Philosophical Significance". *Journal of Philosophy* 76, 57-83.

Warnken, B. and Samuels, E. (1997), "The Types of Opinions Issued". *Online Academic Support Program for Law Students*. http://www.onlineasp.org/class/case08.htm

Whitehead, A. N. and Russell, B. (1962 [1910]), *Principia Mathematica to *56*. Cambridge: Cambridge.

Wolfram, S. (2002), *A New Kind of Science*. Champaign, Illinois: Wolfram Media, Inc.

Zeilberger, D. (1993), "Theorems for a Price: Tomorrow's Semi-Rigorous Mathematical Culture". *Notices of the American Mathematical Society* 40, 978-81.

Collective Epistemology:
The Intersection of Group Membership and Expertise

Abstract

The idea of collective epistemology is based on the assumption that the isolated individual is not the only locus of decision-making. Instead, there are cases when groups also act and, in these cases, it is the community or collective that are the object of analysis rather than the individuals that make up those groups. In this paper, I examine the relationship between individuals and groups in terms of the distribution of expertise. By distinguishing between those cases where group members do have the necessary expertise and those where they do not, the critical issue of public engagement with science and technology is brought into sharper focus. Whilst the analysis does not lead to any obvious solution to this problem – indeed it suggests it may be intractable – it does, nevertheless, serve to clarify the challenge faced by those who argue that mass participation in technical decisions is necessary.

1. Introduction

'The [UK] Government believes that, based on the significant evidence available, the lifecycle carbon emissions from nuclear power stations are about the same as wind generated electricity with significantly lower carbon emissions than fossil fuel fired generation'

Do you agree or disagree with the Government's views on carbon emissions from new nuclear power stations? What are your reasons? Are there any significant considerations that you believe are missing? If so, what are they?[132]

It is now almost a commonplace that policy debates involving science and technology require some element of public participation. Recent examples in the UK include the consultation on nuclear power referred to in the epigraph as well as consultations on nuclear waste disposal, embryology and fertility research, and genetically modified crops. At the time of writing, a public consultation on possible schemes to harness tidal power in the Severn estuary is underway.[133] In each case, the assumption is that members of the public will be able to contribute to taking these decisions and that, in so doing, the epistemic quality of the process will be enhanced. In this paper I want to disentangle the conflation of legitimacy and epistemic quality by examining the relationship between group membership and expertise.

In developing the argument I draw on Science and Technology Studies (STS), which has been a key advocate of more participatory decision-making, as well as more recent work examining the nature and distribution of expertise. From STS I take an understanding of knowledge as social practice and hence start from the assumption that it is the social community that holds knowledge rather than the individual. In this sense, an individual is made up of the social groups in which they participate rather than the groups being made up of the individuals they include. This clearly has a strong resonance with the idea of collective epistemology.

In the case of expertise, I draw on the classification of expertise that is based on this foundation and summarise the typology set out in Collins and Evans (2007). This also draws on the assumption that knowledge is located in social groups but pays more attention that STS has traditionally done to the more negative implication of this, namely that different 'degrees of immersion' (Ribeiro 2007) within social groups give rise to different kinds of knowledge and expertise and, at the limit, no immersion

---

[132] Department for Business, Enterprise and Regulatory Reform (2007) *The Future of Nuclear Power: Consultation Document.* <http://www.berr.gov.uk/files/file39197.pdf> Accessed 30 March 2009. Quote at page 13 (para 45)
[133] <http://www.decc.gov.uk/severntidalpower> Accessed 12 August 2010.

means no expertise. This, in turn, provides the basis of a simple 2x2 matrix through which I examine what happens when the distribution of expertise either does or does not coincide with membership of the decision-making group. Both these sets of ideas are set out in more detail below before the main possibilities that arise from their combination are discussed.

2. Science, Knowledge and Public Participation

Research in Science and Technology Studies (STS) has done much to promote the idea that public participation in decisions involving science and technology is a good thing. The reason is that STS sees science as a constitutively and fundamentally social practice. For STS, scientific knowledge is developed, confirmed and validated within a scientific community and objectivity is understood as the expression of a collective agreement rather than the outcome of a correspondence theory of truth (Bloor 1976; Collins 1992). If this is accepted, however, then who makes these agreements, and on what basis, becomes a legitimate topic for political debates about the accountability of science and other forms of expertise within democratic systems. In effect, the argument from STS is that scientific knowledge privileges a particular view of the natural world and, in so doing, reinforces the social ordering that goes with such a conception (Irwin 1995; Wynne 1982). Whilst this might have been acceptable in the past, there is no doubt that the transition from a more or less unproblematic 'Modernity' to the contemporary 'Risk Society' has brought the link between 'science' and 'progress' into question (Beck 1992; Giddens 1990).

The most visible outcome of this research programme can be seen in the changing nature of the debates about the relationship between 'science' and 'society.' There has been in a significant increase in the importance attached to soliciting opinions from stakeholders, concerned citizens and the wider public (e.g. RCEP 1998; House of Lords 2000; POST 2001; Gerold and Liberatore 2001; OST 2002; Wilsden and Willis 2004; CST 2005). The reasoning behind this development draws directly on the social scientists' emphasis on science as social institution or culture. Firstly, the epistemological status of science is reduced by emphasising that it is a community of practice based in a particular socio-historical context. As such, the traditional reason for deferring to science – i.e. that is was a distinct and superior kind of knowledge in every respect – is negated. Secondly, the epistemological status of local or indigenous knowledge is raised for the same reason, namely that these too are communities of practice based in particular socio-historical context. The outcome is then a call for dialogue between partners rather than the more traditional 'top-down' model in which scientific expertise sets the parameters within which policymakers and citizens may live out their preferences.[134]

In advocating the inclusion of traditionally excluded communities STS was offering a solution to what Collins and Evans (2002) subsequently called the 'Problem of Legitimacy'. In essence, the Problem of Legitimacy arises because of the unreflexive attempt to generalise scientific knowledge in complex and/or open systems (cf. Funtowicz and Ravetz 1992). As predictions fail and the uncertainty of science becomes more visible so public scepticism about the ability of science to provide definite answers, or even to define the correct questions, increases. In response, a more inclusive decision-making process is required that reflects the diversity of available knowledge and values. As Brian Wynne (2003: 411) puts it:

> "To the extent that public meanings and the imposition of problematic versions of these by powerful scientific bodies is the issue, then the proper participants are in principle every democratic citizen and not specific sub-populations qualified by dint of specialist experience-based knowledge."

---

[134] This is not to say that politicians and others may initiate public consultations as a way of heading off public controversy and with no real intention of listening to the outcome. This does not undermine the argument made in this paper as the claim of STS is that publics, stakeholders and other users *should* be listened to. Consultations that do not listen are thus rightly seen as 'bad consultations' and not as a refutations of the process of public dialog.

Whilst there is no doubt some truth in the claim that scientific institutions have tended to dismiss critics as 'not understanding the science' rather than as raising legitimate doubts, it is equally clear that simply increasing participation in all cases cannot be a sensible solution either. As Steve Miller puts is, writing in the journal *Public Understanding of Science*:

> "If there is not a gap between what scientists and members of the general public know about science, then something is very wrong. We do not want a public understanding of science political correctness in which the very idea that scientists are more knowledgeable than ordinary citizens is taboo. Scientists and lay people are not on the same footing where scientific information is concerned, and knowledge, hard won by hours of research, and tried and tested over the years and decades, deserves respect." (2001: 118).

There is, then, a cost to solving the Problem of Legitimacy by increasing participation and this is what Collins and Evans (2002) call the 'Problem of Extension'. The Problem of Extension refers to the difficulty created when it becomes impossible to rank different knowledge-claims according to their epistemic worth. For traditional STS this is not a problem as its aim is primarily descriptive. If, however, the concern is with making decisions within real-time then the epistemological levelling of STS becomes a problem: if all knowledge is valid within its social context, how then can we rank or exclude the competing claims of different social groups? Whilst being more inclusive has its merits, treating every knowledge-claim from every community as equally relevant seems certain to result in undesirable combination of paralysis and populism (Collins et al. 2010).

The practical challenge of holding science accountable requires therefore some way of deciding how far to extend participation in order to address the Problem of Legitimacy without going so far as to create the Problem of Extension. Put more simply, if the Problem of Legitimacy is solved by giving everybody a voice, the Problem of Extension is solved by listening only to those who 'know what they are talking about'.

Studies of Expertise and Experience (SEE)

Clarifying what it means to 'know what you are talking about' is the central problem of the 'Third Wave' of science studies or 'Studies of Expertise and Experience' (Collins and Evans 2002; 2007; Collins 2007). The basic idea behind SEE is very simple: if knowledge is acquired by socialisation, then expertise can only be acquired through a prolonged period of interaction within the relevant community. This makes expertise 'real' in the sense that those without the appropriate level of expertise will be seen as making mistakes by the more expert members of the community. It also explains how the Problem of Legitimacy arises: if expertise is seen as 'social fluency' within a worldview then it will necessarily include both facts and values.

Seeing the acquisition of expertise as a process of socialisation within the experiences of specific social groups makes it possible to see that different kinds of expertise can be distributed in different ways. For example, some sorts of experience (e.g. speaking a natural language) will be so widely distributed as to make the expertise they give rise to ubiquitous within a specific society. Others, like milking cows or growing stem cells, will be restricted to small groups and so will be seen as esoteric expertises. From a SEE perspective, however, the expertises are of the same quality, only their distribution is different. This, in turn, provides a resolution to the Problem of Extension: if specialist expertise is called for, then it can only be found amongst those with experience of the relevant social groups. The size of those groups, however, will vary.

This is not to say, however, that only those with specialist expertise have a legitimate stake in decisions or that such specialist experts are the only ones able to decide. The opportunity cost imposed by the necessity for specialist socialisation means that that, even if everyone can be an expert in something, no-one can be expert in everything. There must, therefore, be a way of dealing with experts that does not involve acquiring sufficient ex-

183

pertise to become a member of their peer community. The key idea in this context is that of trust. Knowing how to recognise a trustworthy expert is one part of a more complex set of meta-expertises (i.e. expertises about expertise) that individuals have and which they can use to make decisions about who to trust. Based on this social judgement (i.e. who to believe) a technical judgement (i.e. what to believe) is then made possible.

Applying these twin ideas of specialist expertise (i.e. socialisation into the practices of a specific community) and meta-expertise (i.e. the ability to make judgements about experts whilst remaining an outsider) gives rise to the classification of expertises set out in Table One. The main features of this table, which is explained at length in Collins and Evans (2007) are as follows:

UBIQUITOUS EXPERTISES				
DISPOSITIONS			Interactive Ability	Reflective Ability
SPECIALIST	*UBIQUITOUS TACIT KNOWLEDGE*			*SPECIALIST TACIT KNOWLEDGE*
EXPERTISES	Beer-mat Knowledge	Popular Understanding	Primary Source Knowledge	Interactional Expertise / Contributory Expertise
			Polimorphic	Mimeomorphic
META-	*EXTERNAL*		*INTERNAL*	
EXPERTISES	Ubiquitous Discrimination	Local Discrimination	Technical Connoisseurship	Downward Discrimination / Referred Expertise
META-CRITERIA	Credentials	Experience		Track-Record

Table One: Periodic Table of Expertises   (source: Collins and Evans, 2007)

In the row labelled specialist expertise, an individual's expertise can range from 'beer mat expertise', which corresponds to knowing the kinds of facts that might be put on the coasters provided in bars, to contributory, which corresponds to being able to contribute fully to the work of the relevant community. Within this scheme, the two most important distinctions are the distinction between primary source knowledge and interactional expertise and between interactional expertise and contributory expertise:

- The distinction between primary source knowledge and interactional expertise marks the transition from expertises that rely on widely distributed tacit knowledge to expertises that rest on tacit knowledge specific to the group in question. Primary Source Knowledge is thus restricted to what you can learn from written texts and without ever meeting a contributory expert. In contrast, interactional expertise requires sustained interaction with the relevant expert community and is marked by conversational-style fluency in that domain; individuals with Primary Source Knowledge lack this ability.

- The distinction between interactional and contributory expertise corresponds to the distinction between being able to talk fluently about a domain of expertise and being able to contribute to it in practical ways. Interactional expertise is thus acquired by learning the discourse of a domain, contributory expertise by mastering the practice of a domain. The relationship between the two is transitive and asymmetric, so that contributory experts have both conceptual and practical expertise whereas those with only interactional expertise have linguistic fluency but are unable to complete practical tasks. The distinction matters because, where interactions rely on talk rather than practice, an interactional expert would be indistinguishable from a contributory expert. The difference can be illustrated by considering the difference between a criminological researcher and a criminal. The criminologist should understand the conceptual world of the criminal (i.e. have interactional expertise) but does not have to commit crime (i.e. develop contributory expertise) in order to do so as linguistic socialisation (e.g. social science fieldwork) is sufficient.

The second row of the table describes the meta-expertises needed to make judgements about the substantive expertise of others. As with specialist expertises, there is an important distinction between meta-expertises that do not presume any knowledge of the particular specialist domain and those that do:

- External meta-expertise enables judgements to be made even in the absence of any socialisation within the relevant expert community. In effect, these refer to the application of more or less ubiquitous standards to specific substantive domains. The idea of local discrimination highlights the case in which some communities will have experiences that will shape their views about the trustworthiness or credibility of specific experts that are not widely shared even though the criteria invoked draw on social rather than technical knowledge.
- Internal meta-expertise refers to judgements based on some kind of socialisation within the community. Thus, the judgements labelled Technical Connoisseurship, Downward Discrimination, and Referred Expertise all require the person who exercises them to appreciate the criteria used by those they judge. Thus, for example, technical connoisseurs might be familiar with the techniques of the domain being judged even though they were not practitioners in much the same way as wine connoisseurs would be familiar with the techniques of winemaking even though they are not be expected to be wine makers. Downward discrimination refers to the ability to identify a mistake and hence identify someone with less knowledge. Referred Expertise highlights the

capacity to use expert experience in one domain to inform judgements in another domain. The different types of internal meta-expertise thus highlight the different ways in which those outside the expert community of practitioners can, nonetheless, become more highly skilled consumers of that knowledge.

3. Expertise and Participation

Using the categorisation of expertise set out in the Periodic Table of Expertises the problem of public participation can be seen as closely linked to the question of collective epistemology. If decisions are to be made by groups, and groups are constituted by the knowledge they share and hold, then an understanding of expertise is an essential component of collective epistemology. In the case of public participation, the connection lies in the relationship between the expertise held within the group and the expertise needed to address the task in hand. As an initial model we can envisage four possible outcomes, as shown in Table Two below.

	Expertise needed is esoteric	Expertises needed is ubiquitous
Epistemic community is large	'Knowledge gap' problem	Civic epistemology
Epistemic community is small	Standard scientific community	Untrained sample

Table Two: Epistemic Communities and Expertise

Table Two uses the distribution of expertise to characterise the different kinds of epistemic groups that might arise. The cells in the table represent the different situations created by the intersection of the following two dimensions:

- **Group size**: whilst there is no attempt made to pin down the quantitative point at which a small group becomes a large group difference between small and large is nonetheless clear at the extreme ends. For the purpose of this exposition, a small group can be considered to be one in which hierarchies are relatively flat and members generally known to each other. In contrast, large groups are those where some form of bureaucratised organisation is needed to solve the problem of co-ordination created by the number of group members.
- **Availability of expertise**: again no attempt is made to pin down the boundary condition at which an expertise shifts from being ubiquitous to esoteric. As with group size, however, the distinction is clear at the extremes. Thus a ubiquitous expertise is one that is widely shared within a society and, in the limit case, consists only of those expertises that ALL members must have in order to live in that society (e.g. speaking a natural language). In practice, however, some expertises (e.g. like driving a car in Western Societies) are so widespread as to be practically ubiquitous. Esoteric expertises, in contrast, are those that remain the property of distinct and well-bounded social groups.

Combining these two dimensions produces a 2x2 classification in which the key concern is the extent to which the expertise needed to resolve the problem is available *within* the epistemic group. Each of the four cells is described in more detail below, but most attention is given to the top row as this is where much public participation work is located. I begin, however, by discussing the bottom row as by understanding why small epistemic groups work it is much easier to see what the problems are in the top row.

Small group, esoteric expertise: standard science

The standard example of a small community dealing with an epistemic question that requires esoteric expertise is a scientific community. Here all the participants have contributory level expertise in their disciplinary base and some level of interactional expertise in the cognate sciences of their collaborators. These expertises, as the quote from Steve Miller (cited above) indicates, are the product of hard work and many years experience and, crucially, include the tacit knowledge particular to that community. In the case of science this will include the practical craft skills needed to carry out practical work, the intellectual skills needed to recognise a 'good' question or a 'neat' solution and the social knowledge needed to make judgements about contested scientific data (Collins 1992).

Even though the scientific community is the proto-typical example of this activity it is important to stress that the scientific community is not its only manifestation. Indeed, by showing how much scientific practice draws on everyday kinds of reasoning it becomes possible to see how non-scientific communities can, nevertheless, legitimately be seen as expert communities. The most famous examples are probably the Cumbrian sheep farmers (e.g. Wynne 1992) and the farm workers concerned about the safety of the herbicide 2,4,5-T (described in Irwin 1995). Less well documented examples, which make the same point but in a way that carries less academic baggage, include any specialist group or community such as, for example, patient activist groups, bee keeping associations or scuba diving clubs. In each case, what matters is that the social groups have their own distinctive set of experiences that give rise to an expertise that is as esoteric as any science and, in its own domain, just as relevant.

The implications of this for collective epistemology turn on the domains of expertise that are relevant. So long as the expertise needed is found within the membership of the group then it is appropriate that the decision-making also takes place within that group. For example, in the case of bee keeping, it is the bee keepers themselves who must take responsibility for ensuring that hives are correctly sited and maintained. Similarly, one expects that diving instructors are themselves competent divers with at least some experience and so on. In the case of science, this same point seems more controversial but it follows from the argument given above that, if the *epistemic* quality of scientific research is to be assessed, then it should be assessed by those with expertise in the relevant science.

The alternative way to make the same point is to say that, where the expertise required is esoteric and the epistemic group that holds it is small, there is no particular role for those outside this group. Again, bee keeping provides a relatively uncontroversial example – most lay citizens and non-bee keepers would, I imagine, be happy to leave the inspection of bee hives to those with specialist expertise and be concerned if such inspections were to be carried out by individuals with no specialist training or knowledge. Similarly for diving instructors where, again I imagine, most novice divers would prefer their instructors to be certified and trained by other professional divers and not by sheep farmers or sociologists.

In the case of science, things are more complex. In some cases, the priority given to expert evaluation remains. For example, in high energy physics lay citizens seem willing defer to scientists in the interpretation of data generated by the Large Hadron Collider. In other cases, however, the boundary of the epistemic community is more contested and what seems to be useful expertise (e.g. that of farm workers, patients or others with relevant experience) is ignored. In these cases, the argument for inclusion seems strongest in order to avoid what Miranda Fricker (2007) terms a 'testimonial epistemic injustice' in which a bona fide speaker (i.e. one with relevant contributory or interactional expertise) is unfairly excluded. Note, however, that this formulation does not imply that mass participation is required, or that public opinion should determine what a scientific research project had discovered. The implication is only that those with *relevant* specialist and esoteric expertise should be heard and given due credit.

In summary, therefore, small epistemic groups working with esoteric expertise should contain within themselves the resources needed to solve the epistemic problem at hand. Whilst some disputes might occur around the boundaries of such groups these typically turn on the relevance of additional expert knowledge and not the need to respond to popular sentiment. Indeed, to the extent that public opinion, which is necessarily based on ubiquitous rather than esoteric expertise, begins to dominate then the group is arguably failing in its epistemic duty as it is no longer relying on its own specialist expertise and hence no longer acting as an expert group.

Small group, ubiquitous expertise: Untrained Sample

Small groups can also be formed when the expertise required is ubiquitous rather than esoteric. Again, the assumption is that the group contains within itself the resources needed to resolve its epistemic problem but, unlike the previous case, there is no presumption that specialist training or socialisation is required. Instead, any competent and properly socialised member of the society can take part (i.e. expertises needed are ubiquitous) even if, in practice, relatively few actually do participate (i.e. the group is small in size).

Perhaps the most well known application of this kind of epistemic group is the jury trial. In the UK, the jury in a legal trial consists of 12 citizens chosen at random from the electoral register and charged with determining the guilt or innocence of the accused. With some exceptions related to previous criminal convictions and current mental health issues, the assumption is that everyone is able to act as a juror. As the trial progresses, the jury hear and see the evidence related to the particular case and, using their everyday experiences and expertise, reach a collective decision that becomes the formally recorded verdict. For the purpose of this argument the key point is that jurors arrive with all the competences and skills needed to reach a verdict.

As with small groups based on esoteric knowledge, small groups relying on ubiquitous knowledge possess the resources they need within their own membership and are similarly self-sufficient. There is a difference in the extent to which others can participate – as the expertise required is ubiquitous, then in principle the group could increase in size until it included everyone. At this point, although the social experience of being a member of that group would undoubtedly have changed (see next section), the expertise required to participate within it would not.

Large group, ubiquitous expertise: Civic Epistemology

If the 'small and esoteric' corner of the table represents the home of legitimate expert decision-makers then the 'large and ubiquitous' corner is where democratic social institutions are located. In this case, the presumption is not only that all members of the epistemic group can participate but that they *should* participate. As this happens, however, the more informal organisation of small groups becomes increasingly formalised and bureaucratised in order that individual contributions can be collected, aggregated and reconciled.

This is not to say that democratic institutions and processes are homogenous. A simple survey of democratic cultures in Europe and the US is enough to reveal the different ways in which these ideas have been developed in different national and historical contexts. In this context, however, the differences are less important that the fact that, in each case, some mechanism has been developed that allows citizens to express their views and see them being taken into account. The fact that the individual systems differ is probably to be expected (Jasanoff 2005) as institutional mechanisms develop in the context of culturally shared values and so come to embody these 'local' commitments and concerns. One manifestation of this is, then, the differing ways in which expert groups are allowed to exercise their autonomy (Porter 1995).

In this context, the Problem of Legitimacy and the STS call for increased public participation can be seen as a response to the historical tendency for 'small and esoteric' epistemic groups to resolve problems that are now seen as falling outside their remit. As explained above, the problem arises because esoteric experts are almost inevitably unrepresentative when judged against standard demographic or cultural criteria. As such, when problems relate to questions of value and preference their ability to speak 'for' others is invariably brought into question. The solution is, therefore, to re-situate the problem within the 'large and ubiquitous' corner of the table and, in so doing, to raise the importance of other kinds of expertise. In so doing, however, the nature of the decision also changes as, although participants may be asked to make judgements about the epistemic authority that should be granted to different expert communities, they do so as members of a wider society and not as domain experts.

Within STS, this interlinking of expert knowledge with its broader interpretation and reception, is often referred to using the idea of 'civic epistemology'. As Yaron Ezrahi (2008: 180) explains in a review of Sheila Jasanoff's *Designs on Nature*, in which the idea of civic epistemology is central, the idea refers to:

> "... the lay mode of balancing causality and morality, of empowering normative popular orientations to edit and frame notions of causality and responsibility with which they are compatible. In some respects democratic civic epistemology reverses the entrenched modern relations between the ethical and the ontological. It represents a shift from the primacy granted to 'objective reality' in fixing the constraints imposed on how far social and political reality can be adapted to ideal principles of freedom, equality and justice to the primacy granted to multiple and often incoherent values and principles to decide which notions of reality and causality will be acceptable as coordinators of social behaviors and public policies."

Although the priorities may be very different, as may the processes involved, there is a key similarity between the idea of civic epistemology and the discussion of the previous two cells in the table. This is that the resources needed to participate within the epistemic group are available within its membership. If civic epistemologies reflect a society's deep-rooted cultural values then these norms are not just instantiated in the design of legal and parliamentary structures but are also, and more importantly, part and parcel of the every day discourse of public reason and debate. What it means to act 'fairly', 'reasonably' may vary from place to place, as does what counts as 'natural' and 'real', but within any given culture these norms are shared and understood. For the STS purist, therefore, increasingly large amounts of science policy, if not actual research, deserve this kind of public scrutiny where what is at stake are the kinds of ontological objects (e.g. what is an 'embryo') that are allowed to exist.

Large group, esoteric expertise: Knowledge Gap Problem

The final cell in the table is the most contested and complex. Whilst the other three cells correspond to identifiable practices in the real world, populating this box is more difficult. The reason is that it is founded upon a contradiction – that there exist large groups possessing esoteric expertise. Almost by definition, however, expertise that is widely distributed is ubiquitous rather than esoteric, so why then does the category matter so much?

The answer is that it is precisely this box that many public participation exercises appear to be orientated towards, at least in part. For example, the consultation document quoted at the start of the paper (BERR 2007), and which is just over 200 pages long, concerns the future development of nuclear power. The report is divided into sections and, in the one concerning carbon emissions, the government's view is summarised as follows:

> "The Government believes that, based on the significant evidence available, the lifecycle carbon emissions from nuclear power stations are about the same as wind generated electricity with significantly lower carbon emissions than fossil fuel fired generation. As an illustration, if our existing nuclear power stations were all replaced with fossil fuel fired power stations, our emissions would be between 8 and 16MtC (million tonnes of carbon) a year higher as a result (depending on the mix of

gas and coal-fired power stations). This would be equivalent to about 30-60% of the total carbon savings we project to achieve under our central scenario from all the measures we are bringing forward in the Energy White Paper. Therefore, the Government believes that new nuclear power stations could make a significant contribution to tackling climate change. We recognise that nuclear power alone cannot tackle climate change, but these figures show that it could make an important contribution as part of a balanced energy policy." (para. 45, p. 14)

Respondents are then asked, based on the preceding discussion of empirical and simulation studies to carbon emissions, wind power, fossil fuels and nuclear power whether or not they agree with the government's view. They are also asked to give reasons and to highlight any 'significant considerations' that the report's authors might have missed.

The obvious problem posed by these questions is how, and on what basis, are citizens to make these judgements? Clearly the consultation document provides some information but how are citizens to know whether the information presented is a fair and accurate summary of the balance of opinion within the relevant expert community?[135] Assuming the consultation document, perhaps supplemented by other written material garnered from the internet, is their principal course of information then, at best, citizens approach the task with Primary Source Knowledge or, more likely, rely on Popular Understanding. In neither case, however, can they have access to the specialist tacit knowledge possessed by the domain experts. What is more, so long as their learning remains remote (either in the form of text or multimedia information) citizens can never acquire the specialist tacit knowledge that comes from interaction with experts (Collins and Evans 2007; Collins 2010).

There is therefore a mismatch between what citizens *need* to answer such questions (i.e. the specialist tacit knowledge that enables expert judgement) and what they are *able* to know (i.e. explicit knowledge from

---

[135] Unsurprisingly there were some complaints that the information was not fair and unbiased but that is not the issue here. Rather the point is to raise the question of what benchmark citizens could use in order to decide whether or not charges of bias and/or selective citation could be justified.

published sources and supplemented by some more general meta-expertise). In what follows I argue that much of the discussion around public participation misses this fundamental point and the difficulties arise precisely because they seek to import processes – mass or public participation and citizen juries or consensus conferences – that work in one cell of the table and apply them to this, very different, problem.

The mass participation route is the one implicitly favoured by much of the STS community in the sense that it does not recognise the Problem of Extension and, as the quote from Brian Wynne makes clear, the claim is that the relevant population is all enfranchised citizens. In effect, this position argues that the mechanisms developed for large-group-ubiquitous-expertise settings can be imported into an epistemic problem in which esoteric expertise is required.

Applying the analysis set out above, however, suggests that this approach, which reached its highpoint in the UK with the GM Nation? debate (DTI 2003) is only suited to those questions where preferences rather than propositions are at stake as preferences are ubiquitous but the specialist tacit knowledge needed to judge propositional questions is, by definition, not widely available.. The difference between these two can be made clear by contrasting the conditions laid down by Wynne with the questions posed by the DTI. According to Wynne, the participation of every democratic citizen is required when the issue at stake is:

"public meanings and the imposition of problematic versions of these by
powerful scientific bodies" (2003: 411)

In contrast, however, what the DTI actually asks the public to comment on are not 'public meanings', by which Wynne means a more inclusive debate about 'which propositional questions [and knowledges] are salient' (2003: 402), but a specific propositional question about the carbon footprints of competing technologies. It is this difference that gets to the heart of the Problem of Extension. Whilst the ubiquitous expertises of that make up a civic epistemology are ideally suited to the kind of problem Wynne outlines, they are not at all suited to the problem the DTI sets. Of course,

Wynne would no doubt argue that this reflects the prior commitments of the policy community in presuming a need/desire for a nuclear powered future and hence that the policy document suffers from all the traditional Problems of Legitimacy. Whilst I would not want to rule this possibility out, such considerations are orthogonal to the point being made here, which is that even if the scientists and civil servants who constructed the policy document had acted with complete integrity and impartiality in sifting the available expert evidence there is no way a lay citizen reading the document could know that.

To put the same point in a slightly different way, what the analysis set out above suggests is that, whilst it is clearly appropriate to consult with publics about the meanings they attach to particular objects, technologies and imagined futures, and the criteria against which these things should be judged, it seems rather less appropriate to ask them, on the basis of no specialist expertise, to judge what the correct outcome of complex scientific modelling exercises should be. The implication this latter point is, of course, that the interpretation of the empirical data belongs in the small-group-esoteric-expertise setting where contributory experts (scientists and others) resolve the propositional question as best they can.[136]

The development of Citizen Juries and other deliberative methods of seeking public opinion represents a more direct way of addressing the lack of esoteric expertise amongst the general population (Evans and Plows 2007). In this case the problem is effectively translated into a small-group-ubiquitous-expertise setting in which a small group of citizens is selected and provided with the opportunity to interact with specialist experts in order to reach a more informed decision. As with the legal jury, however, the presumption is that citizens arrive fully equipped to make the decision (i.e.

---

[136] This introduces a third option – 'just trust the experts' – for dealing with propositional questions. Strictly speaking, however, this does not belong in this cell as it is a small-group-esoteric-expertise problem. The difficulty with STS is that there is a tendency (the Problem of Extension) to see all problems as being large-group-ubiquitous-expertise type problems and hence to empty the small-group-esoteric-expertise cell. In fact, as argued later, it is the large-group-esoteric-expertise cell that should be emptied.

ubiquitous expertises are enough) but require a more wide-ranging knowledge base on which to exercise these abilities. In other words, just as a legal trial assumes that juries will come to understand evidentiary rules, legal distinctions and forensic science, so too a citizen jury assumes that its participants can come to understand enough of the expert discourse to reach a reliable conclusion. Again, as with the legal jury setting, there is no expectation that the citizens will become members of the expert groups they are asked to judge (i.e. just as legal jurors do not leave as qualified barristers or scientists, so citizen jurors do not leave the jury process as expert scientists or environmental activists) although it might be hoped that their future actions will be influenced by knowledge gained as a result of the process.

Whilst this method makes perfect sense in terms of expertise in that members of the group are now being asked to make judgments based on expertise they actually possess, it does raise questions of political legitimacy. In particular, because the sample is small and often self-selecting in important ways, the extent to which the small group represents the large group from which it is drawn is problematic.[137] In jury trials this is less of an issue, not least because the methods are a deeply entrenched part of the UK's legal civic epistemology. In the case of science, however, the same cannot be said with the result that Citizen Jury research remains vulnerable to critiques about the extent to which it generalises. Again, in part this may stem from the way in which it is legitimated in terms of esoteric expertise rather than the more widespread ubiquitous expertises that unite rather than differentiate citizens.

As with the civic epistemology approach, the need to pay attention to the framing of the question remains important. Given their brief and limited interaction with a wide range of heterogeneous communities, Citizen

---

[137] Sampling in Citizen Juries is difficult because participation requires a substantial commitment over an extended time period. This often leads to a relatively high non-response rate and a tendency for people with a particular interest in the topic to be over-represented amongst the final sample.

Jurors are not in a position to make judgements about propositional statements in the same way that domain experts can. On the other hand, and unlike the participants in a mass consultation, they do have the advantage of some intensive training and interaction. What they enact, therefore, is not freshly acquired interactional or contributory expertise (even if their level of specialist knowledge will have increased) but more finely honed meta-expertise based on a more in-depth understanding of the social fields within which the expert controversy is located. In this sense, they enact a civic epistemology but do so from privileged position in comparison to their lay colleagues.

In summary, citizen participants, whether 'broad and shallow' or 'narrow and deep' cannot solve the knowledge gap problem created when large groups are asked to solve epistemic problems for which they do not possess the expertise. Although both can work in different contexts, they work by translating the problem back into different cells of the table. In many ways this is how it should be given that the idea of a widely dispersed esoteric expertise is an oxymoron.

4. Conclusions

This paper has examined the functioning of epistemic groups in terms of the expertise they need to perform the task at hand. The key issue has been the whether or not the expertise needed is ubiquitous or esoteric.

In the case of ubiquitous expertises it has been argued that, whatever the group size, the resources needed for it to act can be found within the group members. As a result, whilst epistemic groups in these two cells of the table might suffer from 'local' difficulties in organising their interactions in a way that participants find satisfactory this has nothing to do with a lack of expertise and so, in this regard, such groups can be regarded as 'fit for purpose'.

In the case of esoteric expertise, the situation is more complex. For small groups, where the boundary of the social group coincides with the boundary of relevant expertise(s) there is again no problem. In this case, as with ubiquitous expertises, the resources needed to solve the epistemic problem are available within the group and it is, therefore, able to act as a collective epistemic agent. Again, this is not to say there will not be disagreements and difficulties within the group as evidence is disputed and synthesised, but it is to insist that the resources needed to undertake this task are to be found within and not outside the group. In this sense it is, like the epistemic groups based on ubiquitous expertises, 'fit for purpose'.

More problematic is the case that arises when a large group is asked to make a decision that requires esoteric expertise. Now the isomorphism between group membership and expertise breaks down as esoteric expertises are, by definition, not widespread. The implication of this observation is that public participation exercises around science and technology that seek to solve technical or propositional problems by putting them out to popular consultation are fundamentally flawed because they are based on a contradiction. More positively, however, reconceptualising public participation in terms of ubiquitous expertises brings the goals of participation back in line with the abilities of citizens, making some forms of citizen participation in science and technology policy both possible and desirable. Citizen Juries seem particularly promising in this regard as they allow time for learning but more broadly based exercises can also be worthwhile.

Finally, it can also be seen that the tension between the Problems of Legitimacy and Extension describes the relationship between the small-group-esoteric-expertise cell and the large-group-ubiquitous-expertise cell. The Problem of Legitimacy arises when too much weight is given to the small-group-esoteric-expertise cell; the Problem of Extension when too much weight is given to the large-group-ubiquitous-expertise cell. As the above analysis has hopefully made clear, the solution to these problems is not in collapsing the table to a single cell but in recognising the importance of distinguishing between different epistemic challenges and formulating a response that is appropriate to the problem at hand.

Bibliography

Beck, U. (1992), Risk Society: Towards a New Modernity. London: Sage.

BERR - Department for Business, Enterprise and Regulatory Reform (2007), *The Future of Nuclear Power: Consultation Document*. http://www.berr.gov.uk/files/file39197.pdf [accessed 30 March 2009].

Bloor, D. (1976), *Knowledge and Social Imagery*. London: Routledge and Kegan Paul.

Collins, H. M. and Evans, R. J. (2007), *Rethinking Expertise*. Chicago, IL: The University of Chicago Press.

——— (2002), "The Third Wave of Science Studies: Studies of Expertise and Experience". *Social Studies of Sciences* 32, 2, (April), 235-296.

Collins, H.M. (1992), *Changing Order: Replication and Induction in Scientific Practice*, 2nd Edition. Chicago/London: University of Chicago Press.

——— (ed.) (2007), Studies in History and Philosophy of Science. Special Issue – Case Studies of Expertise and Experience 38, 4, 686-97.

——— (2010), *Tacit and Explicit Knowledge*. Chicago, IL: The University of Chicago Press.

Collins, H.M., Weinel, M. and Evans, R.J. (2010), "The Politics and Policy of the Third Wave: New Technologies and Society". *Critical Policy Studies* 4, 2, 185-201.

CST – Council for Science and Technology (2005), *Policy Through Dialogue*. London: CST. Available online at www.cst.org.uk/reports [accessed 27 September 2005].

DTI – Department of Trade and Industry (2003), *GM Nation?: The Findings of the Public Debate*. DTI: London. Also available at: http://www.gmpublicdebate.org.uk/docs/gmnation finalreport.pdf [accessed 6 May 2004].

Evans, R. and Plows, A. (2007), "Listening Without Prejudice? Re-Discovering the Value of the Disinterested Citizen". *Social Studies of Science* 37, 6, 827-854.

Ezrahi, Y. (2008), "Review of Sheila Jasanoff, Designs on Nature". *Metascience* 177-82.

Fricker, M. (2007) *Epistemic Injustice: Power and the Ethics of Knowing*. Oxford, UK: Oxford University Press.

Functowicz S. .O. and Jerry R. R. (1993), "Science for the Post-Normal Age". *Futures* 25, 739-755.

Gerold, R. and Liberatore, A. (2001), *Report of the Working Group 'Democratising Expertise and Establishing Scientific Reference Systems*. Brussels: European Commission. Available online at: http://europa.eu.int/comm/governance/areas/group2/report_en.pdf [accessed 4 July 2002].

Giddens, A. (1990), *The Consequences of Modernity*. Cambridge: Polity Press.

House of Lords (2000), *Science and Society*. Select Committee on Science and Technology, Session 1999-2000. Third Report, HL Paper 38. London: HMSO.

Irwin, A. (1995), Citizen Science: A Study of People, Expertise and Sustainable Development. London and New York: Routledge.

Jasanoff, S. (2005), Designs on Nature: Science and Democracy in Europe and the United States. Princeton: Princeton University Press.

Miller, S. (2001), "Public Understanding of Science at the Crossroads". *Public Understanding of Science* 10, 115-20.

OST – Office of Science and Technology (2002), *The Government's Approach to Public Dialogue on Science and Technology*. London: OST. Available online at http://www.ost.gov.uk/ society/public_dialogue.htm [accessed 27 September 2005].

POST – Parliamentary Office for Science and Technology (2001), *Open Channels: Public dialogue in science and technology*. Parliamentary Office of Science and Technology, Report No. 153, London.

Porter, T. (1995), Trust in Numbers: The Pursuit of Objectivity in Science and Public Life. Princeton, N.J.: Princeton University Press.

Ribeiro, R. (2007) *Knowledge Transfer*. PhD thesis, Cardiff University.

RCEP – Royal Commission for Environmental Pollution (1998), 21st Report: Setting Environmental Standards Cm 4053. London: HMSO.

Wilsden, J. and Willis, R. (2004), *See-Through Science: Why Public Engagement Needs to Move Upstream*. London: DEMOS, Green Alliance, RSA and Environment Agency.

Wynne, B. (1982), *Rationality and Ritual: The Windscale Inquiry and Nuclear Decisions in Britain*. Chalfont St. Giles, Bucks: British Society for the History of Science.

—— (1992), "Misunderstood misunderstanding: Social identities and public uptake of Science". *Public Understanding of Science* 1, 3, 281-304.

—— (2003), "Seasick on the Third Wave? Subverting the Hegemony of Propositionalism". *Social Studies of Science* 33, 3, 401-417.

Experimentation versus Theory Choice: A Social-Epistemological Approach

MARCEL WEBER

1. Introduction

The question of how scientists choose theories from a set of alternatives is an old one. Traditionally, it was assumed that there are *decision rules* or *methodological principles* of one sort or another that guide such choices. Furthermore, it was assumed that when a *community* of scientists chooses a theory, this must amount to the application of these rules or principles by each *individual* scientist in the community, or at least by a majority of them. I am at a loss for a good name that ends with "-ism" for the first view, but the second is described well by "methodological individualism". Both views prevail to this day, mutually supporting each other, so it is time to question them and also to think about alternative views.

In my view, the strongest challenge to both of these views still comes from Thomas Kuhn. In the well-known postscript to *The Structure of Scientific Revolutions*, Kuhn wrote:

> "There is no neutral algorithm for theory-choice, no systematic decision procedure which, properly applied, must lead each individual in the group to the same decision. In this sense it is the community of specialists rather than its individual members that make the effective decision." (Kuhn 1970, S. 200)

The reason for this non-existence of a systematic decision procedure according to Kuhn is that there exist different criteria for theory choice and these criteria tend to pull into different directions. For example, one theory may be simpler than another, but at the same time less predictively accurate, e.g., like the Copernican and Ptolemaïc world systems initially. Kuhn has coined the term "incommensurability" for this kind of inter-theoretic relation (see Hoyningen-Huene 1993: § 6.3, for the development of Kuhn's view of incommensurability). The chief feature of incommensurable theories from a methodological point of view is the fact that rival theories may all have their merits and their shortcomings, but it is not possible to *weigh* these and aggregate them into a single measure. Kuhn (1977: 321f.) cites a standard set of criteria for theory appraisal, namely **accuracy**, **consistency**, **broad scope**, **simplicity** and **fruitfulness**. He then argues that in most interesting cases of rival scientific theories, these criteria do not determine a unique choice. The reason is that individuals in a community of scientists may weigh these criteria differently and thus arrive at different choices with respect to theories. Since Kuhn observed that scientists do sometimes *do* choose between different theories or frameworks, this leads him to a second claim, that such choices are made by the *community*:

> "In the absence of criteria able to dictate the choice of each individual, I argued, we do well to trust the collective judgment of scientists trained in this way. 'What better criterion could there be,' I asked rhetorically, 'than the decision of the scientific group?'" (Kuhn 1977: 320f.)

This passage even suggests, in addition to the rejection of what I called methodological individualism, that Kuhn considers such collective choices to be *rational*. It is the combination of these claims of that I would like to focus on in this paper. My central question is how *communities* of scientists *rationally* decide between alternative theories or frameworks, which, according to Kuhn, seems to be something that is impossible at the *individual* level. Scientific rationality emerges at the community level; this view makes Kuhn a social epistemologist.[138] However, there has been little discussion of how this remarkable feat should be possible, either within Kuhn's framework or within the framework of other social epistemologies. This paper aims at precisely such a discussion. However, my discussion will not address the issue in its full generality; it will be restricted to experimental science, in particular experimental biology.

---

[138] Kuhn has no need for postulating collective epistemic subjects, as some authors do (e.g., Gilbert 1987). Neither do I, at least for the argument of this paper.

I shall proceed as follows. In the next Section, I would like to discuss an interesting reconstruction of Kuhn's argument in terms of social choice theory, which is due to Samir Okasha (forthcoming). This reconstruction renders the problem in sharper terms. In the Third Section, I shall discuss two more recent attempts to defend scientific communities as the proper agents of scientific decision-making. Such attempts are typically part of social epistemologies. In the Fourth Section, I shall suggest a *social mechanism* for the selection of a theory or framework by scientific communities that is inspired by what I take to be Kuhn's view. The Fifth Section will address the question of *what* exactly is selected. For it is not clear that theories alone are the appropriate units that are being selected. This will be illustrated on the example of experimental biology. Section 6 summarizes my conclusions.

2. Okasha's Reconstruction of Kuhn Using Social Choice Theory

Okasha (forthcoming) reconstructs theory choice problems as social choice problems. Traditionally, social choice problems involve a social group of people with different preference rankings. The problem is then to find a way of aggregating or integrating these preferences such that the group as a whole chooses from a selection of alternatives on the basis of the individuals' preferences. In general, such problems are only well-defined if certain constraints are specified. These constraints are typically rules that any acceptable solution to a choice problem must satisfy. In Kenneth Arrow's (1963) classic treatment, the following rules are supposed to constrain the space of rational solutions:

(**U**) **unrestricted domain**: any individual preference ranking is admissible as an input into the social choice

(**P**) **weak Pareto**: If all individuals in the group prefer x over y, then the group as a whole should also prefer x over y

(**N**) **non-dictatorship**: there cannot be an individual whose preference ranking with respect to any two alternatives determines the group's choice with respect to these alternatives. In other words, no-one's preferences can trump or over-ride what the group as a whole chooses

(I) independence of irrelevant alternatives: this conditions says that the group's choice between alternatives x and y can only depend on the individuals' preferences with respect to x and y, not on their preferences with respect to other alternatives. If I want my community to build a new concert hall rather than a theatre, then the group's preference of a concert hall over a theatre or vice versa can only depend on my preference between these two options and not, say, my preference of a theatre over a casino.

The problem now is to find a preference ranking for the whole group that satisfies these four constraints. Arrow (1963) has examined the conditions under which this kind of problem is solvable. A famous result is *Arrow's impossibility theorem*. It states that there is no way of integrating so-called *weak* preference orderings under the four above-mentioned conditions for more than two alternatives. These are preference orderings such that ties are permitted, i.e., individuals are allowed to be indifferent with respect to alternatives.

Could Arrow's theorem possibly be relevant to theory choice problems in science? Okasha suggests a scenario how they might be. He first construes Kuhn's different criteria that are supposed to inform theory choices as *individuals*. Under this construal, each of these criteria will return a preference ranking of a set of alternative theories. Thus, simplicity might favor theory 2 over theory 1 and 3, while accuracy prefers theory 3 over 1 over 2. Consistency could rank all at the same level, while fruitfulness prefers theory 1 over 3 over 2, and broad scope as well. Arrow's theorem now says that there is no algorithm or decision procedure that obeys the conditions unrestricted domain, weak Pareto, non-dictatorship and independence of irrelevant alternatives and that returns an unique overall ranking for the three theories, taking into account how Kuhn's values rank them. It should be noted that the five rankings are associated with individual *criteria*, not individual *scientists* in Okasha's reconstruction of the problem. Thus, it is not strictly a social choice problem in Okasha's account. It is merely an application of social choice *theory* to a structurally similar kind of decision problem. Nonetheless, perhaps it could be transformed into a *bona fide* social choice problem by assuming that individual scientists rank theories by applying only one of Kuhn's values. Thus, I could be Mr. Simplicity (obviously), while you are Mr. or Mrs. Accuracy or Mr. or Mrs. Consistency (whichever you prefer!). This would mean that I only look how simple theories are when ranking them, while you only look at how accurate or how consistent they are. But such a social choice scenario is not necessarily a part of Okasha's argument.

Could this be a formal proof for Kuhn's incommensurability thesis by application of Arrow's impossibility theorem? This is not quite Okasha's goal, even if he sees important parallels. First of all, it should be noted, as Okasha does, that Kuhn's claim is not that there is *no* algorithm that can yield a unique choice, there are *many*. Thus Kuhn's claim is different, which, I suppose, is why Okasha's paper is subtitled "Kuhn *versus* Arrow". These differences notwithstanding, Kuhn's thesis (many algorithms) and the Arrow-Okasha thesis (no algorithm) seem just as devastating for the possibility of rational theory choice, at least if there is no way of overcoming these difficulties. Fortunately, there is, at least for experimental sciences, as I will try to demonstrate.

Second, Arrow's theorem does not apply if there are only two alternatives. Perhaps there is a reason why the grand historical debates in science are typically about two alternative theories or frameworks (e.g., Copernicus vs. Ptolemy, phlogiston vs. oxygen chemistry, relativistic vs. classical mechanics or quantum theory vs. classical mechanics). Third, Arrow's theorem only applies to an *ordinal* ranking of theories, in other words, a ranking that does not contain any information about the *strength* of the preferences or the differences in preference. This is good news for Bayesian confirmation theorists and other kinds of formal epistemologists. For according to Bayesianism, theories are not merely ranked ordinally by scientists, they receive a probability value. Arrow's theorem does not apply to such a quantitative ranking. Okasha (forthcoming) suggests various ways of how the Arrovian impossibility result can be avoided, the Bayesian approach being one such way.

I would like to suggest an altogether different way out of the Kuhn-Arrow-Okasha predicament concerning theory choice.

I begin by pointing out that in scientific decision-making, it is not at all obvious that Arrow's condition of **non-dictatorship** applies or ought to apply. While in democratic decision-making, which is what Arrow was concerned with, there are *constitutive* reasons for giving all individuals equal weight when aggregating their preferences, there is no reason why science should be committed to weigh all theory choice criteria equally. As for Kuhn himself, there are indications that he granted **fruitfulness** a special role. Here are two relevant passages that support this view:

> "At the start, a new candidate for paradigm may have few supporters [...]. Nevertheless, if they are competent, they will improve it, explore its possibilities, and show what it would be like to belong to the community guided by it. And as that goes on, if the paradigm is one destined to win its fight, the number and strength of persuasive in its favor will increase. More scientists will then be converted, and the exploration of the new paradigm will go on. Gradually, the number of experiments, instruments, articles and books based upon the paradigm will multiply. Still more men, convinced of the new view's **fruitfulness**, will adopt the new mode of practicing normal science, until at least only a few elderly holdouts remain." (Kuhn 1970: 159, emphasis mine)

This revealing passage suggests that the reasons why an *individual* scientist joins a new paradigm (and thereby, a new theory, see below for more on this) may vary. That is, which of the five criteria for theory choice (if any) influence an individual choice varies, as does the weight that any of the criteria may have. Kuhn captures this aspect of theory choice by suggesting that it's *values* rather than *rules* or *algorithms* that form the basis for such choices (Kuhn 1977: 330f.). The difference is that, while the latter determine a unique choice, the former are subject to interpretation and judgment. I take it that such interpretation and judgment also include a weighing of criteria, should these be in conflict with respect to a specific choice. At any rate, **simplicity, accuracy, consistency, broad scope** and

fruitfulness appear as values that *influence*, but do not *determine* theory choice at the *individual level*.

But things look entirely different when it comes to the *community level*. The passage from *The Structure of Scientific Revolutions* cited above suggests that what the community chooses is the paradigm that is most prolific in turning out "experiments, instruments, articles and books based upon the paradigm". These are precisely the marks of a fruitful paradigm, and I claim that Kuhn's position is that fruitfulness ultimately dictates the community choice.

An obvious objection to this view (whether or not it's actually Kuhn's) must be addressed right away. Doesn't this view put the cart before the horse in suggesting that fruitfulness alone informs community choices? Paradigms don't reproduce like rabbits do (i.e., all by themselves), it's the *scientists* who proliferate it *by means of* "experiments, instruments, articles and books based upon the paradigm". And don't they reproduce a paradigm-associated theory only if it satisfies the criteria of theory choice? Well, not according to Kuhn they don't. On his account, the grounds for judging a new puzzle solution as successful or unsuccessful are provided *directly* by the *similarity relations* to the exemplary problem solutions (Kuhn 1970: 45). Rules or criteria of theory choice such as our five candidates are simply irrelevant for judging something a successful puzzle solution in line with a specific paradigm.[139]

Thus, if Kuhn is right, a choice among incommensurable frameworks or theories is possible on the basis of the *problem-solving capacity* of these frameworks. In other words, problem-solving capacity, which I take to be

---

[139] Of course, there may be a standard of **accuracy** associated with a paradigm, but such standards are highly variable. It is worth noting that judgments about the success or failure of problem solutions are only possible from *within* the paradigm, as it were. Outsiders who have not acquired the salient similarity relations cannot judge whether or not some problem solution conforms to the paradigm. This is a result of Kuhnian incommensurability, which precludes translation into the lexicon of another theory. However, it is always possible to introduce outsiders to the practice such that they acquire this competence.

the same as **fruitfulness**, can be viewed as dictator in theory choice according to Kuhn. This, in my view, is the main reason why Arrow's theorem is not an obstacle to rational theory choice. At the same time, this is the main reason why Kuhnian incommensurability does not imply incomparability.

I find Okasha's analysis helpful because it forces us to reflect on the conditions that constrain theory choice situations. However, I would like to press a different construal of theory choice as social choice. In doing so, I shall remain true to Kuhn's idea that the choice of theories or frameworks does not boil down to choices made by individual scientists, but by the whole community. In other words, even if problem-solving capacity or fruitfulness is the criterion that dictates the choice of a research framework in science, it is not the case that each and every scientist, or a majority of them, make this choice deliberately. Instead, I will suggest there is a *social* mechanism that effects this choice. This mechanism will be the subject of Section 4. But first, I will draw out a connection to other views in social epistemology.

3. Social Groups as Agents of Scientific Decision-making

Some social epistemologists argue that groups are proper subjects, or even the *only* proper subjects, of knowledge. There are different kinds of social epistemology, some are veritistic or truth-directed, others not. Furthermore, we can distinguish between approaches that accord a central role to *deliberation* and approaches that don't. An example of the first kind is the social epistemology of Helen Longino (Longino 2002). On Longino's view, a group can be said to know something if it has engaged in a suitably organized process of deliberation. "Suitably organized" means that the group must be committed to certain procedural norms such as providing public forums of criticism and temperate equality of intellectual authority. Her approach is perhaps best encapsulated in her definition of *epistemic ac-*

ceptability, which plays the role that justification has in standard epistemologies:[140]

> "Some content A is epistemically acceptable in community C at time t if
> A is supported by data d evident to C at t in light of reasoning and back-
> ground assumptions which have survived critical scrutiny from as many
> perspectives as are available to C at t, and C is characterized by venues
> for criticism, uptake of criticism, public standards, and tempered equality
> of intellectual authority." (Longino 2002: 135)

It should be evident in this account that Longino sees a major role for deliberation in scientific decision-making; for what it means for some content
to "survive critical scrutiny" is to be accepted by the group after an exchange of arguments. Longino does not specify how we should think of
group acceptance, whether this involves acceptance by a majority, or if
group acceptance is something over and above the acceptance by individual members (as, for example, Gilbert 1987 argued). At any rate, it has re-
mained controversial as to whether deliberation really plays a role in the
choice of theories by scientists.[141]

An example of a social epistemology that does not see deliberation
as constitutive for knowledge is Miriam Solomon's social empiricism (Solomon 1994). According to Solomon, individual scientists cannot possess
knowledge in isolation because their beliefs are always biased. However,
scientific collectives nonetheless may be said to possess knowledge, because they sometimes choose theories that are empirically more successful
than others. In other words, scientific collectives are *responsive* to empirically successful theories (p. 339). This responsiveness provides that a certain kind of counterfactual claim is true, namely claims from a kind of
which the following claim is an instance: "Physicists would not have accepted quantum theory if it had not been empirically successful." Solomon
argues that this responsiveness is due to the fact that different individuals
in the community are *differently* biased. Thus, even though every individu-

---

[140] The role of truth is played by a concept called "conformity", the satisfaction conditions of which are context-dependent (unlike classical correspondence truth).
[141] It should be noted that there is no reason to think that Longino's deliberators will
not run into the difficulties associated with Kuhnian incommensurability.

al scientist has some personal reasons for preferring one alternative, and these reasons may not always be cognitive in nature, these personal reasons are variable in the community and will cancel each other.

Solomon thus opposes a widespread consensus in the philosophy of science according to which personal biases by individual scientists, while they exist, are more often overruled by a general preference for empirically successful theories than not. Using examples such as the case of plate tectonics in earth science, she shows that scientists do not assess a theory's empirical success in an unbiased way. Only the community as a whole can make an unbiased choice, i.e., a choice that depends solely on the theories' empirical merits.

In that she does not rely on deliberation doing the magic, I find Solomon's view more realistic than Longino's. However, I also think that there is something missing in Solomon's account. What's missing is some plausible story how a community that consists of biased individuals can be "responsive" to a theory's empirical success. This responsiveness is the cornerstone of Solomon's theory. She needs some account of how this responsiveness arises in communities. And this account had better not see groups as responsive because of some property that each individual in the community has. If it were suggested that, even though individual scientists exhibit personal biases, they have nonetheless an individual propensity to select empirically successful theories, this would make the social epistemology collapse into an ordinary individual epistemology. I would also find it unsatisfactory if it were suggested that a preference for empirically successful theories is the only bias that does not cancel out in the community, while all other biases do so cancel out. For this would make scientific knowledge a lucky coincidence. Thus, what we need is a truly *social* mechanism for theory choice, a mechanism that explains how the community as a whole selects empirically successful theories. This is what I turn to now.

4. A Social Mechanism for Theory Choice

The solution I wish to propose is strongly inspired by Kuhn's account. The starting point is provided by passages such as the one from *Structure* (p. 159, cited above) where Kuhn describes how a paradigm is established in the community. ("Gradually, the number of experiments, instruments, articles and books based upon the paradigm will multiply".) We should also remember that Kuhn was *very* serious about there being a strong analogy between scientific change and *biotic evolution*.[142] Just as certain types of organism enjoy more reproductive success than others as a consequence of some heritable characteristics, some theories are propagated more rapidly than others because they give rise to more successful problem solutions:

> "The resolution of revolutions is the selection by conflict within the scientific community of the fittest way to practice future science. The net result of a sequence of such revolutionary selections, separated by periods of normal research, is the wonderfully adapted set of instruments we call modern scientific knowledge." (Kuhn 1970: 172)

Theories reproduce, as it were, by being successfully applied to new cases. Furthermore, scientific specialties that are guided by a paradigm may give rise to new specialties by a process that is like *speciation* in biotic evolution:

> "[B]reakdowns in communication do, of course, occur: they're a significant characteristic of the episodes *Structure* referred to as 'crises'. I take them to be the crucial symptoms of the speciation-like process through which new disciplines emerge, each with its own lexicon, and each with its own area of knowledge." (Kuhn 1994: 100f.)

I contend that Kuhn's account, while it's not intended as an application of evolutionary theory, contains a truly *social* mechanism for theory choice.

---

[142] This analogy has recently been criticized by Renzi (2009) and defended against Renzi by Reydon and Hoyningen-Huene (2010). In a nutshell, Renzi criticizes Kuhn for using evolutionary and ecological concepts that are inadequate on biological grounds. Reydon and Hoyningen-Huene argue that this is irrelevant because Kuhn's use of evolutionary theory is not an application of evolutionary theory. It's just what Kuhn says it is: an analogy.

Scientific communities are socially organized to propagate theories that have a high problem-solving capacity. An important part of this social organization is the *professional reward system*, the system that allocates credit to members of the community. Anyone who has ever worked in a laboratory (as I have) knows that a scientist can only get credits for "positive results", that is, successful problem solutions. "Negative results", i.e., failures to solve some problem in the expected way, are hard to sell, be it to learned journals, funding agencies, tenure committees, even Ph.D. thesis committees (though a Ph.D. student may get away with producing only negative results if it is evident that he or she worked really hard and demonstrated skill and that it is therefore not his or her fault that there were no positive results, just bad luck or poor supervision).

This social characteristic of the scientific profession ensures that theories with high problem-solving capacity (i.e., fruitfulness) out-reproduce theories with lower problem-solving capacity.[143]

The social mechanism that I have just described has the following features:

(1) It can only operate at the community level. In other words, it is not what individual scientists *believe* about a theory, for instance, whether or not it is empirically successful that determines the community's response. Nobody cares what Professor Bloggs or Dr. Muller *believe* about a theory. It's what they *do* that's of interest to the community. Specifically, it is when they present a solved problem that the community responds. It responds by giving Bloggs and Muller credit for what they did, which allows Bloggs to land a research grant to continue her research, or Muller to get tenure, or someone else to receive a Ph.D. The results are presented at conferences, published in an A-journal, and perhaps end up in the textbooks. Thus, the theory reproduces. If a theory does not or only rarely gives rise to

---

[143] A similar evolutionary account can be found in Hull (1988), which focuses on different systems of biological systematics. In contrast to the present account, Hull seemed to view his approach as a bona fide application of evolutionary theory to scientific development. I prefer to stick closer to Kuhn's account, according to which biological evolution is at best analogous to science as a process.

solved problems, it goes extinct. And it would go extinct without anyone ever *deciding* or even *believing* that it is false. Theories are not refuted, they just cease to be pursued because they fail to provide professional rewards to those who pursue it.

(2) The social mechanism of theory selection explains why scientific communities are *responsive* to a theory's empirical success in the sense of Solomon (1994). I define "empirical success" broadly, as any kind of solved problem. Unlike in Solomon's account, this responsiveness is not a coincidental feature of the community. It is the social mechanism that warrants such counterfactual claims as they are made by Solomon: The community of physicists *would* not have accepted quantum theory, *had it not* been empirically successful.

(3) This account does not depend on deliberation, yet it is social in a thoroughgoing way. In particular, it cites *non-cognitive factors* as instrumental in the scientific community's ability to reach its *cognitive goals*. It is not the otherwise disinterested, noble quest for truth that determines the community's behavior, but the selfish career interests of individual scientists. The postulated social mechanism ensures that it is nonetheless a theory's *empirical* credentials (at least fruitfulness) that determine its fate. Thus, my account is *social* but not *externalist*, in other words, it doesn't have to invoke extra-scientific factors to explain scientific change. In this, I follow Kuhn's rejection of externalist sociological accounts of science such as the "strong programme" (Kuhn 1992).

(4) The social mechanism also explains why Okasha's condition of non-dictatorship doesn't hold, and why it's fruitfulness that dictates a theory's fate. The scientific community is socially organized to select empirically successful theories, no matter what methodological preferences scientists have. They all want to advance their own careers, and they belong to communities that ruthlessly select for theories that are fruitful. There is also no conflict between the claim that scientists are driven by their career interests and the idea that science exhibits epistemic rationali-

ty, so long as selecting the most empirically fruitful theories counts as an epistemically rational practice.

So far, I have been speaking as if scientific communities chose "theories". In the following section, I will argue that, in reality, they select something more inclusive.

5. What Exactly is Selected? Lessons From the New Experimentalism

"New Experimentalism" is a label for a very loose family of views in philosophy of science that sail under Ian Hacking's famous slogan "experiments lead a live of their own". What exactly this slogan means, of course, depends on the specific brand of New Experimentalism we are talking about. I am here particularly interested in a version that has been popular especially in the historiography of biology. The best known and also most developed account is by Hans-Jörg Rheinberger (Rheinberger 1997). The core of this account is the idea that what Rheinberger calls "experimental systems" plays a major role in biological research. Often, new experimental systems have been at the beginning of major developments in molecular biology. An example is a so-called in vitro system for protein synthesis that was used in the 1960s to crack the genetic code and subsequently to figure out the mechanism of protein synthesis. This system consists basically of a cell extract from either bacterial cells, yeast cells, or mammalian cells (normally immature red blood cells, because they have a very high rate of protein synthesis that they need to make hemoglobin). If such a cell extract is fed with the right chemicals, it will synthesize protein in the test tube. In the early days, this was detected by adding radioactive amino acids and then measuring the incorporation of the radioactivity into protein.

In his book, Rheinberger details how much experimental work was organized around this system rather than around some theory. One of the core postulates of Rheinberger's theory is that experimental systems are "the smallest integral working units of research" (1997: 28). Biological research, on Rheinberger's account, "begins with the choice of a system rather than with the choice of a theoretical framework" (p. 25). Furthermore, he characterizes experimental systems as "systems of manipulation designed to give unknown answers to questions that the experimenters themselves are not yet clearly to ask" (ibid.). Thus, according to Rheinberger, experimental research in biology does not usually start with a theory, or with well-formulated research questions.[144]

Experimental systems may precede the problems that they eventually help to solve. What is more, experimental systems do not just help to *answer* questions, they also help to *generate* them. Where this process leads is impossible to predict; experimental systems give rise to unexpected events. Thus, Rheinberger draws our attention to the unpredictable, open-ended nature of the research process – an aspect that seems so fundamental about basic science.

I found much to agree with in Rheinberger's account. A major problem, however, is the obscurity of the term "experimental system". Not unlike Kuhn's term "paradigm", it is sometimes this, sometimes that, and the term does different kinds of work. I will not attempt to remedy this situation by providing a conceptual analysis or a refined definition, I will only make two points of clarification.

First, experimental systems are not merely collections of material things (as Rheinberger makes it sound sometimes). Experimental systems also include *instructions for action* (sometimes documented in lab manuals). These include recipes how to prepare the biological materials, how to measure certain parameters, how to analyze the data, and so on. More than anything else, experimental systems are *ways of acting in a laboratory*. They may even include ways of acting collectively, where experiments are

---

[144] Note the stark contrast to Popper (1959: 107): "The theoretician puts certain definite questions to the experimenter, and the latter, by his experiments, tries to elicit a decisive answer to these questions, and to no others. All other questions he tries hard to exclude."

performed by more than one person. Importantly, there are ways of acting associated with such a system that are not documented anywhere, that can only be learnt by doing. To sum this point up, experimental systems consist of certain kinds of materials *and* certain ways of acting. Note also that this already implies that they must be associated with *concepts*, for action is not possible without concepts. Roughly speaking, action is behavior guided by concepts.

Second, experimental systems are closely intertwined with *theory*. New Experimentalism arose as a movement to counter the extreme theory-centrism that has dominated classical philosophy of science, where experiments entered at best in the form of an "observation sentence *o*" or "evidence *e*". But as usual, welcome attempts to redress the balance sent the pendulum to the other extreme, leading to a discourse about science that completely ignores theory. It is time to emphasize that theory and experiment are equally important and deserving of philosophical and historical scrutiny. What New Experimentalists have tended to overlook is that experimental systems always come with *theoretical interpretations* of what happens in an experiment. The aforementioned in vitro system for protein synthesis would not be operational without various theoretical assumptions, the most important one being that what the system does is to make protein from amino acid building blocks and nucleic acid instructions in the same way as a living cells makes proteins. Furthermore, the *outputs* of the system or its *inscriptions*, as some people would say, need to be interpreted. In Rheinberger's case study, for example, it is a *theoretical* claim that the amount of radioactivity in some extractable protein fraction represents the system's protein synthesis activity. Such assumptions used to be called "auxiliaries" in classical philosophy of science. No experimental system could function without them.

To sum this point up, experimental systems are complex structures that include research materials and instruments as well as ways of acting, concepts and theories.

With this concept of experimental system in mind, I wish to defend the claim that, at least in experimental biology, scientists select a more inclusive structure than just a theory. What gets selected is usually a theory or theoretical framework *together* with an experimental system, or perhaps a set of such systems (nobody knows yet how to count them).

A similar view has already been put forward by Kuhn, albeit in somewhat different terms. It is clear from his account that what is selected in science is usually not a theory, but a *paradigm*. Kuhn uses this term in more than one sense, but in one sense he means "the entire constellation of beliefs, values, techniques, and so on shared by the members of a given community" (Kuhn 1970: 175). This is quite similar to my characterization of experimental systems.

To sum this section up, scientists do not select theories on the basis of their fitting a given body of evidence, at least in experimental biology. They select a conglomerate of theory, concepts, research materials, techniques, instruments, and ways of doing experiments. As it were, theories reproduce by giving rise to successful experimental work (an experiment is a theory's way of making another theory, and vice versa). In other words, theories reproduce by making scientists *act* in certain ways. As I have argued in the previous section, scientific communities are built to reward certain successful actions. These actions, because they are rewarded, then give rise to similar actions and are thus selected by a social mechanism. Theories merely piggyback on the actions that are selected by the community by this social mechanism; this is how "theory choice" works.

I suggest that a beautiful example for this claim is provided by *classical genetics*. This will be elaborated a little in the final section.

6. The Case of Classical Genetics

Genetics as we know it was established early in the 20th century, after the rediscovery of Mendel's experiments in peas. In these experiments, Mendel had discovered two regularities, known as the "law of segregation" and the "law of independent assortment". These laws concern organismic traits that occur in two different states, known as "dominant" and "recessive". The first law states that in crosses of two pure lines, the recessive trait will disappear in the first generation. In the second generation, it reappears with a ratio of 1:3 to the dominant trait. The second law states that two traits will segregate and assort independently. The different combinations of the dominant and recessive traits occur in the ratio 9:3:3:1, which is simply the binomial expansion.

Mendelian genetics is intimately tied to doing this kind of crosses on different varieties of some species. It turned out that this kind of experiment can be done on plants as well as on animals. One of the most productive systems for doing such experiments turned out to be the fruitfly *Drosophila melanogaster*. Thomas Hunt Morgan and his associates crossed thousands of naturally occurring mutants of this fly. From the beginning, they found scores of exceptions to Mendel's rules. Many of these "exceptions" gave rise to new defined inheritance patterns, such as sex-linked inheritance, for example (Morgan 1910).

If there was such a thing as a genetic *theory*, it was closely tied to these crossing experiments (Waters 2004). It was noticed that the original Mendelian pattern can be explained by assuming that the stable heritable factors causally responsible for the visible trait differences are located on sister chromosomes. Other inheritance patterns found in Morgan's lab could be explained by assuming factors that are located on the very same chromosome. Detailed genetic maps were constructed that showed the locations of hundreds of genes on the *Drosophila* chromosomes, it was a whole industry or a "system of production" or "breeder reactor", as Robert Kohler described it (Kohler 1994). Needless to say, it also qualifies as an experimental system in the sense that I outlined in the previous section. In this system, theoretical principles such as Mendel's laws are tightly interwoven with certain ways of doing experiments. You can't understand the principles of classical genetics without understanding how to do such experiments, and you can't do these experiments without understanding the principles of genetics.

By the end of the 1920s, the ways of the Morgan school were widely accepted as a sophisticated new science of genetics.

How did classical genetics become established? To see this, it is important to appreciate that there were *rival approaches* at that time. Around the turn of the century, for example, there was the biometric school founded by the English statisticians Karl Pearson and Raphael Weldon, which was heavily influenced by the ideas of Darwin's cousin Francis Galton, who is also known as the father of eugenics. The biometric school attempted to provide a quantitative theory of genetics that was mathematically much more sophisticated than Mendelian genetics with its simple rules. They argued that genetic theory must be based on precise quantitative measurements of an organism's traits, not merely qualitative trait differences as they feature in Mendelian crossings. Of course, the biometricians were aware of Mendel's laws, but they did not think they were very relevant. The biometricians followed Darwin in thinking that what matters in evolution is *gradual* variation, for it allows the finely tuned adaptation of organisms to their environment.

Other biologists that time, too, thought of Mendelian genetics as some kind of laboratory artifact that may be interesting, but not relevant for understanding evolution or development. How was this initial opposition eventually overcome by the proponents of the new genetics? I suggest that they achieved this not so much by presenting their theory and some supporting evidence, but by simply doing what they were best at: *by breeding fruit flies*. Their enormous output of experimental results that were successful by classical genetics' *own* standards started to attract funding and gifted young people to the enterprise. They filled the spaces of the leading journals with their genetic maps and new puzzling cases. The alternative schools in genetics did not stand any chance of matching this productivity. That's how the *community* selected the experimental systems complete with the theoretical principles of classical genetics as the dominant paradigm of genetics. There was nothing like a discourse weighing different theories by methodological criteria, and if there was such a discourse, it was at best epiphenomenal.[145]

It is time now to summarize my conclusions.

7. Conclusions

At least in experimental science, there is bluntly put no such thing as philosophers call "theory choice", at least when this is taken to mean that scientists choose theories on the basis of their fit with a *fixed* body of evidence and possibly other criteria such as **simplicity, accuracy,** and so on. Experimental scientists pick a more inclusive entity that includes theories as well as investigative methods, experimental procedures, sometimes also certain research materials such as model organisms. I have argued that the entity in question is pretty much what Rheinberger calls an "experimental system". I have further shown that experimental systems are *conceptual* entities as much as they are *material*, i.e., they mainly consist in certain ways of acting in a laboratory, which is not possible without concepts and theories. I have tried to use the case of classical genetics as evidence for these claims.

I have not only argued that scientists select more inclusive structures than just theories, I have also tried to take seriously Kuhn's claim that the selection of what he calls "paradigms" is not made by individual scientists but by the entire community. This claim makes Kuhn a social epistemolo-

---

[145] Radick (2005) has made a strong case for the view that the displacement of the biometric by the Mendelian school was a contingent event; geneticists were not inevitably drawn to the Mendelian Truth, as it were. I agree with Radick insofar as there is not one Truth that science inevitably homes in on. However, I maintain that *given* the social organization of 20th century science there was some necessity in the Mendelian's winning, because that organization selects for a certain kind of productivity that only post-Morganian genetics exhibited. In particular, the approach of the Morgan school was fruitful not just for the goals of transmission genetics itself, but also for neighboring disciplines such as evolutionary biology (Weber 1998) or developmental biology (Weber 2005). This might also be Kuhn's spawning of new specialties.

gist. I have contrasted this idea to two more recent social epistemologies, namely Helen Longino's and Miriam Solomon's. Longino's approach is committed to deliberation as the salient choice procedure. I think that's an over-idealization, to say the least. Scientists may sometimes deliberate, but major decisions about research directions are not effected in this way. So I was leaning more towards Solomon's approach, according to which scientific communities as wholes are responsive to empirically successful or – as I prefer – fruitful theories, which overrides any personal biases that individual members of the community may have, which may also include apparently rational biases such as preferring simple theories, or theories with broad scope.

I have amended Solomon's account by a social mechanism that explains *why* scientific communities as a whole select empirically successful or fruitful research programs. The social mechanism has to do with the reward system of professional academic science, which mainly rewards so-called "positive results", which I take to be successful problem solutions. I have not said much as to what counts as a successful problem solution, but I do not think there is a general answer to this question. This strongly depends on the theory and set of investigative procedures in question. This reward system leads to a proliferation of the approach in question by a social mechanism that is akin to natural selection. Like Kuhn, I mean this merely as an *analogy*, as I am not a big fan of "meme theory", which holds that there is a generalized selection theory that applies to genes as well as to human ideas or "memes". I have argued that it is such a mechanism that supports counterfactuals of the kind that Miriam Solomon holds to be true, claims such as: the physics community would not have adopted quantum theory had it not been empirically successful.

Finally, I think that my approach solves the puzzle that raised by Samir Okasha's application of social choice theory to theory choice problems. Okasha's problem only arises under Arrow's assumptions concerning social choice situations. These assumptions include a condition called "non-dictatorship". In social choice theory, it means that no-one's preferences can override those of other members of the community. In our present context, this condition means that no single criterion for theory choice can override the others in cases where different criteria of theory choice pull into different directions. *That* the criteria of **accuracy**, **consistency**, **fruitfulness**, **simplicity** and **broad scope regularly** cannot be aggregated such as to effect a unique choice is also the heart of Kuhn's incommensurability thesis. My account, I hope, shows why this does not matter in scientific practice, because fruitfulness or problem-solving capacity always dominates, given the way science as a profession operates.

Bibliography

Arrow, K. (1963), *Social Choice and Individual Values*, 2nd edition. New York: John Wiley (first edition 1951).

Okasha, S. (forthcoming), "Theory Choice and Social Choice: Kuhn versus Arrow". *Mind*.

Gilbert, M. (1987), "Modelling Collective Belief". *Synthese* 73,185-204.

Hoyningen-Huene, P. (1993), Reconstructing Scientific Revolutions. The Philosophy of Science of Thomas S. Kuhn. Chicago: The University of Chicago Press.

Hull, D. (1988), Science as a Process: An Evolutionary Account of the Social and Conceptual Development of Science. Chicago: University of Chicago Press.

Kohler, R. E. (1994), Lords of the Fly. Drosophila Genetics and the Experimental Life. Chicago: University of Chicago Press.

Kuhn, T. S. (1970), *The Structure of Scientific Revolutions*, 2nd ed. Chicago: The University of Chicago Press.

———— (1977), "Objectivity, Value Judgment, and Theory Choice", in: T. S. Kuhn (ed.), *The Essential Tension. Selected Studies in Scientific Tradition and Change*. Chicago: The University of Chicago Press, 320-339.

———— (1992), *The Trouble with the Historical Philosophy of Science*. Cambridge/Mass.: Harvard University, Department of the History of Science, Preprint.

———— (1994), "The Road Since Structure", in: T. S. Kuhn, *The Road Since Structure. Philosophical Essays, 1970-1993*. Chicago: The University of Chicago Press, 90-104.

Longino, H. E. (2002), *The Fate of Knowledge*. Princeton: Princeton University Press.

Morgan, T. H. (1910), "Sex-Limited Inheritance in Drosophila". *Science* 32,120-122.

Radick, G. M. (2005), "Other Histories, Other Biologies", in: A. O'Hear (ed.), *Philosophy, Biology and Life*. Royal Institute of Philosophy Supplement, 56. Cambridge: Cambridge University Press, 21-47.

Renzi, B. G. (2009), "Kuhn's Evolutionary Epistemology and Its Being Undermined by Inadequate Biological Concepts". *Philosophy of Science* 76,143-159.

Reydon, T. A. C., Hoyningen-Huene, P. (2010), "Discussion: Kuhn's Evolutionary Analogy in The Structure of Scientific Revolutions and "The Road Since Structure"". *Philosophy of Science* 77, 468-476.

Rheinberger, H.-J. (1997), Toward a History of Epistemic Things: Synthesizing Proteins in the Test Tube. Stanford: Stanford University Press.

Solomon, M. (1994), "Social Empiricism". *Noûs* 28 (3), 325-343.

Waters, C. K. (2004), "What Was Classical Genetics?". *Studies in History and Philosophy of Science* 35 (4),783-809.

Weber, M. (1998), Die Architektur der Synthese. Entstehung und Philosophie der modernen Evolutionstheorie. Berlin: Walter de Gruyter.

―――― (2005), *Philosophy of Experimental Biology*. Cambridge: Cambridge University Press.

Gilbert's Account of Norm-Guided Behaviour: A Critique

Caroline M. Baumann

1. Introduction

Norm-guided behaviour is viewed as a serious challenge in the economic literature. In particular, rational-choice theorists who try to explain behaviour in terms of selfish interests are facing problems in making sense of norm compliance. For example, we cooperate in prisoner's dilemma type of situations even if there are no benefits for doing so; or we act honestly or politely even if it is not in our selfish interest to do so. In an attempt to cope with these shortcomings, alternative accounts have been offered. This paper focuses on Margaret Gilbert's proposal on norm-guided behaviour.

Gilbert argues that it is rational for people to act according to social norms irrespective of their individual preferences. This is so because the normativity of social norms is grounded in a joint commitment and rationality requires people to enact the joint commitments they are parties to. Gilbert provides a very elaborate and - despite the technicalities - rather simple picture of norm-guided behaviour. While her proposal has been taken up favourably by some authors (see, for example, Elisabeth Anderson 2000), it has not yet been thoroughly analysed. In this paper, I argue that Gilbert's attempt to overcome the problems inherent in rational-choice explanation of norm-guided behaviour is unsatisfactory. Gilbert does not provide sufficient reason for believing that it is indeed rational to act according to one's joint commitments irrespective of one's individual preferences.

2. Social norms and joint commitments

Let me begin by outlining Gilbert's analysis of social norms. According to Gilbert, social norms are social phenomena that are grounded in joint commitments.

A joint commitment (JC) is a commitment of two or more people. Two people might be jointly committed to paint a house or to go for a walk together. A key aspect of JCs is that they involve obligations and rights (see, for example, Gilbert 1989; 2002a/b). Most importantly, the parties to the JCs have the obligation to act in conformity with the JC unless or until the JC is rescinded, where a JC can only be rescinded by all parties involved. For example, if two individuals John and Bill are jointly committed to paint the house together, John has the obligation to paint the house together with Bill until both John and Bill change their mind and rescind or abandon the JC. John cannot just stop painting without violating a right Bill has toward John to continue paint the house.

JCs are formed when individuals openly express their willingness or readiness to participate in the relevant JCs. There are three basic conditions for the creation of a JC (Gilbert 1989: 222-223). First, there has to be an *intention* to participate in the JC (Gilbert 2002b: 81). Second, to enter a JC there must be an *open expression* or manifestation of one's intention to participate. In other words, potential parties to a JC must, for the JC to be created, *communicate* in some way their intention to participate in the JC. Consider the following example given by Gilbert (2002b: 88): Bob says to Lily "shall we dance?" and Lily responds "Yes! Let's". According to Gilbert, during this interchange, Bob and Lily explicitly express their readiness to dance together. Third, Gilbert posits a *common knowledge* condition: the manifestation of willingness must be common knowledge to all participants of the JC. To summarise, individuals John and Bill are jointly committed to paint the house together if and only if it is common knowledge between them that both have expressed that they intend to be jointly committed to paint the house together.

Having clarified the concept of a JC, let me turn to Gilbert's account of social norms. Note first that Gilbert prefers the notion of 'social rule' or 'social convention' over 'social norm'. However, I take it as uncontroversial that Gilbert's view of social rules and social conventions applies also to social norms[146]. In the following I shall ignore the differences between the notions 'social rule', 'social convention' and 'social norm' and use them interchangeably. According to Gilbert, a key characteristic of social norms is that they are essentially normative: social norms tell us how we 'ought' to act. Typical manifestations of the normativity of social norms are reactions of social approval and disapproval (Gilbert 1989a: 349-351). Further, social norms are special in that their normativity is essentially grounded in the attitudes people take towards them; social norms exist only to the extent that they are supported by a group of people (Gilbert 1989: 351-352).

Based on this understanding of social norms, Gilbert argues that their normativity is grounded in JCs. More precisely, on Gilbert's (1989: 377; 1998) account our everyday concept of a social norm is that of a jointly accepted principle of action or rule. A social norm exists in a population if and only if all members of the population have openly manifested their willingness to be jointly committed to accept the norm or simply to jointly accept the norm (1989: 373). The normativity of a social norm comes down to the binding nature of the JC to accept the norm: someone is bound by a social norm if and only if he has openly expressed his readiness to jointly accept the norm. A party to the joint acceptance of a social norm ought to act accordingly unless he is released from his obligation by all parties to the joint acceptance.

---

[146] Arguments for this claim can be found in my paper ‚Reconsidering Gilbert's account of social norms', forthcoming in the proceedings of the founding conference of the European Philosophy of Science Association, 2007.

3. Gilbert on the rationality of acting according to JCs

The question to what extent the JC approach solves collective-action problems does not seem to be a core concern of Gilbert's overall project. Her main ambition is to understand what social norms consist in and not why people act in accordance with them. Nevertheless, at least in her later writings (2003; 2007), Gilbert suggests that her account of plural-subject phenomena helps to overcome collective-action problems and to explain why people follow social norms even if it is not in their selfish interest to do so.

Gilbert defends this stance by arguing that, in becoming party to a JC, a person has *reason* to act in conformity with the JC (Tollefsen 2004: 10).

> "... I am assuming that the parties to a joint commitment *have reason* to conform to it as long as it is not rescinded. So, all else being equal, rationality would require conformity." (Gilbert 2007: 271, emphasis in the original)

In other words, all else being equal, it is rational for people to act on the JCs they are parties to. We must be clear that Gilbert (2003: 56) does not have in mind rationality in the sense of the maximisation of one's payoffs but rather rationality in the broader sense of according with the dictates of reason. Human beings who are members of a plural subject possess the following important capacities (Gilbert 2007: 271): First, they make their decisions, form their plans and act in light of these; second, they are capable of considering the reasons that apply to them for acting one way or another, of evaluating which reasons outweigh or 'trump' other reasons, and of acting in accordance with what reason dictates. Insofar as they act within the bounds of reason, they will be acting rationally in an important, intuitive way.

How does the reason created by a JC relate to other reasons? Or, in terms of the above quote: what on Gilbert's account needs remain fixed for rationality to require conformity to JCs? What definitely needs to subsist is the JC itself: the reason to act according to the JC exists as long as the JC has not been rescinded. As long as a JC stands, its parties have reason to enact the JC independently of their individual desires. In situations where personal inclinations, urges or promptings are opposed to a JC, commitments of the will 'trump' inclinations with respect to what reason dictates (Gilbert 2007: 271-272). Consider again the example of A and B being jointly committed to paint the house together. Given the JC, A has reason to continue painting the house together with B even if A has changed his mind and would prefer to stop painting the house and may be no longer individually committed to do so. As long as the JC to paint the house stands A has reason to act accordingly.

Insofar as reasons explain why individuals act in a particular way, the JCs can *explain* why individuals act in a particular way (Tollefsen 2004: 10).

> "The JCs which lie at the base of plural subjects are powerful *behavioural constraints*. This is due to the *normative force* of all commitment in conjunction with special features of JC." (Gilbert 2003: 56, emphasis in the original)

To the extent that JCs trump inclinations with respect to what reason dictates, Gilbert holds that her account may well help to overcome collective-action problems as, for example, the problem of explaining why we follow social norms.

> "Suppose ... that reason says one maximize inclination satisfaction, all else being equal. If a commitment always 'trumps' an inclination, as it may be the case, then...an appropriate joint commitment will settle the issue. If this is indeed so, then we can see how agreements, or other joint commitment phenomena...can lead to relatively good outcomes for all in collective action problems of all kinds, including the notorious 'prisoner's dilemma'." (Gilbert 2007: 275)

To summarise Gilbert's stance: people are bound by social norms to the extent that they jointly accepted them; the joint acceptance of social norms *makes it rational* for the individuals who are part of the joint acceptance to enact them and at the same time *explains* why they enact them.

4. Further clarifications of the rational force of JCs

I am doubtful whether Gilbertian JCs do indeed provide a reason that could help to explain why people follow social norms. Particularly, Gilbert's argument to that effect is not convincing. I shall argue that the normative requirement of Gilbertian JCs is not a rational 'ought' in Gilbert's broad sense of rationality. In this section, I further elaborate on the reason-giving nature of Gilbertian JCs.

To begin with, it is important to clarify to what extent Gilbert's explanation of norm-guided behaviour goes beyond rational-choice explanations, that is, explanations in terms of prudential rationality. Following rational-choice theory, actions are to be explained in terms of motivating reasons that consist in pairs of desires and means-end beliefs of individuals. Explanations of action in terms of reasons other than desire-belief pairs remain suspect. Two assumptions underlying rational-choice explanations may be distinguished:

(i)   actions are explained in terms of motivating reasons, that is, occurrent mental states of the agent, and not normative reasons;

(ii) for a motivating reason to explain an action, it needs to consist in particular occurrent mental states of the agent, namely of a desire and a means-end belief.

(i) Motivating reasons are distinguished from normative reasons. According to Smith (1987: 37-41), the characteristic feature of a motivating reason to φ is that in virtue of having such a reason an agent is in a state that is *potentially explanatory* of his φ-ing. And what makes a reason potentially explanatory of his behaviour is that his having such reasons is a fact about *him*, such that it seems natural to suppose that an agent's motivating reasons are *psychologically real*. On the other hand, to say that someone has a normative reason to φ is to say that there is a normative requirement that he φ's. Rational choice theory provides explanations of actions in terms of motivating reasons, that is, mental states of individuals. To be clear, rational-choice theorists do not deny that there are normative reasons; they merely hold that in order to explain human actions, a reason must be motivating, that is, the reason must be grounded in the psychology of the individuals.

While Gilbertian JCs are best viewed as normative reasons, they involve motivating reasons. Consider Gilbert's account of the reason one might have when acting according to a social norm. The reason to act on a social norm grounds in a JC to accept the norm: I have reason to conform to a social norm if and only if it is common knowledge that I have expressed my intention to jointly accept the norm. What is essential for me to be party to a joint acceptance of a norm is that at some point in time I expressed my intention to jointly accept the norm, that there are other individuals who jointly accepted the norm and that it is common knowledge among all members to the JC that I jointly accepted the norm. Now, a past expression of my intent, other people's expression of their intent, and other people's knowledge of my expression of intent are facts that go beyond occurrent psychological states of an agent subject to a joint acceptance of a norm. This suggests that Gilbertian JCs are normative rather than motivating reasons. Nonetheless, they involve motivating reasons. On Gilbert's account, to be part of a joint acceptance of a social norm one needs to be in a particular state of mind. Gilbert's (1989a: 12-13) account of group phenomena is intentionalist: to be part of a joint acceptance of a social norm and to have a reason to act accordingly one must conceive oneself as being part of the joint acceptance. The conception or belief that one is subject to a joint acceptance is a psychological fact about the agent and therewith a motivating reason on Smith's account.

(ii) While Gilbertian JCs involve motivating reasons to act accordingly in Smith's sense, these reasons are not of the right kind to satisfy rational-choice theorists. The mental state that is implied by being part of a JC is a belief. Rational-choice theory assumes that beliefs are insufficient to motivate and therewith explain actions. For a reason to motivate action it need consist of a *desire*-belief pair. However, it is a key feature of Gilbertian JCs that the underlying obligations and reasons stand independently of whether one desires to act accordingly or not. Suppose that after having expressed my intention to jointly accept a social norm and while being aware that I am bound by the joint acceptance, I change my mind and desire to be no longer committed. Would my being jointly committed to the social norm still help to explain why I obey the norm? According to rational-choice theory, it would not explain my acting in conformity with the norm. If the JC is no longer anchored in one's desire to be thus committed, one is no longer motivated to act accordingly.

Gilbert is well aware of the fact that JCs are not reason-giving in the prudential sense of the term. As outlined above, she explicitly defends a concept of rationality that goes beyond prudential rationality. It involves not only acting in function of one's desires but also being able to make plans, take decisions and act on these as well as the capacity of evaluating which reasons trump others and of acting in accordance with what reason dictates. Gilbert's idea is that if we assume this broader sense of rationality, the 'ought' of JCs is a rational 'ought' and JCs to accept social norms can explain why rational agents follow them. I think that this claim is unwarranted: Gilbert's argument to the effect that the 'ought' of JCs is reason-giving in this broader sense of reason is unsatisfactory.

Gilbert defends the claim that the normative requirement underlying JCs is a rational requirement in the broad sense of the term by holding that JCs are commitments of the will and, *qua* reasons, commitments of the will 'trump' inclinations. Her argument goes as follows (Gilbert 2007: 271-272). Commitments are made to overcome contrary inclinations. If commitments did not trump inclinations at the level of reasoning, it would be hard to see how they are supposed to operate in order to produce conformity to them. Consider the relation between a *resolution* and inclinations. Suppose a regular smoker resolves to stop smoking. This resolution is supposed to help him to overcome strong contrary urges. If the commitment to stop smoking would not provide one with a reason to act against the urges to smoke, why would he bother committing himself to not smoking? Or consider the relation between *decisions* and inclinations. Inclinations suggest particular actions. Decisions trump inclinations in that the decision is supposed to be the last word on a subject. Once a decision is taken, it is rational to act accordingly whatever contrary inclinations there are. The fact that we often act against our resolutions or decisions by following our inclinations does not undermine the claim that resolutions and decisions trump inclinations at the level of reasons; it merely shows that human beings often behave irrationally. Based on the analysis of the notions of resolutions and decisions, Gilbert concludes that JCs give reasons for actions that trump inclinations.

> "Each is committed through the JC, and therefore already has a reason to act of the type that a personal decision would give." (Gilbert 2003: 57)

Before proceeding, an additional clarification needs to be made with respect to Gilbert's use of rationality in the context of resolutions, decisions and JCs. When holding that rationality requires us to act on our resolutions, decisions and JCs whatever our inclinations might be, it is implicitly assumed that we do not hold on to relevant resolutions, decisions and JCs irrationally. Gilbert is interested in the reason-giving force of resolutions, decisions and JCs irrespective of the reasons we might or might not have to hold on to them. In her argumentation, she treats resolutions, decisions and JCs as bedrock without further analysing them in rational terms.

5. Is it rational to act on JCs in the broad sense of the term?

One way to undermine Gilbert's understanding of the matter is to reject the view that commitments of the will trump inclinations at the level of reasons. This strategy would need to make plausible the contention that actions against one's resolutions or decisions are not irrational. This is not the line of argument I follow here. Taking for granted that commitments like resolutions and decisions do indeed give reason for action which trumps inclinations, I argue that we may still reject that it is rational to act according to JCs. I hold that the analogy between resolutions and decisions on the one hand and joint commitments on the other is unwarranted. Let me draw attention to three problems.

First, a core element of what seems to make it that resolutions or decisions trump inclinations at the level of reasons is not present for joint commitments. Reconsider the examples Gilbert provides in support of the claim that JCs give reason for action. Both, resolutions and decisions, are instances of *individual commitments*. How are we to make sense of the contention that it is rational to act on one's individual commitments? We could try something along the lines of Edward F. McClennen's account of the dynamics of choice behavior (1990; 1997). McClennen provides an argument for the claim that it is rational to act in accordance with plans formed in the past. Thus, McClennen tries to provide rational grounds for acting on a plan in instrumental terms. He defends a version of rule-utilitarianism according to which people are overall or holistically better off if they act on their plans than if they do not. To the extent that plans are types of individual commitments as Gilbert understands the latter[147], McClennen may be taken to support Gilbert's stance. However, I doubt that Gilbert could sail in McClennen's slipstream. First, Gilbert explicitly argues that the defence of the rationality of JCs has to go beyond standard accounts of rationality. She holds that the rationality of acting in accord with JCs is not to be accounted for in instrumental terms: it is not to be explained in terms of prudential considerations – be they situational or procedural. Second, what McClennen's argument proves is not only that it is rational to act according to one's plans as long as they are upheld, but that it is rational to act according to one's plans, period. Gilbert, on the other hand, understands the binding and therewith reason-giving force of decisions or commitments as subsisting only as long as one holds on to the commitment:

---

[147] McClennen does not use the notion of commitment in the sense of a resolution or decision as Gilbert does. According to him, a commitment is a psychological disposition to act according to a plan or rule (McClennen 1997: 211). In his own terms, McClennen argues that commitments are rational. In Gilbert's terms, he argues that it is rational to have a disposition to act on commitments.

> "Given one's decision, one will continue to be bound...unless or until one has carried out the decision – unless or until one rescinds it." (Gilbert 2007: 263)

A straightforward way of making sense of Gilbert's contention that it is rational to act according to one's individual commitments is to conceive of it by analogy to the view that *akrasia*, or weakness of the will, is irrational. Someone is akratic or weak-willed if he does not do x even if he holds that, all things considered, it is best to do x; that is, even if he decides that 'it is in my best interest to do x' or 'all things considered, I definitely ought to do x'. For example, someone who holds that it is in his overall best interest to stop smoking and still smokes is considered akratic. There is a strong philosophical strand holding that akratic behaviour is irrational behaviour (see, for example, Wedgwood 2002). The smoker who concludes that it is in his best interest to abstain from smoking but smokes anyway is considered irrational.

Now, individual commitments, such as resolutions and decisions, on the one hand and all-things-considered judgments on the other are different types of mental states. What powers the analogy between the rationality of behaviour in accord with commitments and the rationality of behaviour in accord with all-things-considered judgements is the following. First, what grounds the rationality of actions in conformity with individual commitments and all-things-considered judgements are not prudential considerations; these actions are considered rational since they are in line with one's will. Second, the binding nature of all-things-considered judgments is similar to the binding of individual commitments. It is rational to act on individual commitments and all-things-considered judgment as long as they have not been abandoned. Finally, in the case of all-things-considered judgments and individual commitments, it is rational to act accordingly as long as one has *not changed his mind*. In other words, the rationality to act on all-things-considered judgements and individual commitments derives from the fact that the agent is in a particular mental state, a mental state that is considered a characteristic feature of the will.

If I am right to think that the contention that acting against one's individual commitments is irrational builds on the idea that akrasia is irrational, the argument from the rationality of individual commitments to the rationality of JCs is dubitable. The reason is that the mental state characteristic of our will that makes up individual commitments is absent in the case of Gilbertian JCs. The latter are reason-giving for a member to the JC independently of his will and, more precisely, independently of the mental states which are characteristic of his will. Remember, the 'ought' of JCs is grounded in the jointness of the commitment and not the commitment alone. JCs are binding as long as we have not been released from it by the other parties to the JCs. The persistence of a JC depends not only on our own will but also on the will of the other parties involved. To be clear, being bound by a Gilbertian JC does depend on being in a certain mental state, namely on conceiving or believing oneself to be so bound. However, this mental state is not generally considered to be characteristic of the will, such as all-things-considered judgments, individual commitments, resolutions and decisions. It is a normal belief about what one ought to do and not a belief about what, all things considered, it would be best to do. It may be countered that in order to be bound by a JC, one must have expressed one's intention to be so bound; and an intention is a characteristic feature of the will similar to commitments, resolutions or decisions: if one intends to do x, it is rational to do x. True, the *creation* of the obligation underlying a JC depends essentially on an individual's intention to be so committed; however, the *existence* of the obligation is independent of the persistence of the intention of the individual.

The analogy between individual commitments, such as resolutions and decisions on the one hand and JCs on the other hand is undermined further if we look at the reason-giving nature of the two: the 'trumping' of inclinations at the level of reasons is more radical in the case of individual commitments than JCs. The particularity of individual commitments, similar to all-things-considered judgments, seems to be that it is rational to act on them however strong the contrary inclinations are. Consider someone who is *resolved* or *decided* to have lunch with a friend. As long as one holds on to this resolution or decision, it is irrational to act differently even if, for example, one hurt oneself badly shortly before lunch and craves to get some pain-killers and to see a doctor instead of going for lunch. The reason-giving nature of JCs, on the other hand, does not seem to be as strong as that. There may well be situations where it is rational to violate a JC. If someone has *agreed* with a friend to have lunch together some other day, it seems that it may still be rational not to honour the agreement if, for example, one has hurt oneself badly shortly before lunch time and craves to get some pain-killers and to see a doctor instead. Considering that individual commitments and JCs seem to have different reason-giving forces, the strategy of deducing the reason-giving nature of JCs from individual commitments seems at least questionable.

Finally, note that the reason Gilbert herself gives for why resolutions and decisions trump inclinations at the level of reasons does not apply in the same way to joint commitments. Remember, Gilbert argues for the reason-giving force of resolutions and decisions by saying: if they did not trump inclinations at the level of reasoning it would be hard to see how they are supposed to operate in order to produce conformity to them. JCs do not face the same dilemma. It is straightforward to see how JCs might operate in order to produce conformity to them even if they do not trump inclinations at the level of reasoning. JCs look much like pre-commitments which figure centrally in Jon Elster's Ulysses and the Sirens (1979) and Ulysses Unbound (2000). According to Elster, pre-commitments involve self-binding devices to protect oneself from passion, preference change and time inconsistency. They constrain future actions in that they remove certain options from the feasible set, by making them more costly or available only with a delay, and by insulating themselves from knowledge about their existence (Elster 2000: 1). For example, in order to be able to listen to the singing of the Sirens without being detained by them, Ulysses pre-commits himself by letting him be bound to a mast while passing the Sirens' island. His being tied to the mast constrains his actions during the passage of the island by removing the option of choosing whether or not to land on the Sirens' shore. Pre-commitment can also take the form of attaching a cost or a penalty to the choice one wants to avoid making. Elster (2000: 11) gives the following example: "if you think you might get too drunk or too amorous at the office party, you can increase the costs of doing so by taking your spouse along." I think JCs are very intuitively viewed as constraining one's future choices by making them more costly. By entering a JC, one subjects oneself to the obligation to act accordingly, an obligation one has towards the other participants of the JC. The disapproval one might suffer by others if one violates a JC motivates one to act according to the JC.

Clearly, this interpretation of JCs falls short of Gilbert's ambition to argue that JCs are reason-giving in the same way individual commitments are reason-giving. It is not *per se* rational to act according to pre-commitments; it is only rational to act accordingly if the constraints to which one subjects oneself by way of the pre-commitment are such that it is rational to act thus. Under the interpretation of JCs as pre-commitments, it is rational to act on a JC only if the desire to avoid being blamed by others for violating the JC is strong enough to rationalise one's action in accord with the JC.

My conclusion is that Gilbert's argument from the rationality to act on individual commitments to the rationality to act on JCs is not warranted and that further arguments would be needed to support the claim that it is rational to act according to JCs.

Bibliography

Anderson, E. (2000), "Beyond Homo Economicus: New Developments in Theories of Social Norms". *Philosophy and Public Affairs,* 29 (2), 170-200.

Elster, J. (1979), *Ulysses and the Sirens.* Cambridge and New York: Cambridge University Press.

——— (2000), *Ulysses Unbound.* Cambridge: Cambridge University Press.

Gilbert, M. (1983), "Notes on the Concept of a Social Convention". *New Literary History* 14 (2), 225-251.

—— (1989), *On Social Facts*. Princeton: Princeton University Press.

—— (1998), "Social norms". In: E. Craig (ed.), *Routledge Encyclopedia of Philosophy*. Retrieved online on October 18, 2006, from http://www.rep.routledge.com/article/R029.

—— (2002a), "Acting Together". In: G. Meggle (ed.), *Social Facts and Collective Intentionality*. Frankfurt: Dr. Hänsel-Hohenhausen AG.

—— (2002b), "Considerations on Joint Commitment: Responses to Various Comments". In: G. Meggle (ed.), *Social Facts and Collective Intentionality*. Frankfurt: Dr. Hänsel-Hohenhausen AG.

—— (2003), "The Structure of the Social Atom: Joint Commitment as the Foundation of Human Social Behavior". In: F. F. Schmitt (ed.), *Socializing Metaphysics*. Lanham, Maryland: Rowman & Littlefield.

—— (2007), "Collective Intentions, Commitment, and Collective Action Problems". In: F. Peters and H. B. Schmid (eds.), *Rationality and Commitment*. New York: Oxford University Press.

McClennen, E. F. (1990), *Rationality and Dynamic Choice: Foundational Explorations*. New York: Cambridge University Press.

—— (1997), "Pragmatic Rationality and Rules". *Philosophy and Public Affairs* 26 (3), 210-258.

Tollefsen, D. P. (2004), "Collective Intentionality". *The Internet Encyclopedia of Philosophy*. Retrieved on October 1, 2007, from http://www.iep.utm.edu/c/collint.htm.

Wedgwood, R. (2002), "Practical Reason and Desire". *Australian Journal of Philosophy* 80, 345-358.